Industrial change

29.6.79

List of Contributors

GYULA BORA	Karl Marx University of Economics, Budapest, Hungary
MAND R. CHAUDHURI	Burdwan University, West Bengal, India
JOHN H. CUMBERLAND	University of Maryland, College Park, Maryland USA
F. E. IAN HAMILTON	London School of Economics and Political Science and School of Slavonic Studies, University of London, England
DAVID E. KEEBLE	University of Cambridge, Cambridge, England
HORST KOHL	Humboldt University, Berlin, German Democratic Republic
BRONISLAW KORTUS	Jagiellonian University, Kraków, Poland
TEOFIL LIJEWSKI	Institute of Geography, Polish Academy of Sciences, Warsaw, Poland
GODFREY J. R. LINGE	School of Pacific Studies, Australian National University, Canberra, Australia
PETER R. ODELL	Erasmus University, Rotterdam, Netherlands
J. OKEZIE C. ONYEMELUKWE	Ibadan University, Ibadan, Nigeria
JOHN REES	University of Texas at Dallas, Richardson, Texas, USA
ALLAN B. RODGERS	The Pennsylvania State University, State College, Pennsylvania, USA
KENNETH WARREN	University of Oxford, Oxford, England
RYSZARD WILCZEWSKI	Institute of Planning, Warsaw, Poland

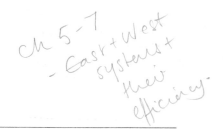

Industrial Change:

International Experience and Public Policy

edited by **F. E. Ian Hamilton**

Longman
London and New York

Longman Group Limited London

Associated companies, branches and representatives
throughout the world

Published in the United States of America
by Longman Inc., New York

© Longman Group Limited 1978

First published 1978

ISBN 0 582 48593 2

Library of Congress Cataloging in Publication Data
Main entry under title:

Industrial change.

Includes index.
1. Industries, Location of – Addresses, essays, lectures. 2. Industry and state – Addresses, essays,
lectures. 3. Industrialization – Addresses, essays, lectures. I. Hamilton, F. E. Ian.
HD58.I47   338'.09   77-11075
ISBN 0-582-48593-2

Typeset in Great Britain by the Pitman Press, Bath
and printed by Richard Clay (the Chaucer Press) Ltd., Bungay, Suffolk.

Contents

Ch 4 + 5

Preface and Introduction

A companion volume, *Contemporary Industrialization*, investigates modern trends in national, regional and urban industrial development, structure and location, in response to changes in technology and organization. The focus is primarily upon the spatial analysis of a variety of aspects of current industrial behaviour, about which governments and other agencies concerned with shaping regional and urban policies ought to be made more aware. This book, *Industrial Change: International Experience and Public Policy*, sets out (*a*) to examine a range of achievements of State regulation of, or influence upon, spatial industrial change in the past and at the present; (*b*) to elucidate shortcomings or deficiencies in government policies; and (*c*) to propose certain lines that public policy should take in the future. Experience regarding the interrelationships between industrial change – especially spatial change or 'movement' – and governmental socio-economic, environmental, regional and defence policies is drawn, in varying degrees, from a diversity of 'industrial environments': two developing African and Asian States, the mixed economies of west European countries, the planned socialist economies of eastern Europe and from 'federal' economies in the New World.

Industrial change is interpreted widely, to embrace alterations, and the consequences thereof, in the 'mix', scale and locational patterns of industries on varying levels – regional, interregional, national and international. Prominence is given to spatial change. Several chapters debate the definition, mechanisms and processes of 'industrial migration'. Some, like Keeble (Ch. 4) interpret migration in the narrow senses of the relocation of productive activities or of the establishment of branch plants. Others, like Hamilton (Ch. 3), Wilczewski, Lijewski and Kortus (Ch. 8), Rodgers (Ch. 9) and Rees (Ch. 13) use the term in the wider sense that includes also differential rates of expansion in various locations or regions, while Onyemelukwe (Ch. 10) argues that developing countries exhibit industrial 'splashing' as a spatial expression at national or interregional level of international migration. Interesting conclusions can be drawn regarding the use of public policy to control or to use industrial migration as a tool of regional socio-economic policies. There is a broad concensus of opinion – from the developing, developed, capitalist, mixed and socialist economies alike – that central governments have greater ability to influence the development and location of heavy industries than of the smaller, more footloose and lighter industries which can finance themselves (even to a degree in the centralized socialist economies) and can thus expand more readily *in situ* without central control or can locate in or near existing urban–industrial nodes or agglomerations. This latter point is related to another broad conclusion: that governments fail to assess properly, or even to realize, the direct and indirect spatial effects – at regional, national or international levels – of broad fiscal or infrastructure-investment policies.

A secondary, but pervasive, theme is the use of quantitative techniques in measuring spatial industrial change. Particular reference is made to the shift-share technique in the chapters on Poland (Ch. 8), the Italian Mezzogiorno (Ch. 9) and the American Sun Belt (Ch. 13), while Keeble (Ch. 4) applies the Theil entropy index in his analysis of interregional and sub-regional industrial migration in the UK.

All the chapters in this book are revised versions of papers presented variously at conferences of the International Geographical Union Working Group on Industrial Geography in London in 1974 and in Novosibirsk, USSR in 1976. They are grouped 'geographically' and commence with Cumberland's global assessment of the consequences of past policies and attitudes towards industrial evolution which have encouraged the present high levels of environmental damage and resource depletion: changes in future policy are recommended. In Chapter 2 Odell examines the locational and policy implications for industry and government in northwestern Europe of the exploitation of North Sea energy resources. Still at the international scale, Hamilton (Ch. 3) outlines the interrelationships between evolving national and Community policies and growth of multinational industrial firms in the EEC. The British industrial economy is investigated from two quite different angles: Keeble (Ch. 4) relates migration of industrial plants to government regional policy while Warren (Ch. 5) makes a critical assessment of the achievements and deficiencies of that policy in encouraging spatial-structural industrial modernization and balance.

Industrial change in socialist countries in Eastern Europe is the subject of Chapters 6, 7 and 8. Kohl (Ch. 6) describes the problems confronting State industrial policy in the German Democratic Republic in achieving regional modernization and interregional redistribution of industry. Bora (Ch. 7) briefly outlines past effects of Hungarian location policy as a background to the development of a spatial job-allocation model which will provide guidelines for future State planning. A trio of Polish authors (Ch. 8) approach industrial shifts in their country from three different angles: the quantitative evaluation of interregional change, the examination of migration types and processes and the study of regional structural shifts in Upper Silesia. Rodgers (Ch. 9) uses quantitative techniques to measure the dispersal achieved by Italian government policies in the Mezzogiorno. Industrial movement in the developing countries is the subject of two chapters. Onyemelukwe (Ch. 10) places particular emphasis on the impact of Nigerian dependence on external industrial control, internal government infrastructure policy and entrepreneurial behaviour, while Chaudhuri (Ch. 11) explains some of the results of Indian national planning on industrial location. Both stress data collection difficulties. Finally, industrial change in the New World is viewed through Australian experience (Linge, Ch. 12), where 'federal' organization combines with small market size, the historical pattern of urbanization and environmental constraints to encourage inertia, and contrasts with the study of the Dallas–Fort Worth area (Rees, Ch. 13) which exhibits both the spatial dynamics of US manufacturing and the cyclical uncertainties of government defence spending.

In conclusion I wish to extend my gratitude to a number of people: first to my family – Justyna, Bartholomew and Michael – for their often tenuous tolerance of the preoccupations of the editor; second, to the secretaries of the Department of

Geography at the London School of Economics & Political Science, for their patience and extremely hard work, under great pressure, in typing and re-typing submitted papers; and third, but not least, to the members of the IGU Working Group on Industrial Geography who made this book and its companion, *Contemporary Industrialization*, possible.

The editor alone, however, is responsible for any errors or omissions.

F. E. Ian Hamilton

Acknowledgements

Dr F. E. Ian Hamilton wishes to express his gratitude to the editor of the *Tijdschrift voor Economische en Sociale Geografie* for permission to reproduce Chapter 3 in shortened and modified form.
Dr J. Rees gratefully acknowledges support for his research from the National Science Foundation, N.S.F. Grant SOC 76-19009.

Chapter 1

Planning future industrial development in response to energy and environmental constraints

John H. Cumberland

Significant contributions to human welfare have resulted from the ingenuity of industrial decision-makers and planners, who organized the labour, capital, materials, energy and technology embodied in such industrial complexes as Novosibirsk, Dnepropetrovsk, Pittsburgh, Gary, Kobi, Manchester and the Ruhr Valley: yet, one of the great human ironies facing planners is that the very success of past industrial development is generating adverse consequences of a magnitude which requires drastic changes in future industrial design. Indeed, for theoretical and practical reasons, current patterns of industrial activity contain an inherent internal logic and set of forces which can be expected, if not corrected, to provide positive incentives and rewards for pollution, depletion and other injury to general welfare. Recent USA–USSR joint space efforts have dramatically illustrated not only the brilliant technical achievements of science and technology, but these scientific findings have emphasized the fragility and delicate balance of the limited biosphere upon which the survival and welfare of all societies depends. A systems approach as shown in Fig. 1.1 combining interrelated concepts such as entropy from the physical sciences, ecology from the life sciences and common property resource management from the social sciences can provide the analysis necessary for improving future industrial planning. Industrial planners now face a major challenge in seeking new patterns of industrial development designed to assure society of the benefits from industrialization while minimizing the adverse effects of efficiency in large scale which cause depletion and pollution. The successful design of viable future patterns of industrial development must be based upon a more complete understanding than in the past of the principles of materials balance, entropy and environmental science.

Major problems of current industrial practices

The problems of resource depletion, energy shortage and pollution associated with current industrial practices result from complex interrelationships between the concepts and processes of economic development which industry is designed to serve. The principal factors involved are as follows.

1. In both industrial and pre-industrial societies, the advancement of human welfare is assumed to depend upon continued, self-sustaining, self-reinforcing economic development.
2. In most societies, economic development is based, at least partially, and in some cases primarily, upon the extraction and utilization of non-renewable material and energy supplies.

1

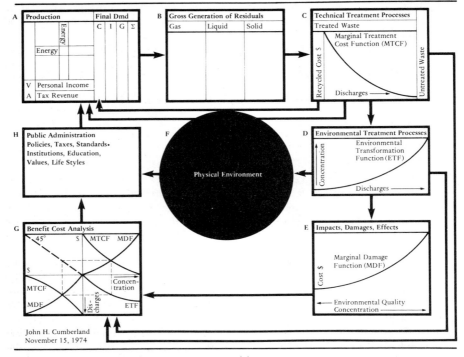

John H. Cumberland
November 15, 1974

Fig. 1.1   An economic environment systems model.

3. In general, the level of economic activity will be accompanied by a proportionate level of waste generation. Current patterns of economic development raise the dual problem of resource depletion on the input side and pollution generation on the output side.
4. Many potentially renewable resources which are treated as common property resources are subject to over-use and extinction.
5. Common property resources, such as air and water, are exploited as the carriers of adverse external effects from one set of activities, regions or groups to others.
6. Current institutions often provide inadequate incentives and opportunities for local, national and international agencies to invest in measures for the protection and management of renewable and non-renewable resources.
7. Current national and international institutions often find little support for measures to protect the interests of future generations, and this concern drops off sharply for generations more than a few removed from the present.
8. In most industrial nations, the military sectors account for a significant share of total economic activity, therefore generating not only a significant share of total resource depletion and pollution, but also pre-empting much economic output which could be used for domestic and international redistribution and welfare improvement.
9. Recent price increases and embargoes by oil-producing nations have drawn attention not only to the unequal global distribution of energy resources, but more important to the global limits on the total supplies of non-renewable energy resources.

10. Rising prices, interrupted deliveries and reduced supplies of international oil are forcing many nations to expand output of economically-marginal and highly-polluting domestic sources of non-renewable energy supplies.
11. Expanding global populations and growing food shortages have revealed severe problems inherent in non-sustainable, current agricultural practices in industrial nations, which absorb more energy from non-renewable fuels, and fertilizers than is returned in food values.

Each of these factors, if uncorrected, raises serious problems for local, national and world planning of industrial development. Their combined effects, if not ameliorated, could lead to the type of social collapse forecast by the Club of Rome (Meadows *et. al.*, 1972). Current patterns of high-pollution industrial production and resource-depleting economic development practised by industrial nations cannot realistically be achieved at comparable per capita levels by large populations in the developing nations, and indeed cannot be sustained indefinitely by currently industrialized nations. Although time spans are difficult to specify, unrealistic efforts to sustain and extend current rates of non-renewable resource depletion and waste generation will at best be unavailing and, at worst, can lead to the types of national and international collapse and disaster predicted in the doomsday literature. Planners therefore must move beyond the closely-held preconceptions of the last few decades concerning the nature and consequences of economic development to new concepts and guidelines which are consistent with the constraints on economic activity imposed by energy, space, non-renewable resources and environmental capacity. Recent advances in the field of environmental economics and related sciences offer guidelines for addressing the problems cited above, for shaping new approaches to the development of sustainable economic growth and for achieving improvement in human welfare. While not all of these problems can easily be solved by industry alone, improved industrial design is a necessary condition for a more responsible global approach to environmental management.

Industrial planning for optimal rates, composition and distribution of economic output

Most present discontent with economic growth arises from failures to achieve (1) optimal or even satisfactory rates of development, (2) an adequate balance in the composition of output, (3) satisfactory distribution of output and (4) control over pollution and other negative side effects of activity.

Common property resources and pollution

The most serious and dangerous side effect of economic growth and industrial complexes is the massive generation of emissions, wastes and pollutants. The design of successful remedies for correcting large-scale pollution threats requires a thorough analysis of the multiple causes of pollution. The most fundamental cause lies in the concept of materials balance or conservation of matter. Since normally matter is not destroyed, all material outputs, whether for further production or for consumption, must eventually become waste (Ayres and Kneese, 1969). Another cause is that the existence of non-priced common property resources, such as air and water, makes it possible for generators of pollution to discharge their wastes at low private cost into commonly-owned environmental transport media, which transfer impacts to other regions, groups and individuals at high social cost.

Plant managers, whether striving to meet quotas in planned economies, or to maximize profits under a market systems, under pressures to shift some of their costs from their own activities, operate under misleading signals because their internal costs do not reflect the full social costs of their activity (for further discussion see Beyers & Krumme in Hamilton, 1974; Murata in Hamilton, forthcoming 1978). Thus, high-pollution activities produce both excessive amounts of outputs and the incorrect mix of output because they have not had to pay the full social cost of their production and consumption processes. Moreover, given current technologies, to the extent that economic growth objectives are achieved, the waste management and pollution problem will increase.

Numerous remedies are available. The most preferable on ethical grounds would be for all producers and consumers to avoid actions which injure and impose costs on others. In practice, this would require industrial complexes to be designed from the beginning to include complete and adequate facilities for internalizing waste, either by recycling it or by rendering it harmless to others. Ideally, this policy would cause the prices of all products to reflect the full costs of their production, and, in a competitive market, result in the optimal rate and composition of all outputs, with efficient resource allocation. Where this condition could not be met, efficiency would require that the product not be produced. In the case of high-pollution activities, prices would rise and outputs would fall, relative to low-pollution activities, resulting in a movement toward a more socially-optimal solution. Where this ideal policy of fully internalizing all adverse spillover effects cannot be achieved, other second best and less satisfactory remedies are available, the most generally recommended being the Pigouvian tax or emissions charge designed to bring the private cost of production into line with the full social cost.

Properly-designed emissions charges or pollution penalties can have several constructive effects. First, consumers, having to pay higher prices to cover the full costs of production, reduce their purchases from high-pollution activities. Second, taxation of emissions provides production managers with strong positive economic incentives not only to reduce pollution, but to use their ingenuity and special knowledge to find the least-cost methods and combinations of methods for reducing pollution. Third, incentives are also provided for developing low-pollution technology. Fourth, money obtained from emission charges can be used for monitoring pollution, compensating those injured by it and supporting research on pollution control (Cumberland, 1972).

Some of these relationships are illustrated in Fig. 1.1. Setting optimal emission charges requires knowledge of treatment cost functions (lowest-cost methods and combinations of methods for obtaining incremental reductions in pollution) and damage functions (which require interdisciplinary social science, life science and earth science research). These factors vary locally, and require extensive research to identify. Environmental management of an estuary, for example, or an international ocean, could be achieved by giving a national or international body the right to set emission charges, and to use the revenue collected to monitor the results and conduct the research needed to identify damage functions, and to enforce environmental protection standards.

In theory, the use of environmental regulations, emission standards or subsidy payments can achieve results comparable to those resulting from emission charges. Also, in theory, the same type of research on damage functions, treatment cost functions and local environmental transformation function is needed for optimal management, whether by regulation, taxation, subsidy or some combination. However, these alternative policy measures do not provide the same economic incentives as emission charges for minimum cost pollution abatement, economic efficiency and development of improved technology.

In practice, the use of emission charges can aid in the management of an industrial complex if the overall management has the authority to establish, and collect emission charges. Greatest efficiency will be achieved by establishing the charges at optimal levels which equate marginal treatment costs with the marginal damages from pollution (Cumberland, 1974) as shown in Fig. 1.1. The effect of a set of optimal pollution charges imposed by the managers of an industrial complex would be to keep pollution down to appropriate levels, minimize the damage imposed by one producer upon others, encourage the socially-desirable composition of outputs, establish efficient price structures, minimize costs of pollution treatment processes and stimulate the development of new low-pollution technologies. In cases where the external, spillover effects of the industrial complex are confined to a single management area or a single political region, the establishment and collection of emission charges can be straightforward. Where spillover effects spread over additional political areas and national boundaries, the management problem becomes more complex. This becomes serious as the number and types of industrial spillover effects begin to approach global proportions, as with oil spills, nuclear radiation, thermal pollution and weather modification. However, the concept of using internationally-administered emission charges by non-political, cooperative environmental protection agencies to provide funds for monitoring, research and protection of the global environmental resources has great potential appeal. The emergence of regional, national and international environmental management agencies with authority to tax and regulate emissions can be viewed as a corrective device, necessary to moderate the otherwise wasteful and destructive use of global environmental resources, which if not managed in the public interest will, because of their common property nature, be wastefully over-used eventually to the point of extinction and depletion.

The most important theoretical aspect of pollution penalties and emission charges is that by encouraging movements toward Pareto optimality, a properly designed set of charges can help solve simultaneously two major economic–social problems, i.e. both the proper rate of economic growth, and the optimal mix of outputs within the growth rate, as the result of correcting for uncompensated external diseconomies.

Energy and entropy

Just as the materials balance concept is fundamental to the task of pollution control in the design of future industrial processes so the entropy concept is basic to the role of energy in economic growth. Current industrial processes are based heavily upon massive use of non-renewable energy concentrations for which economical substitutes are not readily available (Georgescu–Reogen, 1975). Recent reductions in supplies of petroleum from the Middle East have drawn widespread attention to a phenomenon which had already become far advanced, namely the emerging shortage of petroleum. More than two centuries of the industrial revolution succeeded by decades of exponential economic development since the Second World War have depleted much of the known easily-accessible, high quality global reserves of oil. Even with continuing new discoveries and improved extraction techniques, low cost supplies of liquid hydrocarbons cannot prudently be assumed to last for more than a few generations. This fact poses major problems for the design of industrial complexes, which typically consume vast quantities of petroleum both as a source of energy and of petrochemicals.

Economists have traditionally assumed that physical resource depletion was not a major source of concern because price effects and financial incentives would continue to encourage discovery of new sources, development of substitutes, emergence of new technologies and the improvement of conservation practices. These corrective phenomena worked well in the past, but are subject to constraints. Whatever may be the full extent of undiscovered petroleum, its total availability on a finite globe is limited, and its rate of replacement is negligible. The large global reserves of coal may serve to some extent as a substitute, or as a raw material for liquid fuels but the conversion process requires large quantities of water, and generates large quantities of highly polluting residuals. Nuclear fission processes may eventually be improved, but currently pose serious problems of reliability, pollution, safety, security and long-term storage of hazardous wastes. Even if inexpensive, totally safe sources of energy from fusion or other technologies could be achieved, the problem of global increases in temperature and disastrous weather modification resulting from energy use would impose ultimate limitations on the growth of industrial complexes of conventional design.

The vast majority of the world's industrial plant has been designed in response to yesterday's misleading signals from energy prices which did not adequately reflect growing world shortages, heat pollution and uneven global distribution of petroleum reserves. As a result, the international economy is saddled with energy-wasting industrial processes, accompanied in many areas by uneconomic worker-commuting patterns and wasteful transportation systems. Unrealistically-low energy prices of the recent past have disguised the finite limits of non-renewable energy supplies and the fact that today's energy waste will deprive future generations of the supplies now being consumed. Continuation and growth of current patterns of exponential increases in consumption of non-renewable energy supplies is hardly viable for many more generations.

Future industrial planning will eventually have to be designed to conserve energy through greater heat economies, recycling, insulation, conservation and greater use of renewable energy supplies. Solar energy flows in its many forms of sunlight, agricultural crops, tidal forces and meteorological phenomena will eventually have to be substituted for dwindling fixed energy stocks.

Economic growth rates and inter-generational equity

In most economies, intensive efforts are being devoted to maximizing rates of economic growth as a result of international rivalry. Yet idealistic and altruistic elements are also involved in efforts to generate output for aid to developing nations and to the assembly of vast aggregations of capital equipment from which the output will primarily benefit futurenerations.

Ironically, many such sacrifices by present generations to benefit future generations may not be the optimal policy for benefiting any group. Sacrifices made to achieve high rates of capital formation assume that this capital can be either used to produce the types of outputs or converted into the types of capital which will be demanded by future generations. Unfortunately, consideration of ecological balance, materials balance and entropy suggests that the most important and basic forms of capital are non-renewable environmental resources, and that some forms of damage to them may be irreversible. Thus, future generations, which will probably have high income elasticities of demand for leisure, recreation and natural environments, may instead find that past generations have sacrificed consumption opportunities to produce, at heavy environmental cost, forms of physical capital which are not wanted in the future and which cannot be used to produce the highest priority goods, i.e. natural environmental life support systems.

This line of reasoning suggests that the welfare of both present and future generations can be advanced if current generations reduce their rates of capital accumulation through investment, and instead shift to higher levels of consumption, especially of education, cultural activities, services, investment in human capital and other goods and services having low environmental impact. This policy would also greatly benefit future wealthier generations which would inherit less inappropriate physical capital, and more irreplaceable environmental resources.

This long-run re-evaluation of entropy, inter-generational equity and economic growth has a number of implications for the design and operation of industrial facilities and complexes. First, current high rates of utilization of non-renewable energy, environmental and material resources are at the direct expense of future generations. Damage to future generations can be reduced in several ways. One important step in responsible inter-generational design of industrial facilities is through life-cycle planning (Cumberland, 1973) involving comprehensive accounting for the full economic, social and environmental effects of development over all phases of its life, including exploration, planning, construction and operation, but with special emphases upon the need for eventually phasing out the project after its useful life is fully amortized, and rehabilitating and restoring the site for future use.

Such planning can be achieved by building into the price of the output of such facilities a return to a trust fund, which is committed to the eventual restoration of the site and disposal of its wastes and facilities. Failure to adopt this type of full-cost life-cycle planning has caused serious, long-term, probably irreversible damage from strip-mining in the USA. These lessons of life-cycle planning and full costing have yet to be assimilated and applied in the rehabilitation of nuclear facilities sites, underground pumping of wastes, damage to the ozone layer of the atmosphere, extinction of threatened species, ocean dumping of wastes, silting of dam sites, storage of nuclear wastes and a growing number of other side effects from industrial expansion. Adoption of life-cycle planning, full costing and establishment of trust funds for site rehabilitation can help minimize the imposition of inter-generational injustice of transferring heavy environmental damage to future generations.

Investment in pollution control and the public goods problem

Investment in pollution control and other environmental management activities at the lowest levels of economic activity (the plant, the local community) can be expected systematically to be at inadequate levels. Failure to invest adequately in the public welfare need not be either accidental or irresponsible but results from the public goods problem of the inability of local agencies to exclude others from the benefits of certain types of programme and from the inability of factories and local areas to capture the full benefits of expenditures on public goods. The usual remedy is for a higher level government body to attempt to identify the optimal level of investment in activities like pollution control for the total community and to make the expenditures, out of public funds, on behalf of the public. This procedure works reasonably well where adequate information is available on the costs and benefits of environmental management within a common political unit, and where the political autonomy of the area is co-extensive with the geographic impact of the problem.

The implications of the global public goods–environment management problem for industrial planning are profound. Nations are unlikely unilaterally to invest heavily to prevent pollution which can be exported beyond these boundaries by air and water common property resources, yet all nations will be heavy losers unless corrective measures can be adopted globally to provide environmental protection against such growing technologies as weather modification, ocean-mining, nuclear proliferation, oil-spills and atmospheric damage. These are obvious potential benefits to all nations which could accrue from some form of global environmental agency.

The function and power of a world environmental protection agency could be linked to the amount of damage involved. At the minimum, such an agency should monitor critical environmental parameters at key spots around the world, using satellites and other advanced technology. At the minimum, it could also conduct benefit–cost studies, publish current environmental indicators and make public recommendations of guidelines for industrial activities having potentially international environmental impacts.

If scientific evidence then indicates growing global damage, then common sense, humanity and environmental economic theory would suggest then that a global environmental agency should be given increasing powers to regulate and manage if internal national efforts are inadequate. International investment in efforts to improve industrial planning could yield large returns to the participants, and to all societies.

Spatial hierarchies in industrial planning

Each of the major problems of industrial planning treated above was observed to have important spatial and geographic dimensions. At the local and plant level, responsible design criteria should be fully planned to avoid detrimental internal and external spillover effects which could damage workers, or residents of local and distant areas. Damage to other activities could also be avoided and internalized by combining plants and enterprises so that the management of each must account its mutual effect on the other. Wastes and residuals of various activities should be re-used constructively as inputs to other processes. Local administrative bodies will be necessary to improve welfare through changing the composition and growth of economic activity by enforcing optimal rates of environmental management and economic activity through regulation, bargaining, merger or simulating optimal market system through subsidies, or preferably, emission charges. This objective function and trade-off is illustrated in Fig. 1.1. Optimal activity levels derived from this analysis can be achieved by a variety of control measures.

Where industrial activity generates detrimental impacts which flow over interregional boundaries or within a nation, optimal control problems are more difficult than where they are confined within a region: interstate river basins are an example (Kneese and Bower, 1968). Inter-governmental regulatory agencies, based upon water sheds, air sheds or other impacted area boundaries are necessary to avoid environmental imperialism, which seeks economic gain by exporting pollution. If these agencies are given the authority to apply enforceable controls, expenditures or emission charges they can bring internal costs into line with full social costs, and reduce pollution and other spillovers to optimal levels.

National industrial design is also necessary for managing nationwide industrial side effects. National planning agencies can use controls, subsidies and charges (Fig. 1.1) to achieve national balance in environmental balance which might not result from sectoral or local planning. An example is the unique Lake Baikal whose remarkable purity and beauty, as the result of national recognition of its value to all Soviet citizens, present and future, was protected by regulation from detrimental externalities caused by cellulose production. This same desirable goal might also have been achieved by high emission charges or by State subsidies to technological improvements for high level pollution control.

The most difficult case of adverse spillover from industrial activity is where pollution spreads beyond national boundaries. Many potential remedies are available in international laws, organizations, agreements and cooperation, not only to avoid environmental imperialism, but to achieve mutual international benefits (O.E.C.D., 1972). Though some encouraging international agreement on fisheries resource management have been achieved, many problems make inter-national environmental management more intractible than intra-national environmental management: different languages, enforcement authority, differing national value systems and culture all lead to divergent views on damage functions and intergenerational discount rates. However, despite this the formation of international environmental management agencies with enough power to apply depletion charges to oceanic resources and to impose emission charges on wastes flowing across national boundaries and into international air and water, offers several attractions. Self-generated revenues can be used to support monitoring, enforcement and investment in environmental protection which would not otherwise be undertaken because of the public goods problem.

A modest proposal

Because of economic pressures to minimize internal costs of production, meet production quotas, maximize profits and to export damaging wastes, industrial planners currently have strong positive incentives to locate facilities where air and water currents transfer wastes outside national boundaries. In many cases, altruism or a long-run view of global environmental responsibility imposes restraints, but these factors cannot always withstand the growing pressures of large-scale technology and waste generation, and are weakened proportionally as the beneficiaries of the sacrifices are perceived to be more distant in time and space.

Though many crucial world problems of environment and energy can be solved, or at least mitigated by improved industrial design, some quite intractible problems remain to be solved at higher political and philosophical levels. Solution of complex human problems of population growth, the widespread belief in material progress as the vehicle for human welfare, the drive for industrial parity by developing nations, the value to be attached to the claims of future generations, and above all, the fearful problem of international military security and rivalry will require wisdom, generosity and insight which are to be sought not exclusively in social sciences, but at the highest levels of human statesmanship and aspirations.

Improved industrial planning can do little to address such ultimate problems of man's tenure on earth as population growth, military rivalry, or interspatial and inter-generational justice.

However, even the modest innovation proposed here for improved global industrial environmental management, in the form of an international body of experts to levy emission charges on harmful pollutants flowing across national boundaries, could provide an initial step towards broader international environmental protection, especially if that body could be largely self-financing, non-political and scientifically objective. The functions of a global agency need not extend farther than monitoring, conducting research, publishing recommendations and collecting emission charges on scientifically-agreed dangerous emissions. The power to tax at very high rates for very dangerous substances, such as plutonium, could approach the power to limit emissions of some substances altogether. Progressive taxation of international emissions hazardous to world population would have the advantage of providing strong incentives not otherwise available for controlling pollution. It would also encourage financially the development of pollution-reducing technology while discouraging consumption of high pollution goods and services. Research and monitoring would be necessary to identify the damage and treatment cost functions needed for setting optimal emission charges, could offer early warning of environmental catastrophe and provide a forum for international discussion and education concerning the environmental integrity of the earth. Initial experience in international scientific measurement and research on conventional industrial pollutants might demonstrate the desirability and wisdom of monitoring and reducing the international environmental damage from the potentially most hazardous and irreversible of all human functions: military preparation and activity.

References

Ayres, R. U. and Kneese, A. V. (1969) 'Production, consumption and externalities', *American Economic Review*, LIX (3), pp. 282–97.

Beyers, W. B. and Krumme, G. (1974) 'Multiple products, residuals and location theory', Chapter 3 in: F. E. I. Hamilton, ed., *Spatial Perspectives on Industrial Organization & Decision-Making*, Wiley, London.

Cumberland, J. H. (1972) 'Establishment of international standards – some economic and related aspects', *Problems in Transfrontier Pollution*, Organization for Economic Cooperation and Development, Paris, pp. 287–314.

Cumberland, J. H. (1973) *Regional Development Experiences and Prospects in the United States of America*, Mouton, Paris, pp. 142–3.

Cumberland, J. H. (1974) *Economic Analysis in the Evaluation and Management of Estuaries*, prepared for the United States Environmental Protection Agency Report to Congress on Estuaries.

Georgescu-Roegen, N. (1975) 'Energy and economic myths', *Southern Economic Review*, 6 (3), pp. 347–81.

Kneese, A. V. and Bower, B. T., eds. (1968) 'Water quality management in the Ruhr: a case study of the Genossenschaften', Ch. 12, in: *Managing Water Quality: Economics, Technology Institutions*, Resources For The Future, Inc., Johns Hopkins Press, Baltimore.

Meadows, D. H. et al. (1972) *The Limits to Growth*, Universe Books, New York.

Murata, K. (1978) 'The limits of regional agglomeration and social cost', Ch. 5 in: F. E. I. Hamilton, ed., *Contemporary Industrialization: Spatial Analysis & Regional Development*, Longman, London.

Organization for Economic Cooperation and Development (O.E.C.D.) (1972) *Problems in Transfrontier Pollution*, Working Document, Environment Directorate, Paris.

Chapter 2

North Sea oil and gas resources: their implications for the location of industry in Western Europe

Peter R. Odell

The spatial interrelationships that evolved in the past between coal-producing areas and the location of industry produced many of the major industrial regions of Western Europe. How and why that symbiotic relationship had been broken down has been widely discussed, yet it has created the present difficulty 'even in stating an hypothesis on the spatial relationships of energy availability and industrial development' (Odell, 1974). Yet one can isolate some of the main elements required in such a hypothesis. These would include (1) attention to the *inertia* in location decisions that generates a continuing geographical relationship between certain industries and their traditional coalfield locations in Western Europe; (2) the inability of coalfield areas to attract new kinds of economic activities by virtue of their having certain characteristics repellent to modern industry; and (3) the idea that some opportunities for industrial growth poles emerge out of the development of locally-concentrated production of energy resources other than coal.

Here only the third element is examined; in the geographical context of Western Europe and in the historical context of a revolutionized outlook for the role of energy in the continent resulting from events in the world of oil power since 1973 (Odell, 1975a). Detailed description and analysis of this revolutionary change is not appropriate here. The change, however, is important for understanding the interrelationship of energy and industrial location since it has undermined much of last two decades' indifference to questions of the supply and price of energy. Indeed, industrial decisions since 1955 were based on the then valid assumption that energy input costs would continue to fall in real terms, a trend which is illustrated in Fig. 2.1. The revolution has also so reduced the likely rate of growth in the demand for energy that the infrastructure capacity to process and to handle the energy that was expected to be demanded through the rest of the 1970s and the early 1980s will not now be needed. This is especially important regarding infrastructure that has been built, projected or planned to deal with oil to be imported in increasing quantities from other parts of the world. Much of this will not now be needed and so seems likely to cause problems in locations where there was, or was planned to be, a heavy concentration of it. Table 2.1 illustrates the magnitude of the possible change in energy demand in Western Europe in the remainder of the twentieth century as the revolution in the world oil power continues to become an increasingly severe constraint on economic development in Western Europe (Odell, 1975b).

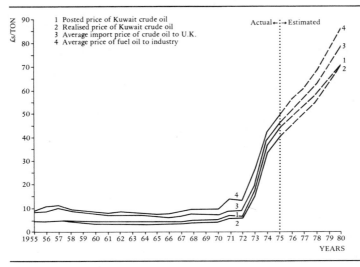

Fig. 2.1 The price of oil 1955–75 and estimates 1975–80 on the assumption that the O.P.E.C. cartel is maintained.

An energy-rich Western Europe

In an environment of changed prospects for energy demand the idea of new areas of concentrated and large-scale energy production in Western Europe is somewhat embarrassing: in organizational and in geographical terms it implies changes in the energy system which will be uncomfortable for the established entities. Yet it is even more surprising in view of the hitherto firmly held 'belief' that Western Europe is an energy-poor continent! Such a belief was never valid in a physical sense – given the continued potential availability of coal resources which remain more than enough to satisfy needs for centuries; but coal which could not be produced competitively in a period of freely-traded cheap energy from other continents. The belief is now, however, also no longer true in an economic sense for indigenous oil and natural gas resources have been proven, or can be reasonably hypothesized as being discoverable and producible in the relatively short-term future, at supply-prices which are far below the price of oil imported from the member countries of the Organization of Petroleum Exporting Countries (O.P.E.C.). Since this oligopolistically-determined price of internationally-traded oil also determines the price of all other possible energy imports (coal, liquified natural gas, even uranium), the long-term supply price of much indigenous oil and gas is also below that of other alternatives.

There are two elements involved in decisions to produce – or not to produce – indigenous oil and gas: (1) the resource base and (2) politics and institutional behaviour which influence production schedules.

How much oil and natural gas can be produced in total from the North Sea basin remains a matter for dispute: the range of estimates extend from a low of 40–45×10^9 barrels of oil and 7×10^{12} cubic metres of gas (roughly the equivalent of another 40×10^9 barrels of oil) to a high some three times greater for both oil and for natural gas. However, given the increasingly wide recognition that the North Sea basin is a major hydrocarbon province by world standards, the

Table 2.1 Conventional and and alternative views on Europe's energy supply, 1975–2000

| | 1975 | | 1980 estimates | | | | 1985 estimates | | | | 2000 estimates | | | |
| | Expected approximate use | | Conventional | | Alternative | | Conventional | | Alternative | | Conventional | | Alternative | |
	mmtce†	%	mmtce	%	mmtce	%	mmtce	%	mmtce	%	mmtce	%	mmtce	%
Total energy	1580	100	2255	100	1850	100	2870	100	2200	100	5425	100	3300	100
Oil – total	920	59	1500	66	785	42	1845	64	800	36			1350	41
Indigenous	30	2	50	2	380	20	195	7	600	27			1100	33
Imported	890	57	1450	64	405	22	1650	57	200	9			250	8
Gas – total	215	13	265	12	575	31	385	14	750	34			1050	32
Indigenous	200	12	215	10	500	27	300	11	600	27	not available		800	24
Imported	15	1	50	2	75	4	85	3	150	7			250	8
Coal – total	400	26	280	12	310	17	310	11	350	16			500	15
Indigenous	360	23	205	9	230	12	220	8	250	11			400	12
Imported	40	3	73	3	80	5	90	3	100	5			100	3
Primary electricity	45	3	210	10	180	10	330	12	300	14			400	12
Total indigenous	635	40	680	31	1290	69	1045	37	1750	80			2700	81
Total imported	945	60	1575	69	560	31	1825	63	450	20			600	19

Sources: O.E.C.D., E.E.C. and various national estimates prior to the oil crisis of future energy supply patterns form the basis of the conventional estimates. The alternative estimates are the author's own – March 1974.

† million metric tons coal equivalent

‡ Columns do not necessarily add to 100 because of 'rounding'

differences between the estimates of its potential resource base have been narrowing and now much of the gap that remains reflects contrasting views over the percentage of technically-recoverable oil and gas which can be extracted in various politico-economic environments.

Ultimately recoverable reserves figures (roughly 50×10^9 barrels) declared by the oil companies take their expectations of costs, prices and taxes into account. On the other hand, a simulation model of the potential availability of oil† assumed that all possible oil-bearing structures (as revealed by seismic work) would be tested – so implying a high-cost complete exploration process – and that all oil discovered and *technically* recoverable would be recovered irrespective of the increasing marginal cost curve for such an intense exploitation effort. With these assumptions the model indicated a mean ultimate resource base of 109×10^9 barrels of oil.

These different interpretations of the availability of recoverable oil are, however, of greater concern to the medium to longer term outlook. Governmental and company policy decisions which are taken in recognition of either the opportunities or the uncertainties offered by the possibility for energy resource developments in the North Sea will be more important in determining the rate of exploration – and hence the discovery of new reserves – than in determining the actual rate of production of oil and gas in the next five to ten years. For this shorter period the main determinant of production is the exploration success so far achieved – though, of course, short-term economic and political factors do influence the amounts and rates of production of already discovered oil and gas.‡ It is in relation to the oil and gas production patterns that have been established, or those that will be established over the next few years, that changes in industrial location and regional development patterns in western Europe are being initiated – so generating possibilities for a longer term restructuring of the continent's economic geography.

North Sea basin oil and gas and industrial development

Figure 2.2 describes the developments to the end of 1976 in the North Sea oil province. It is also useful in indicating the geography of possible changes, both positive and negative and direct and indirect, in West European industrial structures arising out of future oil and gas production patterns. The southern basin largely produces gas: most of the larger fields lie offshore between England and the Netherlands and their exploitation necessitates, as shown in Fig. 2.3, only relatively short-distance pipelines to close or convenient landfalls. This already well-developed system of off-shore energy production and transport (which will, on full development, ultimately be capable of producing the annual equivalent of more than 100 million tons of coal) seems unlikely, however, to lead to clearly distinguishable industrial growth zones – for two reasons. Firstly, the landfalls of the

† This model was developed in the Economisch-Geografisch Instituut, Erasmus Universiteit, Rotterdam (Odell and Rosing, 1975).

‡ Variability in the degree to which discovered oil is recovered depends upon costs, prices and tax rates in relation to the three-dimensional spatial structure of a field. This has been investigated by the Economic Geography Institute in Rotterdam and the first results indicate that current economic conditions are significantly depressing the quantities of oil which the companies will be able to recover on a commercial basis from any given field (Odell and Rosing, 1976).

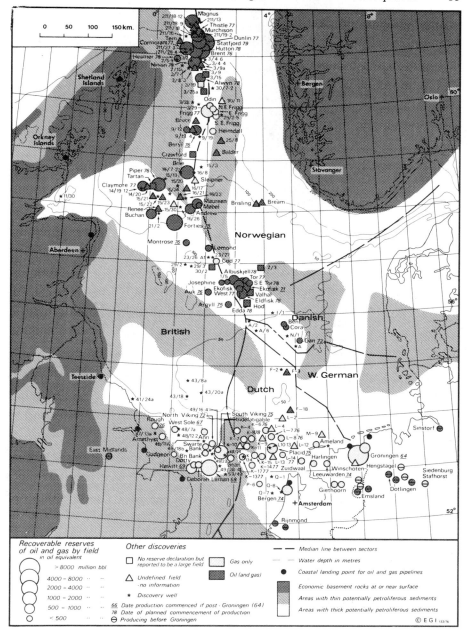

Fig. 2.2   Oil and gas fields and discoveries in the North Sea oil province to December 1976.

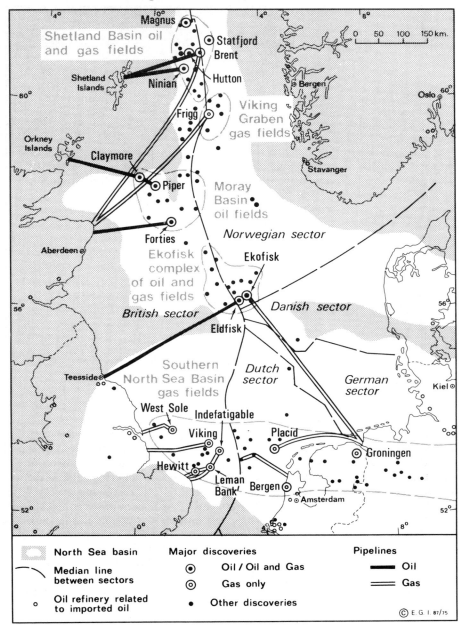

Fig. 2.3   North Sea oil and gas pipelines in operation or under construction, December 1976.

short sea-to-shore pipelines are relatively close to long-standing industrial areas (such as Tees-side, London, the English Midlands and Randstad) to which the gas can be cheaply transported. Secondly, in both the UK and the Netherlands gas has to be delivered to nationalized gas companies (the Gas Corporation and Gasunie, respectively) which, as a matter of principle, relate prices to types of users rather than to the location of customers. Thus, these institutions eliminate, by the process of the 'geographical averaging' of the price, any industrial location pull to the points of initial entry of the energy (Odell, 1966). Nevertheless, one significant industrial development has emerged from these southern North Sea basin gas resources. This arises from the development of the massive Groningen gasfield with resources of up to 2500×10^9 cubic metres of gas and a production potential of over 100×10^9 cubic metres per year – the equivalent of about 105 million tons of coal per year – so making it the largest single energy-producing location in Western Europe (Odell, 1969).

Though energy-intensive industry is economically attractive at resource locations given a spatially variable gas pricing policy which takes transport and distribution costs into account, this did not apply at the Groningen field for reasons outlined above. Instead, industrialization of the Ems estuary adjacent to the Groningen field has arisen essentially from Dutch governmental intervention in spatial pricing policy for gas. In order to encourage the dispersal of heavy industry from the Rotterdam region (where it has been concentrated since 1950), types of industry new to the Netherlands were given access to their gas supplies at prices 5 per cent below the regular price on condition that they located in Groningen, or in another specified province. The result has been the establishment of metal-processing (notably aluminium smelting) and various chemical industries and they collectively constitute an industrial growth pole of significant dimensions in the Dutch economy. Its development potential has also, moreover, been enhanced by the decision, which had to be taken for political reasons, that the province of Groningen should benefit from above-normal government expenditure on physical infrastructure projects in the region, in recognition of the increasing importance of revenues from gas production in the central government's finances. Indirectly, therefore, Groningen is being made *relatively* more attractive, compared with other locations in the Netherlands, for other-than-energy-intensive industries than would have been the case in the absence of gas exploitation in the Province.

Energy-based industrialization in Groningen is thus significant in the context of the geography of the Dutch industrial structure and the experience in this case seems to indicate clearly the processes which will be at work in determining industrial location vis-à-vis north North Sea oil exploitation. Figures 2.2 and 2.3 depict the spatial pattern of oil-finds, production plans and the transport system as developed and projected at the end of 1976. The greatest regional oil impact will be in north-east England, Scotland and the Orkney and Shetland Islands. To date no oil-related activities have emerged elsewhere, apart from supply bases at Stavanger and Bergen in Norway and platform-construction facilities at several coastal sites in north-western Europe generally. By the early 1980s there may be an oil line direct from the Statfjord field (the largest so far discovered in the North Sea) to Norway and another to mainland Denmark but both these possible developments will, however, produce essentially the same associated industrial and related activities as in areas of the UK to which oil is already flowing, and for the same reasons.

By the early 1980s Tees-side will handle up to 100 million tons, Sullum Voe (Shetland) over 150 million tons (to make it Europe's largest crude-oil terminal by far) and the Orkneys and Cruden Bay well over 50 million tons of oil per year each. Given that (*a*) oil from the North Sea will largely substitute oil which has hitherto flowed to Western Europe from distant producing areas to feed individual company's refining and distributing systems built up over the last twenty five years (Fig. 2.4 shows the 'Shell system' as it has been developed in Western Europe); and (*b*) the overall demand for oil now seems unlikely to increase very quickly (see Table 2.1), then the optimal economic behaviour of most producers would be to channel North Sea crude oil to their pre-existing refineries – though suitably re-equipped to handle the different type of crude oil involved (Odell, 1976). Thus Shell, for example, would take oil from its share of the Brent, Cormorant and other fields, via the Sullum Voe terminal, to its refineries in Rotterdam, Scandinavia, England, West Germany and France, where capacity is more than adequate for Shell's expected share of the limited growth of oil demand to 1985 (Fig. 2.4). Only oil companies which have found North Sea crude oil and which have not previously had refining or distributing facilities in Western Europe will have an immediate and economically justified motive for considering refining and associated development at the terminals of the off-shore pipelines – that is, if they choose to deliver North Sea oil as refined products to European and other destinations rather than to ship their crude oil to mainland and refining locations. (Over such relatively short distances mammoth tankers do not offer any scale economies and thus there are few transport cost savings in shipping crude rather than oil products: see McGill, 1975.) Such necessary refinary decisions are thus likely to be amongst the earlier processing industry developments which will be related geographically to North Sea oil.

However, oil companies with pre-existing refineries in other West European locations seem unlikely to be able to choose patterns of development which are optimal for their own systems because they will be subjected to pressures and restraints obliging them to invest in new refining and petro-chemicals facilities at points in space politically related to their North Sea oil production. The broad lines of such pressure are already very evident, for both Britain and Norway have insisted on North Sea operations by international oil companies being made recognizably separate from the companies' other operations. The objective of this separation so far as been to enable governments to levy appropriate rates of tax on all profits arising from the North Sea producing operations as such, but the powers taken could also be applied to the oil itself and to the facilities required to handle it. Moreover, both British and Norwegian governments have indicated that they expect their North Sea oil to be used to generate investment and jobs in refining, petro-chemicals and associated activities – a process already under way at the new Mongstad refining and petro-chemicals complex in western Norway. (Norwegian oil produced from the Ekofisk group of fields and piped to Tees-side in England will be held in bond there, prior to being transported back across the North Sea by tanker to Mongstad for processing.) This same process will be unavoidable in Britain given a governmental policy which reserves the right to require between 66 and 75 per cent of all British oil to be refined in the UK. Moreover, both Norway and Britain have created state oil companies – Statoil and B.N.O.C., respectively – with immediate access to North Sea oil, by virtue of the interests they have been given in discovered fields, and with rights and responsibilities for 'downstream' operations which must or will, of course, be located at home.

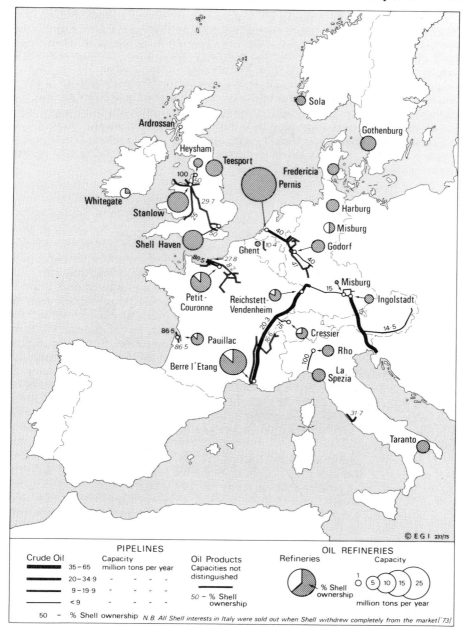

Fig. 2.4   Shell Petroleum's refining and distribution system in Western Europe.

Thus, political and institutional factors – and some economic factors in the case of oil companies without previous processing facilities in Western Europe – constitute a powerful motive for industrial development in locations around the northern North Sea where, before the discovery of oil, little refining and pipeline capacity had been located (Fig. 2.5). Yet refining locations which did develop in the period of oil industry expansion in Western Europe from 1948 to 1974 often became highly developed, capital-intensive industrial centres. Rotterdam was the leading example (Fig. 2.6). In light of the increasing relative importance of North Sea oil in the now near-stagnating oil industry of the continent, the likelihood of any further developments at these existing locations seems remote. Indeed, there may even have to be retrenchment in the event of new capacity being built at new locations related to North Sea oil production.

The longer term issues

The important open question for the longer term is the degree to which one, or more, of these new locations can progress towards a complex and relatively diversified centre of industrial activities. Though the new locations are relatively remote from market centres in Western Europe and generally have inadequate or outdated infrastructures (compared with regions which have enjoyed post-war oil-based development), they will quickly become the relatively most wealthy areas of Western Europe in both individual incomes, as a result of local competition for scarce resources, particularly labour, and in terms of the wealth of local authorities which are negotiating special royalty arrangements with oil-producing companies for the use of local facilities. For example, the Shetland Islands, with fewer than 20,000 people, are certain of oil industry royalties of £76 million as payment for Sullom Voe terminal (*The Observer*, 1975). Norway, as a result of increased revenues from the production of oil and gas (over 90 per cent of which will be exported), will be the wealthiest country in Western Europe on a per capita income basis by 1980. Forecasts such as these lie behind the pressures for Scottish independence.

If, as seems increasingly likely, Europe decides, or is forced, to rely on North Sea oil because of deteriorating or more expensive supplies of O.P.E.C. oil, then oil wealth will bring power to the northerly parts of Western Europe, including the power to 'buy' industrial activities which are either oil-related or energy-intensive. This appears to be the only practical alternative to having such developments located outside Western Europe altogether in oil-producing States seeking to diversify their economies away from simple dependence on revenues earned from crude oil exports and hence insisting on 'downstream' and energy-intensive industries being located at home – as is planned in Saudi Arabia, Kuwait and in more populous O.P.E.C. countries like Venezuela and Iran. Development plans in all oil-exporting countries are very ambitious and require investment of their very substantial oil revenues in the construction of oil refineries, petro-chemical facilities, steel plants and aluminium smelters (Stauffer, 1976).

Conclusion

The middle 1970s marked a period in which largely specious original 'Club-of-Rome'-type arguments on resources' scarcity combined with much more relevant

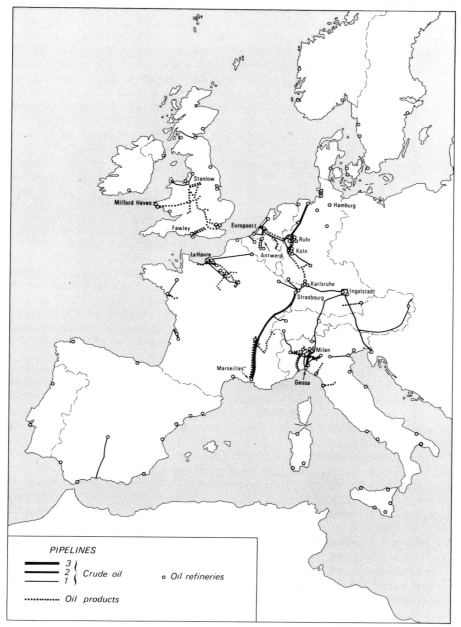

Fig. 2.5   Refinery location and crude oil/oil products pipelines in Western Europe by 1976.

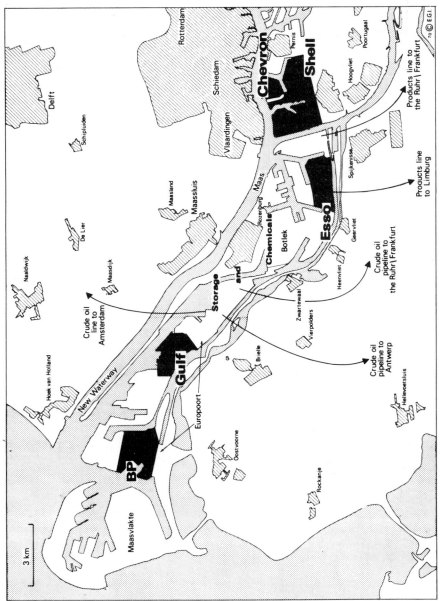

Fig. 2.6 Rotterdam's oil-based industrial complex.

and powerful political and economic forces which effectively constrained energy flows to consuming areas. The traditional industrial centres in Western Europe have constituted the world's single more important region of energy consumption throughout the coal and imported-oil eras of the last 150 years. Further decisions to locate more industry in those regions must now face a high degree of uncertainty. When this changed outlook is seen in conjunction with the powerful political and institutional forces in Western Europe which are potentially available for securing industrial location decisions geographically close to North Sea oil and gas resources, then the likelihood of a significant, trend-breaking shift in the location of industrial activities in Western Europe appears to be a hypothesis which is worth analysis. Though many other factors are involved in the processes at work in creating shifts of location, a fundamental and essential factor in a period of high price and uncertainty over availability is that of the geography of energy supply – suggesting a return to a role for the energy component in industrial decision-taking as important as that which pervaded such decisions in the days of water power and the early exploitation of the readily available coal resources of Western Europe.

References

McGill, J., ed. (1975) *Investing in Scotland*, Collins, Glasgow, Ch. 3.

Odell, P. R. (1966) 'What will gas do to the east coast?', *New Society*, May.

Odell, P. R. (1969), *Natural Gas in Western Europe: A Case Study in the Economic Geography of Resources*, E. F. Bohn, Haarlem, Netherlands.

Odell, P. R. (1974 'Energy resources and regional development in Western Europe', in: *Papers of the I.G.U. Regional Conference*, Budapest, 1971.

Odell, P. R. (1975a) *Oil and World Power: The Background to the Oil Crisis*, Penguin, London, 4th edition.

Odell, P. R. (1975b) *The Western European Energy Economy: Challenges and Opportunities* (Stamp Memorial Lecture), Athlone Press, London.

Odell, P. R. (1976) 'The E.E.C. energy market: structure and integration', in: R. Lee and P. Ogden, eds., *Spatial Perspectives on Integration in the E.E.C.*, Saxon House/D. C. Heath, London.

Odell, P. R. and Rosing, K. E. (1975) *The North Sea Oil Province: an Attempt to Simulate its Exploration and Exploitation, 1969–2029*, Kogan Page, London.

Odell, P. R. and Rosing, K. E. (1976) *The Optimal Development of North Sea Oil Fields*, Kogan Page, London.

'Shetlanders match up to the oil moguls', *The Observer*, 28 December 1975.

Stauffer, T. (1976) 'Energy-intensive industrialization in the Arabian/Persian Gulf: a new Ruhr without water', *Energy Policy*, forthcoming.

Chapter 3

Multinational enterprise and the European Economic Community

F. E. Ian Hamilton

Not all multinational corporations are large: some are small in the international corporate league tables in fixed assets, employment or sales turnover, yet control world-wide markets through high product specialization. Nevertheless, most business transactions and their spatial consequences originate in larger multinationals whether these are defined narrowly by their industrial (extractive and manufacturing) action space (Vernon, 1973) or widely by their commercial action space (Labasse, 1975), so including corporations producing in only one country but selling world-wide. Real evidence for measuring the size and importance of multinational corporations in the European Economic Community (E.E.C.) is fragmentary. This underlines the critical need for the Community to introduce legislation to ensure a full information supply regarding the activities of both western European and foreign corporate (or foreign State-owned) organizations within the Market. Data must be sought on the shares of multinational corporations in investment, employment, wage-bills, value-added and markets within the Community since 1958 and in its nine constituent nations. Even more useful in shaping policy towards foreign enterprise would be full exposure of the flows of materials, services, information and profits that they generate between locations, regions and nations.

What information does exist suggests that the importance of multinational corporations varies significantly both between industrial sectors and between member countries. They are most prominent in 'newer' industries, a factor related to the higher thresholds for achieving scale economies in manufacture existing since the initiation of their product cycles as compared with those of earlier products and industries of the 'industrial revolution'. Such 'new' industries require large-scale investment, use advanced technology and high skill. Either they depend upon bulk inputs of (often imported) materials like oil-refining, petrochemicals, synthetic fibres and non-ferrous metallurgy industries, or they supply final consumer, 'industrial' or 'business' markets with sophisticated products which require frequent, widespread advertising and after-sales servicing, like vehicles and aircraft, electrical and electronics manufactures, film-processing (Precheur, 1976). Large-scale, global and intricate backward and forward linkages from secondary into primary, tertiary and quaternary activities characterize such industries as means of reducing uncertainties both in supply and demand.

'Lead firms' in these industries operate from an expanding domestic market threshold to penetrate overseas economies progressively: (1) by transfer of products, i.e. shipments of manufactures from the 'home' to 'overseas' markets; (2) by subsequent transfer of technology and investment in branch plant production operations overseas; (3) by creating local technology and innovation of new products overseas, a situation which implies a wider range of 'branch' manufacturing activities, research, development and services (O.E.C.D., 1969). A major factor in extending US multinational control in the critical second stage of production-innovation in overseas markets has been that lead firms bring in components or service suppliers of American nationality with which they are linked 'at home' – so penetrating the European market through what, in Schumpeterian terms, are 'clusters of sectors' (Schumpeter, 1939), rather than becoming dependent upon local firms.† This trend is reinforced when oligopolistic 'control' motivates other firms to 'follow the leader' into overseas markets.

In 1970 US corporate manufacturing investment in the nine E.E.C. countries exceeded $14 500 million, the greatest concentration of foreign-owned industrial activity anywhere outside North America (United States *Survey of Current Business*, 1971). It represents a substantial absolute and relative increase from 1964 when US firms produced 5.67 per cent of all European manufactures sold (Hufbauer & Adler, 1968). Figures in 1970 varied markedly among industries, from 1 per cent of paper products sales to 13 per cent of rubber and transport equipment. There are also large national variations within the E.E.C. in the degree of American corporate penetration. Greatest influence by far occurs in UK production with $127 per capita US manufacturing investment in 1970 followed, significantly, by Benelux (Belgium $75 per capita, Netherlands $67), West Germany ($42) and France ($37) and trailing far behind, Italy ($14).

This order remains, though shifts in US investment since 1970 have favoured Belgium, Netherlands and West Germany at the expense of the UK especially and also of France and Italy (Young & Hood, 1976). In 1973, US firms employed 18 per cent of all persons in British manufacturing. Since 1964 when American firms accounted for 10 per cent of UK sales of manufactures (Vernon, 1973) US firms have acquired many British firms and as some export a significant proportion of their output from the UK they do not dominate UK *sales* to the extent they do UK *production*.

The situation varies greatly among industries, too. One American firm (International Business Machines: I.B.M.) controls two-thirds of the E.E.C. market in electronic computers *except* in Britain where domestic firms retain more than half of sales. The 'big three' US vehicle manufacturers (Chrysler, Ford and General Motors) collectively accounted for 26.6 per cent (1 775 000) of total E.E.C. car sales (6 672 000) in 1975, but national figures vary from 38 per cent in the UK and 34.5 per cent in West Germany to only 10.7 per cent in Italy.

Far more research is needed to facilitate accurate conclusions regarding intersectoral balance in the E.E.C. as a whole and in its constituent countries and regions as between multinational corporations owned by United States, West European national and other foreign interests. This need becomes greater when viewed against current trends. Not only has American influence grown, Japanese corporations, though starting late and still small, are expanding rapidly. By 1974 one-quarter of all Japanese overseas investment was located in the E.E.C. Coming at a time of increased sensitivity to multinational enterprise, late entry has illicited Japanese adoption of a three-fold 'behaviour code' involving 'resource diplomacy', 'orderly marketing' and expansion of technologically advanced production (Ballon, 1973). Another new form of multinational enterprise is appearing in the

† A classic case is the spread of American 'rent-a-car' firms throughout Europe with clear linkage to US 'fleet car' suppliers; Avis–Chrysler; Budget–General Motors; and Hertz–Ford.

establishment of joint companies by State-owned enterprises from Eastern Europe with West European firms to derive benefits of advanced technology, established credit marketing outlets, of access to profits in hard currency in return for cheaper production. Ability to use West European know-how and experience is crucial to East European and Soviet managers who have little practical knowledge of the workings of a capitalist system alien to them (Wickham, 1973). Significantly, like American and other multinational firms, these socialist enterprises recruit local managerial expertise.

Why Europe?

Why has Western Europe been so attractive to foreign multinational enterprise? Rapid growth of an affluent market, an abundant and cheaper (than American) supply of labour with good skill qualities and significant transport cost savings from production in Europe compared with transhipment of products from the USA are powerful reasons (Blackbourn, 1974), but not enough. First, since the 1870s US and latterly Japanese firms have penetrated Europe by initiating new product cycles or by more successful application of European inventions. Second, short- and long-term consequences of the Second World War induced more American corporations into Europe directly or indirectly through information feedback: Marshall Aid, N.A.T.O. rearmament and US troop occupation of West Germany.

Third, very important has been entry by many US firms into Europe as an oligopolistic response to a perceived competition threat from European manufacturers (Wilkins, 1970). Large and expanding markets in Europe provide thresholds for growth overseas by European corporations which could threaten the stability and profitability of American corporations 'at home' as well as overseas: such threats could be checked only by significant American penetration of the Europeans' home market. In theory, this can work both ways. In practice American corporate expansion of 'industrial' and 'commercial' space alike into Europe is great in scale and in relative importance. By contrast, European penetration of the US market is considerable commercially but is very limited in US-located subsidiaries of European firms producing manufactures: in 1972 American investment in industry in Europe was nearly four times greater than European (combined E.E.C. and E.F.T.A.) investment in manufacturing located in the USA (Hellman, 1973).

The explanations lie in the contrasting geographical, historical and politico-economic environments of the United States and the European Common Market. The US became a transcontinental political and economic union ninety years before the signing of the Treaty of Rome: from 1869 when, following *political* union, the first railway linked east and west coasts. Not only did this permit American enterprise to exploit fully the commercial advantages and scale economies of huge, diversified natural resources and of the revolutionary technologies evolved in those decades, but it generated rapid, large-scale functional and spatial concentration of finance and management unimpeded by world events, creating a 'transcontinental' business mentality. Wide spatial separation of major resources, cities and markets, and adjacency to the easily-penetrated expanding Canadian economy all induced mental thresholds for thinking 'intercontinental' once imported resources and markets overseas became a necessary ingredient to sustain business activity at home, especially during and after the Second World War.

By contrast, political and national fragmentation of Europe, deepened by two world wars 'on the ground', has had a myriad of negative impacts on West European business. Differences in national outlook, language, conscience and military involvement on opposing sides, have nurtured 'national' and more 'inward looking' corporate policies, discouraging transactional manufacturing *within* Europe (though not 'the Empire'), even transnational associations of firms. Tariffs, limiting markets to nations a fraction of US size, have further stunted corporate growth. In any leading industry, many more firms serve the West European than serve the American market. In 1958 five US firms supplied the larger American market while twenty-eight firms (twenty-four of them European) supplied the much smaller aggregate Western European market with cars and trucks (Law, 1974). That by 1974 the number active in Western Europe had decreased to thirteen (three American) is a measure of the impact of economic union upon industrial organization. Yet, except for Leyland and Volkswagen greatest integration in the E.E.C. vehicle industry has been achieved by American rather than by European firms.

Spatial behaviour in the E.E.C.

Interest is growing rapidly in the spatial functioning and dynamics of multinational manufacturing activity in the E.E.C. Studies have focused upon (1) the behaviour of US firms in the Market (Blackbourn, 1974; Dunning, 1973; European Economic Community, 1969); (2) the pattern of foreign industrial investment in specific countries (De Smit, 1966; Dunning, 1958, Forsyth, 1972; Irish Development Authority, 1970; and (3) selected European corporations (Battiau, 1973; Beaud, Danjou & David, 1975; Derrieux-Cecconi, 1973; Gorgé, 1975; Jansen, 1972; Krumme, 1970; Wolfowski, 1972). But research is still very meagre and yet to combine all three approaches in a spatial analysis through time. The ensuing tentative observations are thus open to close scrutiny, critique and verification.

Aggregate patterns

Broadly, multinational industrial firms are more localized than aggregate manufacturing and facilities of US firms are more concentrated spatially than those of their European multinational counterparts. Fewer aggregate facilities and their larger average scale partly explain why multinational units are less dispersed than industry in general. Most tend to be located in or near major cities and ports offering cheapest, easiest or quickest connections with *international* supplies of inputs and information, *international* marketing outlets for products and for *international* executive personnel contacts. Though a significant proportion of larger 'national' or smaller 'regional' and 'local' firms is similarly located to process imports or to gain agglomeration economies, much 'European' industry is dispersed among the medium- and small-sized towns of the continent; or it is localized in old industrial areas relatively unattractive to new multinational enterprise because of their poor 'built environments': pollution, declining coal or textile industries and their tendency to localize growth in heavy industries which, for reasons of national need or security, are under 'national' corporate or State ownership.

Noticeable differences occur between the spatial distribution of American and of European multinational firms. Tendencies are very strong for US firms to develop in or near major metropolitan, port or regional centres – the major areas of growth: a northwestern group comprising the London and Paris regions, the Ghent–Antwerp–Liege triangle and Randstad Holland, and, to the east, an arc of favoured city regions from Hamburg through the Ruhr, Rhineland and south German cities to Munich. Outliers are Milan, Rome and West Berlin. Of course, many European multinationals show a similar aggregate distribution, but many have offices and key production facilities in second- or third-order provincial, subregional or industrial towns which are far less favoured, not considered, or even avoided by US firms. Classic examples are the 'company towns' such as Billingham (I.C.I.), Clermont-Ferrand (Michelin), Eindhoven (Philips) and Wolfsburg (Volkswagen), but so, too, are larger cities like Birmingham (Cadbury-Schweppes, Leyland, Lucas), Lyon, Toulouse and Turin. Greater 'eccentricity' in the spatial pattern of European multinationals is explained by their successful survival and growth in the more 'random' locations of their 'founding fathers' (Hamilton, 1974, pp. 6–13).

European 'national' versus American 'transnational' corporate expansion paths

Yet wider dispersion of European corporate functions also clearly expresses their greater average longevity, aggregate scale and complexity *in Europe*. Attention must thus focus upon the dynamics of their spatial expansion paths. Each E.E.C. country is the home and 'core' of varied numbers, scales and types of 'autochtonous' multinational corporations – though sometimes two States form the joint home of 'allochtonous' corporations (Jansen, 1972) like the UK and the Netherlands do for Royal Dutch Shell and Unilever. By contrast, all E.E.C. countries lie in the 'periphery' of every US corporation. The implications are both quantitative and qualitative.

European-based multinationals have evolved, or have acquired over time, an integrated spatial functional system comprising head, divisional and regional offices, parent and branch plants, distribution and servicing units which are located variously over several or many locations and regions. Operations of American (or other non-European) corporations are commonly confined to one or a few branch plants, especially among new entrants to Europe of highly-specialized smaller firms. However, such operations do also span the entire range up to those of the largest US firms long active in Europe (like Eastman-Kodak, Ford, General Electric, General Motors, I.B.M., ITT, Monsanto, Singer, Westinghouse, and oil companies like Continental, Gulf, Mobil, Phillips, Standard Oil and Texaco). These have developed fairly autonomous European sub-systems comprising many vertically and horizontally-linked facilities subordinate in strategy to the US system but autonomous in operation by virtue of the large scale of the European market, the high costs of supply from the USA, or the need to import materials (like oil) from other world regions.

The spatial–functional structures of the largest American and European multinationals merit greater study, yet it is this which apparently differentiates the two types most sharply. The industrial action space of most European firms is dominantly 'national' (Hanappe, 1974). Except for a few assembly and components-manufacturing plants, the overwhelming proportion of Leyland activity and employment is in the UK; Citroen, Peugeot and Renault in France; Volkswagen, Mercedes and B.M.W. in West Germany; and Fiat, Alfa Romeo and Lancia in Italy. Other industries may provide exceptions, especially huge chemicals firms like Bayer, B.P., Courtaulds, Hoechst, I.C.I., Pechiney-Ugine-Kuhlmann and Royal Dutch Shell which have port and estuarine installations located in most E.E.C. countries: for example, less than 10 per cent of all jobs in Unilever and Royal Dutch Shell was located in the Netherlands in 1971 while the comparable figure for Philips was 27 per cent (Jansen, 1972). Figures should be higher for 'home' jobs in firms based in larger economies like Italy, West Germany or the UK but, overall, the generalization still holds.

Large US multinationals, by contrast, have developed more truly international 'European' networks of facilities which are dispersed among E.E.C. member countries and are interdependent across national frontiers, but are usually sited near large cities. Enlargement of the E.E.C. in 1975 has intensified integration and interdependence, especially among firms like Ford, G.M. and I.B.M. Long established, they had previously expanded in a divided Europe and until the 1970s had retained essentially distinct E.F.T.A. (mainly British) and E.E.C. (mainly German or French) productive sub-systems.

These contrasts result largely from distinct geographic expansion paths, themselves reflecting different managerial perceptions of industrial and commercial action space within overall corporate objectives. Once parent sites became congested, most European firms expanded by developing new branches or by acquiring and modifying existing facilities in medium or small towns nearby, mostly within 150 km of head office. This created a spreading, yet still compact, regional industrial action space centred on a national or provincial metropolis or port; within it the 'core' of corporate administration, research, production, storage and servicing is still clustered, as with French auto industries in the Paris Basin and Massif Central, and Leyland in Midland England. Indeed, firms prefer to expand as near as possible to their main operations, as in West Germany (Law, 1974), though in the UK and Italy State regional policies have required them to expand in more distant 'development areas'.

Wide dispersion even within one nation is thus constrained by European managerial 'short distance experience', an attitude fed by national or parochial opinions but biasing perceptions of regional attributes (Labasse, 1975). Moreover, such images are often perpetuated since the firm can usually supply the European market competitively from its regional industrial action space since distances and costs of access are low and delivery frequencies can be high: 'foreign' production sub-systems within other E.E.C. member countries are not economically necessary unless bulky products (like chemicals) are involved. An exception was expansion by British and Swedish firms (e.g. Leyland, Volvo) into 'The Six' to obviate tariff barriers between the E.E.C. and E.F.T.A. and higher trans-shipment costs of supplying the larger mainland E.E.C. market 'across the water' from 'offshore' production sites.

Decisions on the location of expansion through time reflect both a continuing learning process among managements and changing external environments. Historically, most European firms expanded abroad within the politico-economic space (empires) in which their national language and laws were 'international' and their host countries' attitudes 'preferential' (dominions) or 'non-influential' (colonies). British firms expanded commerce and sometimes also production into

Canada, Australia, British areas of South-east Asia, Central America and Africa (e.g. I.C.I., Leyland) while French corporations established facilities in French North and West Africa, Madagascar and French S.E. Asia (e.g. Pechiney–Ugine–Kuhlmann). The longest German and Italian firms have vied for 'economic territory' in Latin America (e.g. Fiat in Brazil) where Spanish and Portuguese activity has been weak. European integration and 'decolonization', however, have worked in a push-pull fashion to modify the perceptions that shape corporate spatial strategy, so that even 'for directors who have become internally-minded, the scale of reasoning is constantly European, rarely international' (Labasse, 1975, p. 121).

American managements of all large and many smaller US corporations perceive industrial and commercial action space globally. They fit their European operations, though at varying levels, into a world-wide trade jigsaw. Thus, once expansion of US industrial action space into Europe has been decided, entry by establishing branch facilities is not bound by local traditions. Managements are as free as they wish to be in choosing the country and the region of operations. Their choice reflects American managerial attitudes to, and perceptions of, the comparative advantages of several, potential host countries. Though these may be coloured by 'ancestral national sentiments', undoubtedly corporate commercial and political objectives have dominated the assessment of host-country attributes. The UK loomed most favourably in such assessments until the 1960s: hence, the greater prominence of US firms there. Common language and 'heritage' were major assets in initial American entry into Europe via Britain, though the strength of German cultural ties should not be underestimated. Yet Britain offered the political stability and insularity from upheaval which Germany did not until the 1960s. Economically, the UK was (and is) a leading European market, but offering additional advantages of greatest geographic and cultural 'proximity' to America, a great shipping tradition, a high reputation in export markets and access – via UK subsidiaries – to British Commonwealth markets.

Initial operations in Britain were also favoured by the long-term strategy of the US firm to progress from branch plant production or assembly towards the formation of a semi- or fully-autonomous European functional sub-system. Operations in Britain, giving trade contact with mainland Europe, offered American management learning experience as a springboard for expanding manufacturing into the more diversified consumer, cultural, legal, linguistic and political environments of mainland E.E.C. (and non-E.E.C.) countries. An inevitable result of this process is the relative decline in the British share of American activity in Europe. Prior to formation of the E.E.C. the UK produced 57 per cent of all sales in Europe by American subsidiaries: by 1968 this was down to 41 per cent and today is little more than 25 per cent. Similarly, while the percentage of US overseas investment located in Britain rose from 7.8 in 1958 to 10.4 in 1971, that located in 'the E.E.C. Six' increased simultaneously from 7.0 to 15.8 per cent (Dunning, 1973).

Such a shift undoubtedly results from the opening of facilities in other E.E.C. States by U.S. firms already owning subsidiaries in the U.K. Young and Hood (1976) argue that firms tend to develop their first or major mainland European operations outside the UK in or near the 'Golden Triangle', the economic heart of the E.E.C., comprising Belgium, southern Netherlands, northern France and the western German Federal Republic. Contemporary entrants into Europe wishing to 'leap-frog' the UK are also likely to locate there. Later, if costs of goods transport or personal contact with markets require, further units in an evolving European sub-system are set up also in the 'peripheral' E.E.C. particularly Italy, and in the Iberian, Scandinavian and Balkan 'peripheries' of Europe.

Not uncommonly, though, American firms have entered Europe by acquiring or by developing complementary facilities in two or more countries at the same time – like the 'splashing' effect referred to by Onyemelukwe (Ch. 10). Ford, G.E.C., I.T.T., Singer and Westinghouse provide good examples which pre-date 1930. The countries preferred – Britain and Germany (less so France and Italy) – were chosen for their larger market thresholds for future corporate expansion. But the strategy of distributing related facilities among several nations underlies all evolving European production sub-systems of American firms. It eloquently expresses an economic response to the politics of multinational corporate objectives: (1) Their concern is to minimize both overt presence in the economy, and dependence upon the goodwill, of one country. (2) Their desire is to maximize corporate 'economic muscle' in bargaining with the government of each (and every) country, so restricting real national sovereignty. (3) Their needs are for flexibility in the organization of the functional roles and relationships of the constituent units in the sub-system and (4) for maximizing the advantages and for minimizing the disadvantages from long-term trends and short-term fluctuations in international patterns of comparative costs, labour relations, market conditions and currency exchange-rates. Such international sub-systems offer foreign firms in Europe opportunities for quantitative and qualitative changes and substitutions unrealizable by European firms with very few units or with highly localized 'national' or 'regional' clusters of units.

Large US corporations have thus been *able* to shift a greater volume of their European activities progressively from Britain into the 'economic heart' of the mainland E.E.C. via three parallel processes: (1) by more rapid expansion of production-innovation, research and administration at their existing German or French facilities than at British units; (2) by greater specialization of production among European units but with *trends* towards higher-value 'up-market' production in Germany and France and correspondingly greater relative emphasis on 'down-market', or components manufactures, at British plants; and (3) by developing 'intermediate' components or 'middle-to-lower market' products assembly in new facilities situated spatially between the British and German systems, particularly in Belgium, the Netherlands, France or the Saarland. This pattern – true for trends in the operations of Chrysler, Ford and General Motors – finds its varied analogies in many other industries. It reflects US corporate response to the changing international balance of real and perceived advantages within the E.E.C. in the 1970s: greater relative and absolute market growth in 'the Six' than in the UK; better labour relations and less inflation in Benelux and West Germany; more rigid governmental control of location or stronger socialist tendencies in Britain, France and Italy.

E.E.C. policy and multinationals

Policy-makers face many difficulties in deciding the objectives and in shaping the strategies of the E.E.C. towards multinational firms. Such goals and strategies must be formed within the framework of long-term Community economic, political and social goals in general and of financial and industrial policy in particular. The fundamental dilemma is the way in which multinationals both contribute positively to, and conflict negatively with, the process of attaining long-term goals at Community, national and regional levels. Yet disagreement is rife as to the ultimate balance, positive or negative, of advantages and disadvantages offered by the presence of multinationals. Further difficulties arise as real or perceived 'desirability' can differ as between: one period and another; E.E.C.-based and 'foreign' firms; individual corporations; industrial sectors; and between the Community and its constituent national, regional and the urban scales. More research into this 'matrix' of issues is required. Nonetheless their implications demand that Community-level economic, social and governmental policies should be firm and simple, yet flexible enough to satisfy any principles of discrimination which may be deemed necessary between types of corporations. Guidelines are also required to establish to what extent regional and urban policy can, or should, be left to influence multinationals as it is now conceived to shape the behaviour of capitalist enterprise in general.

The pros and cons of multinational enterprise

Multinationals have greatly bolstered the supply of capital for development and growth: almost 30 per cent of overseas US manufacturing investment is located in the E.E.C. Net remittances for reinvestment by European multinationals from raw-materials processing, oil-refining and manufacturing in the Middle East, Africa, Latin America, Asia and Australasia are also substantial. New skills and know-how have been created among European labour and the technology lag behind the USA substantially reduced in some fields. These inputs are not only significant quantitatively in numbers of jobs and incomes innovated in Europe, they are significant qualitatively: most capital from overseas has flowed into diversified finished-manufacturing, including technologically-advanced and research-oriented industries, forming 'clusters' of inter-industry sub-systems of high growth capability and high value-added. The Community has thus benefited far more from multinationals than have Africa, Latin America, Asia, Canada and Australasia, where their investment is more 'resource-exploitative', adding far lower value and creating lower local income.

Against this must be set the negative economic consequences which often interweave with other key issues – the spatial and social distribution of benefits and questions of national and Community political and economic sovereignty. Investment flows generate a return flow of interest rates, dividends from profit and royalties. In 1969, US multinationals spent $3200 million on new investment abroad, re-invested $2200 million from profits earned abroad while total remittances exceeded $7000 million (Vernon, 1973). If this is representative, the US earned 30 per cent more from its foreign operations than it spent, although the rate of financial 'leakage' from the E.E.C. is lower than that from developing countries.

More serious is the challenge to sovereignty. Oligopolistic competition undermined consumer sovereignty long ago: multinationals have further 'internationalized' this process. American business practices have penetrated European life with high-powered, persuasive 'market-creative' advertising, raising barriers to entry and competition (Schmalensee, 1974), restricting ranges of highly identical products and putting a premium on brand loyalty. 'Planned obsolescence' (Le Pan de Ligny, 1975), sales gimmicks and packaging have stimulated energy, consumer and industrial demand beyond necessity, leading to waste of resources and producing a waste-disposal problem which directly or indirectly conflicts with E.E.C. environmental policy (Centre Universitaire d'Etudes des Communatés Européens, 1974). Yet national consumption habits (Oksanen and Spencer, 1973) still persist in European family budget expenditure patterns, a factor which partially sustains E.E.C. firms through 'national brand loyalty'.

Challenges to national and Community sovereignty comes from non-E.E.C. corporations in other ways. Vernon (1973) estimates that 75 per cent of all assets of US subsidiaries are obtained from European sources: acquisition of local firms (e.g. the Chrysler takeover of Rootes and Simca), subsidiaries' profits, or capital raised in London, Frankfurt, Paris, Brussels, Geneva or Milan. Such raising of capital locally has undoubtedly influenced the spatial pattern of US corporate facilities in Europe (Labasse, 1975). On average only 25 per cent is provided by the American parent corporation, so 'a relatively small number of US enterprises control a huge pool of liquid foreign assets whose management . . . could greatly affect the . . . positions of [European currencies]' (Vernon, 1973, p. 155). Thus the relative shift of US corporate activity from the UK into the economic heart of the E.E.C. has added to other factors causing the decline in the value of the £ sterling by comparison with German and Benelux currencies.

Threatening national sovereignty, social dignity, the very roots of political and economic democracy is that many decisions are taken abroad by managements in New York, Detroit, Chicago, San Francisco-Oakland, Los Angeles, Tokyo or elsewhere. Such decisions affect the jobs, incomes and productivities of people, the economic base of cities, the economic 'health' of entire regions in the E.E.C. and do so not only negatively or positively but *differentially*. Once multinational firms penetrate the economy of a city or region directly, or indirectly through sub-contracting, the economic life and social welfare of their people become part of the global design of the corporation, open to discardment or neglect whenever management no longer feels their contribution essential or desirable to world corporate survival, progress or domination. Recent economic recession has led many smaller US firms to withdraw branch operations from the E.E.C. and precipitated rationalization by larger corporations involving actual or threatened closure of major facilities in some countries. Governments have felt obliged to compromise, as the British government did with Chrysler, to maintain reasonable employment levels at home, using local taxpayer's money. So the US 'capital international' has brought even the more centralized west European nations to be *dependent* upon its multinational firms (Dockès, 1975).

'Tension'

Attitude to multinationals within the E.E.C. are closely interwoven with national economic, political and social experience, and impinge heavily upon the issue of policy-formulation. The years 1950 to 1965 were the 'honeymoon period', when the technological and managerial gap between the 'old war-torn continent' and the 'new world' was perceived to necessitate an 'open arms' policy by European nations to US investment. By the 1960s, however, the negative implications of the rapid growth of multinational enterprise within the E.E.C. were becoming more apparent. In 1963 a French call for control over American investment was rejected by her five E.E.C. partners (Hellman, 1973): while Dockès' attitude is typically French in demanding radical Community action it is not universal. Yet there is growing 'tension' between the E.E.C. and multinationals. First, increased foreign business penetration is being matched by increased Community strength, which launched a European policy counter-offensive after 1968. Second, new E.E.C. policy issues have been raised by multinational involvement in O.P.E.C. countries and in the Community's increasingly prominent 'resource-extractive' sector, North Sea oil and gas.

Nonetheless, 'tension' levels between host countries and multinationals vary nationally, hindering formulation of Community control. It is greater between firms and the politically more centralized, 'national' or 'socialistic' states like France, Britain and Italy than in the more 'permissive' or decentralized states like Belgium, the Netherlands and Federal Germany. Such tensions have become 'cumulatively-causal' as US and other corporations concentrate their activities in Benelux and West Germany.

Thus while more radical elements advocate or threaten the nationalization of 'locally-based' (e.g. Leyland) or foreign corporations, others argue that E.E.C. policy must 'steer' multinationals to behave in the Community's interests. Propositions include encouragement to greater investment in higher quality activities involving local skill- and technology-creation combined with the fulfilment of regional policy objectives through E.E.C. control over the location of multinational activities (Van Ginderachter, 1973).

Another source of tension is the awareness that the Treaty of Rome itself contains serious practical deficiencies in industrial policy. These have hindered the creation of truly integrated 'European' multinationals by confining the industrial action space of European manufacturers to their home country. The obstacles are legal, financial, technical and organizational (Balassa, 1974). Complete integration, through takeover or amalgamation, is *legally* impossible between corporations of different nationality while it is also difficult intra-nationally where State-owned and private corporations coexist. This explains why various European (especially French, Swedish and Italian) motor vehicle producers have to achieve rationalization of components via 'cooperation' and do not form mergers. New laws are thus essential to facilitate creation of European (rather than British, Dutch or German) firms under Community control. *Financial* obstacles stem from variations in national taxation policies and from the absence of a free market in capital (which has been primarily opposed by French and Italian governments). Musgrave (1972) suggests that formulae can be devised, which a coordinated E.E.C. taxation policy could incorporate, to ensure retention of a proportion of the profits created by multinationals in each country or region for re-investment under local, national or Community control. This is one objective of recent British government policy for 'partnership' with multinational corporations engaged in extracting North Sea oil. *Technical* standardization also impedes integration. So, too, does a major *organizational* practice: rapid growth in government spending has strongly favoured 'national' firms since contracts are not normally open to tenders from firms of other E.E.C. countries. The Treaty of Rome has thus restricted the growth in the scale and rationalization of European corporations and hence their competitiveness. The problem is somewhat analogous, therefore, to the dilemma facing N.A.T.O.'s European governments that 'standardization and value-for-money usually means buying American'.

Multinationals and the regional policy problem

If the need for defining, coordinating and regulating the interaction between national and Community-level institutions is basic to the formulation of policy towards multinational corporations (Ubertazzi, 1974), it lies no less fundamentally at the heart of the problem of devising and implementing long-term regional policies. Very broadly, such policies must incorporate five types of strategy (Scargill, 1973–6): (1) implantation of non-agricultural and urban functions in dominantly rural regions, like the 'French desert' or the Mezzogiorno, to sustain a viable population, social infrastructure and economy; (2) structural and physical renewal of old urban–industrial (primarily coalfield) regions suffering rapid decline; (3) containment of, and redistribution of growth from, major urban and metropolitan regions like Midland or South-eastern England, Randstad Holland, the Paris Region, middle Rhinelands and northern Italy; (4) management of coastal and offshore regions where port and industrial expansion, based partly on North Sea oil and gas, must be balanced with environmental protection and expansion of tourism; (5) integration of frontier regions which, while being geographically juxtaposed, have experienced different paths of economic and social evolution within the context of contrasting national histories and spatial organization.

All E.E.C. countries contain these types of 'policy region' in some combination and scale. Thus, in line with the Community's overall regional objectives, most national policies attempt to create more 'balanced' spatial development by diverting growth from regions of rapidly expanding economic opportunities or of actual or latent congestion to the less developed, or economically declining, regions. However, the urgency and mechanisms for such strategy vary markedly from nation to nation. Substantial regional disparities – as in Belgium, Netherlands, Denmark, Eire, the UK and more specifically France and Italy – create situations in which localized zones of high growth and very large or dominant metropolitan centres become serious 'inflation leaders', diffusing rising prices and wage rates, weakening national competitiveness and reinforcing inertia in interregional relationships (Cros, 1974). By contrast, the German Federal Republic enjoys a far more 'even' spatial structure: many larger and well-spaced cities counteract the major concentration – the Ruhr – which, in any case, has suffered relative decline and is hence not comparable as an inflation leader with London or Paris. Thus West Germany has benefited from a higher 'efficiency' of spatial organization – the legacy of past disunity, reinforced since 1945, by decentralized government (Gaudard, 1975; Perrin, 1974) – and which is evident also in the smaller size of less developed areas. At regional level this is also an economic strength of Northern Italy and typical of 'l'Europe mediane' (Documentation Française, 1975).

These real spatial problems are partially mirrored in that regional policy has been more rigorous, or at least more overt, in E.E.C. countries other than the German Federal Republic. Yet many deficiencies exist at present. Most regional policies have evolved in *ad hoc* fashion, expressing the progress of a perceived awareness by government of regional problems. Often regional policy is partial, relates only to certain areas of the nation, and is not part of an integrated national spatial policy for regulating all interregional relationships in the interests of regional improvement (Ch. 5). France is perhaps a major exception. Above all, regional policies are designed and implemented nationally – one reason for the neglect of frontier regions. The Community must move towards a supra-national spatial policy, since each and every city and region in 'the Nine' is becoming more interdependent in an evolving economic, social and political union. The roles, structure and organization of each region should be defined by a process of planned evolution towards a 'compromis d'optimisation' (Moran, 1974), between national and E.E.C. optima. International policies must be designed to take into account: interregional and international division of labour; the transnational interrelationships of cities and their functions; economic development along major corridors of transport, communications, water and energy supply within and across national frontiers; and proper 'complementary' development of, and service provision in, the hierarchies of medium-sized and smaller towns lying in, or accessible to, such corridors (Boudeville, 1974; Laget, 1975; Lapetina & Marchesnay, 1975).

The desirability of harnessing multinational firms in regional development still requires verification prior to innovation of Community policies for controlling industrial location, closure or expansion. Undoubtedly, however, multinational firms — when left with open choices — have seriously sharpened interregional economic and social disparities within the present E.E.C., though not without support and encouragement from the 'agglomerative behaviour' of indigenous entrepreneurs.

American corporations were instrumental in assisting rapid industrial growth in and around London in the 1930s: no fewer than 160 US firms opened manufacturing plants and local offices there at that time when unemployment in the structurally-maladjusted coalfields of northern and western Britain varied from 20 to 80 per cent. These firms further perpetuated the interregional economic rift between South-East and 'peripheral' Britain through their diffusion of branch industrial growth to new and expanded towns near London in the 1950s and 1960s — though British government policy also stimulated them. In-migration of US and other European (including British) corporations into northern Belgium (De Smet, 1974) till 1966 aggravated the 'contradictions' too between the Flemish 'growth' region and Walloon 'depressed coalfield' region that expressed themselves in distinct labour market conditions — shortage in Flanders, unemployment in Wallonia (Ville & Leroy, 1973) — and in ethnic conflict. Localization of growth industry in Randstad Holland, especially Rotterdam (Tinbergen, 1962; Fischer, 1975) had hindered development of viable urban and regional economies in northern and eastern Netherlands until Dutch policies towards the Groningen gas field were changed (Ch. 2). Dominance of the Paris region in the spatial pattern of foreign investment in France is exceptionally marked (Bakis, Gribet *et al.*, 1974; Durand, 1974).

Three factors further accentuate regional differentials. First, in-movement of multinationals to major port or metropolitan regions reflects their poorer locational perception of foreign environments and hence their need for uncertainty-and-risk minimization. It also results because other multinationals are locating in the same regions, creating clusters of growth industries offering close inter-industry, inter-corporate linkages (Marnet-Leymaire, 1974) and as an oligopolistic response to competitors in poorly-differentiated product markets. It contrasts with the more 'chance' and functionally unconnected coincidence of multinationals in other, more 'peripheral' areas where impact is often minimal (e.g. I.B.M. at Montpellier). Second, leading European corporations have often created much larger clusters in similar regions. Third, corporations of all 'nationalities' have progressively innovated, ·concentrated or expanded their most rapidly growing functions – administration, research and development – in major metropolitan regions (Evans, 1973; Parsons, 1972). This trend is an integral part of a spatial-organizational process which is expressed in a marked decrease in the average levels of employee skill and in the importance of non-production (i.e. office, research) jobs with increasing distance from the management centre of the corporation.

Recent concern for the *quality* of regional and interregional dispersion of industrial activity (Townroe, 1974), and doubts about its real potential as a growth tool (Pred, 1974), have encouraged the viewing of the *quantitative* migration of industry in new light. Yet such a quantitative shift has been the main objective of industrial location policies applied by governments of E.E.C. countries to foster more balanced regional development. Undoubtedly such policies (e.g. the Barlow Report in the UK and the legislative acts of 1966 and 1970 in Belgium to steer industry into Walloon areas) were promoted to counteract the far-reaching consequences of spatial behaviour by foreign firms.

Only since introduction of regional 'stick-and-carrot' policies, incorporating financial and other incentives (such as infrastructural provision or industrial estates), have multinationals begun to be active in the economic modernization of less developed or depressed areas. That role, however, is full of dilemmas for planners and politicians alike. Managements of foreign corporations have often been more ready to establish facilities in 'new', 'exotic' or 'development' areas than have management of indigenous firms. The reasons and motives are varied: wider spatial experience; greater frequency (and hence confidence) in making location decisions (Hamilton, 1974); less 'parochial' inhibitions and no regional 'attachment'; or a desire to be seen acting in 'national interest' while also reaping State financial 'hand-outs' or concessions.

Experience varies, however. Blackbourn (1974) and Kearne (1974) found in Eire that US corporations preferred Dublin and Shannon airport for easy access to the UK and the USA, while German firms chose to locate plants in more dispersed, rural development districts. The spatial association between grant-aided areas and foreign-investment location in Belgium has also varied: it was negligible in Flanders, strong in Wallonia (Biname and Jacquemin, 1973; Mingret, 1972). Though more research is required on the role of industrial estates in the E.E.C., it appears that French industrial decentralization policy has had limited sucess, among other reasons, because of inadequate provision of such estates by urban planners (Bastié, 1975; Gueniot, 1974). Despite the sharp contrasts often present in adjacent frontier regions in monetary, legal, economic and infrastructure conditions (Van der Auwera, 1975), some border regions have attracted much foreign investment. French frontier areas with labour surpluses have benefited from juxtaposition to the labour-deficient German economy: West German firms have located branch plants both close enough to their side of the border for daily commuting to work by French *frontaliers* and in the French Bas Rhin and Moselle areas of Alsace (Martin, 1973). Italian regional policy has had limited sucess (Ch. 9) despite its dependence upon 'national' enterprise and restricted entry of foreign firms (Solustri, 1975).

The whole objective of steering multinational (and other firms) to 'development' or 'intermediate' areas is to initiate and to sustain regional economic growth and better social welfare. Much doubt now exists as to how far this can be realized by industrial 'implantations' in such areas, as in Languedoc-Roussillon (Blésés, 1974;

Verlaque, 1975). Several issues are relevant here. Very often the scale of units built is small and most are branches linked to a parent located in a high-growth region or abroad. Many lines innovated in branch plants involve simple products with short 'life cycles'. Thus, not only are relatively few jobs created by such plants, but labour training for semi-skilled jobs is minimal and development often short-lived. *Study of the expansion-propensity, death or survival rates of industrial facilities steered to lagging regions is just as significant as study of their initial establishment – if not more so.* Data on this is often unavailable where governments fear criticism of limitations on, or failures of, their policies. Heavy dependence in such policies upon manufacturing as a tool of decentralization (Derieux, 1974) underlines the importance in future of encouraging diversified activities to underprivileged areas to 'cushion' the effects of closures, to convert vacated premises and to train labour. Multinationals are particularly apt to close branches unless they have involved large capital outlays because of their international spatial 'elasticity' in being able to move activities, if necessary, to their 'core' regions.

Even large-scale plants do not necessarily stimulate regional development, unless widespread sub-contracting and local multiplier effects evolve. Detailed study of I.B.M. in France has shown that 'direct regional impact is practically nil since plants form one link in the intra-corporate but international division of labour (Bakis, Gribet *et al.*, 1974). Similar evidence emerges from other studies of the behaviour and impact of large growth firms (Braam, 1972; Erickson, 1974). Moreover, multinationals often 'badger' local communities and central governments with promises of providing hundreds or thousands of jobs and varied services insupportable from public funds so as to obtain precious sites. Very often the multinational gets the site but then builds a capital-intensive plant generating few jobs but promising the community plenty of pollution. Shell's new oil terminal in Anglesey (Wales) is just one case in point. That large firms can behave in this manner is simply explained: they can threaten to go abroad if they feel that they are being too closely controlled.

Such 'muscle' should not be underestimated: *the E.E.C. contains so many and such extensive 'attractive' development areas from Orkney and Shetland to Sardinia and Sicily, all offering plentiful labour, grants, tax concessions, cheap land and utilities, but all competing with each other for the provision of the relatively few new jobs offered by highly mobile firms that not one of them is in any position to bargain.* The time has come for the E.E.C. to reassess the purpose, value and methods of all regional policies and their role in relation to multinational industrial enterprise.

Conclusion

So long as the E.E.C. maintains its faith in capitalist enterprise as a mode of progress it must come to terms with the realities of multinational enterprise and with the difficulties involved in its control. Examination of this problem, however, throws light upon other broad weaknesses in E.E.C. policy, especially with regard to rationalization of European-based corporations and to regional policy. If unity is to proceed satisfactorily, then regional, national and Community goals must be coordinated. Yet measures deemed necessary to control the activities of non-E.E.C. multinational or foreign State-socialist enterprises must also be applied to its own E.EC.-based firms operating abroad. Failure to do so will endanger the Community's relationships with the wider, especially Third, World.

References

Bakis, G., Gribet, M. F. *et al.* (1974) *Recherches de Géographie Industrielle*, C.N.R.S. Memoires et Documents, Paris, Vol. **14**, pp. 131–298.

Balassa, B. (1974) 'Politica industriale nella Communità Economica Europea', *Moneto e Credito*, Rome, **105**, pp. 50–67.

Ballon, R. (1973) 'Japan's investments overseas', *Aussenwirtschaft*, **3–4**, pp. 128–53.

Bastié, J. (1975) 'Industrial activity in the Parisian agglomeration: a study of recent change in location and structure' in: L. Collins & D. Walker *et. al.*, *Locational Dynamics of Manufacturing Activity*, Wiley, London, 1975, pp. 279–94.

Battiau, N. (1973) 'Étude geographique d'une grande entreprise, le groupe Prouvost-Masurel', *Ceres Nord Pas-de-Calais*, March, p. 15.

Beaud, M., Danjou, P. and David, J. (1975) *Une multinationale française: Pechiney-Ugine-Kuhlmann*, Editions de Seuil, Paris, 288 pp.

Biname, J. P. and Jacquemin, A. (1973) 'Structures industrielles des régions belges et grands enterprises: quelques elements d'analyse', *Recherches Economiques*, **4**, pp. 437–58.

Blackbourn, A. (1974) 'The spatial behaviour of American firms in Western Europe', Ch. 9, in: F. E. Ian Hamilton, ed., *Spatial Perspectives on Industrial Organization and Decision-Making*, Wiley, London, pp. 245–64.

Blesés, J. L. (1974) 'Identification des effets de Fos sur le Languedoc-Rousillon', *Economie Méridinale*, Montpellier, **1(89)**, pp. 1–11.

Boudeville, J. R. (1974), 'Integration européene régions urbains et villes moyennes', *Revue d'Economie Politique*, **2**, pp. 252–76.

Braam, J. (1972), *Invloed van Bedrijuen op de Overheid*, Unpublished Doctoral Thesis, University of Gronigen, Netherlands.

Centre Universitaire d'Etudes des Communautés Européens (1974), 'Les problems de l'environment dans le C.E.E.', *Revue du Marché Commun*, **175**, pp. 221–317.

Cros, J. (1974), 'Les deséquilibres geographiques dans le C.E.E. face aux objectifs de l'union économique et monetaire', *Revue d'Economie Politique*, **2**, pp. 145–73.

Derieux, B. (1974) 'La décentralisation des emplois est surtout le fait de l'industrie', *Economie et Statistique*, **62**, pp. 13–35.

Derrieux-Cecconi, R. F. (1973) 'Les espaces de la firme: in case de Creusot-Loire', *L'Espace Geographique*, **1**, pp. 21–36.

De Smet, L. (1974) 'De vestiginsplaats van de buitenlandse industriele investeringen in België', *Tijdschrift voor Economische en Sociale Geografie*, **65(2)**, pp. 102–9.

De Smit, M. (1966) 'Foreign industrial establishments located in the Netherlands', *Tijdschrift voor Economishe en Sociale Geografie*, **57(1)**, pp. 1–19.

Dockès, P. (1975), *L'Internationale du Capital*, Presses Universitaire de France, Vendôme, 287 pp.

Documentation Française (1975) *L'Europe Mediane*, Scheme général d'Aménagement de la France, Paris, 123 pp.

Dunning, J. H. (1958) *American Investment in British Manufacturing*, Allen & Unwin, London.

Dunning, J. H. (1973) 'The location of international firms in an enlarged E.E.C.', *Manchester Statistical Society Papers*, pp. 26–41.

Durand, P. (1974) *Industries et Régions: L'Aménagement Industriel de la France*, Documentation Française, Paris, 211 pp.

Erickson, R. A. (1974) 'The regional impact of growth firms: the case of Boeing, 1963–68', *Land Economics*, **2**, pp. 127–36.

European Economic Community (1969) *Die Elektronische Industrie der Gemeinschafts-Lander und der Amerikanischer Investigionen*, Brussels.

Evans, A. W. (1973) 'The location of the headquarters of industrial companies', *Urban Studies*, **10(3)**, pp. 387–96.

Fischer, A. (1975) 'Recherches sur la croissance industrielle aux Pays-Bas', *Bulletin d'Association Géographique Française*, **424–5**, pp. 121–5.

Forsyth, D. J. C. (1972) *US Investment in Scotland*, Praeger, New York.

Gaudard, G. (1975) *L'Inegalité Économique dans l'Éspace*, Éditions Universitaires, Fribourg, Switzerland, 222 pp.

Gueniot, Y. (1974) *Des Zones Industrielles vers Les Parcs d'Activities: Étude, Réalisation, Evolution des Zones Industrielles*, Editions Berger-Levrault, Paris, 438 pp.

Gorgé, J. P. (1975) 'Une étude du ministère de l'industrie sur la concentration industrielle', *Economie et Statistique*, **68**, pp. 39–58.

Hamilton, F. E. Ian, ed. (1974) *Spatial Perspectives on Industrial Organization and Decision-Making*, Wiley, London, 533 pp.

Hanappe, P. (1974) 'Aspects spatiaux du développement industriel en Europe de l'Ouest Aires economiques et aires politiques', *Metra*, **3**, pp. 357–72.

Hellman, R. (1973) *Weltenternehmen nur Amerikanisch?*, Tübingen.

Hufbauer, G. C. and Adler, F. M. (1968) *Overseas Manufacturing Investment and the Balance of Payments*, US Treasury Department, Washington D.C., pp. 37–8.

Irish Development Authority (1970) *Principal New Industries with Foreign Participation*, Dublin.

Jansen, A. C. M. (1972) 'Enkele Aspekten van het Ruimtelijk Gedrag van Grote Industrië Concerns in Nederland, 1950–1971', *Tijdschrift voor Economische en Sociale Geografie*, **63**, pp. 411–25.

Kearne, K. C. (1974) 'Industrialization and regional development in Ireland, 1958–1972', *American Journal of Economics and Sociology*, **33(3)**, pp. 299–16.

Krumme, G. (1970) 'The international corporation and the region: a case study of Siemen's growth characteristics and response patterns in Munich, West Germany', *Tijdschrift voor Economische en Sociale Geografie*, **61**, pp. 318–33.

Labasse, J. (1975), 'The geographical space of big companies', *Geoforum*, **6**, pp. 113–24.

Laget, M. (1975), 'Les services industriels dans le système économique régional', *Economie Méridionale*, **1(89)**, pp. 11–18.

Lajugie, J. (1974) *Les Villes Moyennes*, Parks (Editions Cujas), 216 pp.

Lapetina, M. and Marchesnay, M. (1975) 'L'apport de l'économie industrielle à l'analyse régionale', *Economie Méridionale*, **1(89)**, pp. 21–8.

Law, C. M. (1974) 'Some aspects of the postwar geography of the West European motor vehicle industry', *K.N.A.G. Geografisch Tijdschrift*, **8(1)**, pp. 5–16.

Le Pan de Ligny, G. (1975) *L'Enterprise et la Vie Internationale*, Editions Dalloz, Paris, 292 pp.

Marnet-Leymaire, D. (1974), 'Les recherches interindustrielles dans le localisation des industries de croissance en France', *Revue Economique Sud-Ouest*, Bordeaux, **1**, pp. 33–95.

Martin, J. E. (1973) 'Industrial employment and investment in a frontier region: the Franco-German example', *Geography*, **58(1)**, **258**, pp. 55–8.

Mingret, P. (1972) 'A factor in the regional evolution of Belgium: the geographical distribution of American industrial investments', *Terra*, **84**, pp. 14–22.

Moran, P. (1974) 'La politique régionale confrontée aux optima nationaux et europeéns', *Revue d'Economie Politique*, **2**, pp. 224–51.

Musgrave, P. B. (1972), 'International tax base division and the multinational corporation', *Finance Publique*, **4**, pp. 394–411.

O.E.C.D. (1969) *Gaps in Technology – Electronic Computers*, O.E.C.D.' Paris.

Oksanen, E. H. and Spencer, B. G. (1973) 'International consumption behaviour: tests of the alternative consumption function hypothesis using national accounting data for twelve countries', *Revue Internationale Statistique*, **1**, pp. 69–72.

Parsons, G. F. (1972) 'Giant manufacturing corporations and balanced regional growth in Britain', *Area*, **4(2)**, pp. 99–103.

Perrin, J. C. (1974), *Le Développement Régional*, Presses Universitaires de France, Paris, 208 pp.

Precheur, C. (1976) 'Diversité des firms multinationales et leur espaces géographiques', in: F. E. Ian Hamilton, ed., *Symposium on Spatial Production Systems, Institute of Economics & Organization of Industrial Production, Novosibirsk, USSR.*, London School of Economics, London, 278 pp.

Pred, A. (1974), 'Industry, information and city-system interdependencies', Ch. 4 in: F. E. Ian Hamilton, ed., *Spatial Perspectives*, op. cit., pp. 105–41.

Saint-Julien, Thérèse (1973) 'Signification géographique des implantations industrielles décentralisees en province', *Annales de Geographie*, **82(453)**, pp. 557–75.

Scargill, D. I., ed. (1973–6) *Problem Regions of Europe*, twenty paperback volumes, Oxford University Press, Oxford.

Schmalensee, R. (1974), 'Brand loyalty and barriers to entry', *Southern Economic Journal*, **40(4)**, pp. 579–88.

Schumpeter, J. (1939), *Business Cycles: A Theoretical, Historical and Statistical Analysis of the Capitalist Process*, New York.

Solustri, A. (1975) 'La politican industriale italiana nell'esperienza di programmazione economica 1966–1970', *Rivista Politica Economica*, Rome, IV, pp. 444–93.

Tinbergen, J. (1962) 'Research on the geographical decentralization of industry in the Netherlands', in: E. Henderson and L. Spaventa, eds., *Guest Lectures in Economics*, Milan, pp. 230–42.

Townroe, P. (1974) 'Post-move stability and the location decision', Ch. 11 in F. E. Ian Hamilton, ed., *op. cit.*, pp. 287–308.

Ubertazzi, G. M. (1974) 'Les sociétés multinationales et les communautés europeens', *Revue Marché Commun*, **180**, pp. 513–17.

United States (1971) *Survey of Current Business*, **51(10)**, pp. 32–6.

Van der Auwera, G. (1975) 'Les régions frontaliers et l'integration européene', *Revue Marché Commun*, **182**, pp. 78–85.

Van Ginderachter, J. (1973) 'Les enterprises multinationales et la politique régionale communautaire', *Revue des Sciences Economiques*, Liège, **174**, pp. 59–76.

Verlaque, C. (1975) 'A propos d'une enquête de geographie industrielle dans le Languedoc-Rousillon', *Bulletin d'Association Geographique Française*, **424–5**, pp. 99–110.

Vernon, R. (1973) *Sovereignty at Bay: The Multinational Spread of US Enterprises*, Pelican, London.

Ville, Ph.De and Leroy, R. (1973) 'Processus et facteurs de l'evolution régionale de l'emploi', *Recherche Economiques*, Louvain, **2**, pp. 219–36.

Wickham, S. (1973) 'Cooperation interfirmes est-ouest et concurrence internationale', *Banque*, Paris, **323**, pp. 965–72.

Wilkins, M. (1970) *The Emergence of Multinational Enterprise*, Harvard University Press, Cambridge, Mass.

Wolfowski, C. (1972) 'Fiat', *L'Information Geographique*, **36(5)**, pp. 244–6.

Young, S. and Hood, N. (1976) 'The geographical expansion of US firms in Western Europe: some survey evidence', *Journal of Common Market Studies*, **14(3)**, pp. 223–9.

Chapter 4

Industrial migration in the United Kingdom in the 1960s

David E. Keeble

Industrial migration, defined here as the complete transfer of productive capacity to, or establishment of a branch factory in, a new location by an existing manufacturing firm, is of growing importance within the United Kingdom. Though the total national stock of manufacturing establishments has been declining recently, the number of migrant plants has been growing. This is clearly illustrated for movement at the broad inter-regional level by Table 4.1, which records total stock, moves and average annual movement rates for four periods between 1945 and 1971.† Movement here relates to the crossing of any boundaries separating the eleven standard regions (see Table 4.4) into which the United Kingdom is divided for statistical and economic planning purposes. The figures thus exclude substantial short-distance within-region movement. They do include all moves in the period specified, whether or not the factories concerned are still operating, and factories set-up in Britain for the first time by foreign companies.

The 1960s witnessed a substantially greater movement rate than that recorded for the late 1940s and 1950s. By the 1966–71 period, nearly 200 manufacturing firms were establishing migrant plants each year in other British regions. Movement is defined in transfers or branches established across any one of the boundaries separating sixty-two sub-regions: no less than 1728 moves were recorded officially by the Department of Industry during this most recent period, giving an annual average total of 298 migrant plants. Unfortunately, this subregional migration figure cannot be compared strictly with data before 1966 as the Department of Industry substantially amended its sub-regional classification in that year. On its old classification, which recognized fifty sub-regions and a similar definition of all the main origin areas, inter-subregional movement between

Table 4.1 Inter-regional manufacturing movement rates in the United Kingdom, 1945–71

	Average annual inter-regional moves	Total UK manufacturing establishments ('000s)	Movement rate, per 1000 UK establishments
1945–51	142	98.6 (1948)†	1.44
1952–59	69	92.8 (1958)	0.74
1960–65	141	89.9 (1963)	1.56
1966–71	186	91.8 (1968)	2.08

Sources: UK Department of Industry manufacturing movement statistics: *Abstract of Regional Statistics*, 1973, p. 69.

† Indicates estimate only.

1960 and 1965 involved 1404 moves, or 234 per annum. This also suggests an increase in industrial migration since the 1950s.

The reasons for the increase are varied. Probably the major influence, operating mainly at the between-region scale, is government regional-development policy. Since the 1930s successive British governments have been committed to a policy of reducing, if not eliminating, economic and social disparities between the more prosperous South East and Midlands and the less prosperous peripheral regions such as Wales, northern England, Scotland and Northern Ireland (Keeble, 1974*a*). Implementation of such policy has focused almost exclusively on encouraging, if not enforcing, the movement of expanding manufacturing firms from central to peripheral regions (Keeble, 1971). Policy has, however, been applied with varying rigour at different times (Turner, in Hamilton, 1974). The 1950s saw only passive regional policy implementation, a fact evident in the low between-region migration rate (Table 4.1). Since 1963 regional policy has attracted increasing attention. Not only have controls on manufacturing growth in the South East and Midlands been more rigorously applied via the Industrial Development Certificate system, but massive government expenditures have acted as incentives to industrial movement to the periphery. Moore and Rhodes (1974) calculate that the gross cost of regional policy incentives to manufacturing industry setting-up in the 'assisted areas' rose from only £5.3 million in the 1950s, to an average of £105.9 million in the 1960s, and to £270.2 million in 1970–1: while recent official estimates give actual regional policy expenditure in 1973–4 as of the order of £314 million, with a forecast of £554 million at 1974 prices by 1976–7 (Keeble, forthcoming). The latter allows for the doubling of the Regional Employment Premium from August 1974. These huge sums are moreover now available, to greater or lesser degree, in a complex hierarchy of assisted areas – Special Development, Development and Intermediate Areas – which together contain over 40 per cent of the United Kingdom's population and cover more than 60 per cent of its land area. These facts suggest that the substantially increased migration rates for the 1960s recorded in Table 4.1 are a significant product of government policy, although other factors are undoubtedly also involved.

This chapter attempts to measure and categorize the impact of recent industrial migration upon the changing spatial distribution of manufacturing activity, emphasizing the relationship between migration and government regional policy. Although the United Kingdom is exceptional amongst the non-centrally planned economies in the length of time during which it has operated such a policy (forty years, commencing with the Special Areas Act of 1934), it seems very probable that increasing migration rates characterize many developed countries at the present time. Berry (1973) found 'accelerated filtering . . . of manufacturing activities into smaller towns and rural areas in the inter-metropolitan periphery' of the USA.

Sub-regional manufacturing employment changes in the 1960s

Quantitative analysis of changes in aggregate sub-regional manufacturing activity levels may give indirect support or otherwise for the hypothesis that regional policy and manufacturing migration have become key determinants of change in the industrial geography of the United Kingdom. Direct analysis of spatial variations in net manufacturing migration permit quantitative assessment of its role as a component in recent industrial change in particular sub-regions.

The first of these approaches is possible for the years 1959 to 1971, using employment data for these two years collected on a detailed local area basis by the Department of Employment and aggregated to the standard Sixty-two sub-region framework. A further manufacturing employment data set for 1966 permits comparison of trends at the sub-regional level with 1959 and 1971. Yet these data are not entirely satisfactory as an index of temporal and spatial variations in manufacturing activity. For example, a spurious growth in manufacturing employment between 1966 and 1967 (only 1.3 per cent in S.E. England, though) resulted solely from reclassification of certain firms from non-manufacturing to the manufacturing industries following introduction of a payroll tax (Selective Employment Tax) on service industry in the latter year. A major change in industrial classification introduced in 1958, and the switch in 1972 to employment data collection via a census of firms as compared with the insurance card exchange system previously in use, were overcome by choosing the 1959 and 1971 terminal dates. Thus generally the data can be regarded as a reasonable index of spatial change in manufacturing activity levels.

Simple calculation of sub-regional rates of manufacturing employment change provides initial support for the basic hypothesis. Throughout the 1959–71 period, no less than seven of the ten sub-regions recording the highest percentage manufacturing employment growth rates were in the government-assisted peripheral areas: conversely, the great industrial connurbations – London and the West Midlands – which dominate Britain's two main prosperous regions both recorded significant absolute decline in manufacturing employment. London, Britain's biggest single industrial centre, in fact recorded the highest percentage fall (23.4 per cent) of any sub-region, losing no less than 360 000 manufacturing jobs: factory building controls and sponsored industrial emigration thus achieved a prime aim of government regional and land-use planning policy (Keeble, 1972a).

The hypothesis receives further support from simple comparison of trends during the two sub-periods, 1959–66 and 1966–71. The marked strengthening of regional policy, dated by Moore and Rhodes (1973) as beginning in 1963, required a time-lag of two or more years to take effect between a movement or investment decision and its physical implementation. A 1966 date is thus a reasonable dividing line between sub-periods of relatively passive and active regional policy. The regional policy/migration hypothesis infers that in the former sub-periods the economically more rapidly-expanding sub-regions would tend to be concentrated disproportionately in the more prosperous regions, as compared with the peripheral areas, while the converse would be true of the latter sub-periods. This is exactly what the figures reveal. Table 4.2 records the distribution

Table 4.2 Sub-regional manufacturing growth and decline, 1959–66 and 1966–71

	Fastest-growing sub-regions		Fastest-declining (or slowest-growing) sub-regions	
	1959–66	1966–71	1959–66	1966–71
Peripheral sub-regions	7	11	10	6
Central sub-regions	12	8	2	6
Remainder of UK	1	1	8	8

Source: Unpublished Department of Employment statistics.

of the twenty fastest-growing and twenty fastest-declining (or slowest-growing) sub-regions in terms of manufacturing employment during each of the two sub-periods.

Henceforth the 'peripheral sub-regions' comprise Wales, Northern England, Scotland, Northern Ireland, Southwest, Merseyside and Furness. The Central Sub-regions include the South East, East Anglia, the East and West Midlands, and Eastern Southwest.

While the peripheral regions did account for 7 of the 20 fastest-growing sub-regions during the earlier sub-period, suggesting, as other evidence corroborates, that this sub-period was one of only *relatively* passive policy, their share during the later sub-period increased significantly, to 11. Exactly the converse characterized the prosperous central regions. At the same time, the number of peripheral sub-regions included in the fastest-*declining* (or slowest-growing) category *decreased* significantly, from 10 to only 6, while the number of central sub-regions in this category *increased* sharply, from only 2 to 6. Of equal note here however is the unusually large proportion of remaining sub-regions (8 out of a total 14), located in the North West and Yorkshire/Humberside, which also recorded unusually low rates of manufacturing employment growth (or even decline) during *both* periods.

Spatial inequality analysis and sub-regional manufacturing change

Simple classification of sub-regions by rates of manufacturing employment change may be supplemented by quantitative analysis, using Theil's entropy index (Theil, 1967) as a measure of spatial inequality in the sub-regional distribution of United Kingdom manufacturing employment. As Martin (1972) demonstrates, this index, derived from information theory, can be used to compare the level of spatial inequality in the distribution of employment at different points in time, providing that exactly the same set of spatial units (sub-regions in this case) is used at each date. Moreover, the index possesses various advantages over other approaches to manufacturing spatial concentration of dispersion (Martin, 1972; Chisholm and Oeppen, 1973, pp. 34–6). The index may be calculated by

$$I(y) = \sum_{i=1}^{N} y_i \log \frac{y_i}{1/N} = \sum_{r=1}^{R} Y_r \log \frac{Y_r}{N_r/N}$$
$$+ \sum_{r=1}^{R} Y_r \sum_{i \, r} \frac{y_i}{Y_r} \log \frac{y_i/Y_r}{1/N_r}$$

where,

$I(y)$ is the overall United Kingdom entropy index of spatial inequality.
y_i is the percentage share of the i sub-region of all United Kingdom manufacturing employment
y_r is the sum of the percentages of all sub-regions in region r.
N_r is the number of sub-regions in region r.
N is the total number of sub-regions in the whole United Kingdom (62).
R is the total number of regions in the whole United Kingdom (11).

The significance of this particular formula for calculating the entropy index is that it is designed to distinguish separately the contributions to the overall $I(y)$ value of 'between-region' inequality and 'within-region' inequality. The former is given by the first term in the main equation, the latter by the second term. The first term thus simply measures the degree of difference in the *regional* percentage shares (Y_r) of United Kingdom manufacturing employment, while the second term measures the degree of difference in *sub-regional* percentage shares within each region, weighting this value by the region's overall share of United Kingdom employment (Y_r).

In the present analysis, $I(y)$ and the respective contributions to it of between-region and within-region spatial inequality were calculated for the three years (1959, 1966 and 1971) for which sub-regional manufacturing employment data were available. Earlier discussion suggested that at least three results might be anticipated. First, the inequality index should fall significantly between 1959 and 1971, as policy-induced industrial migration redistributed manufacturing activity from the prosperous and more heavily industrialized South East and Midlands to the peripheral areas. Second, the overall index should decline more rapidly during the 1966–71 sub-period, when regional policy was more actively implemented, than during the 1959–66 sub-period. Third, perhaps more tentatively, these trends should be most marked at the between-region level, where regional policy primarily operates, rather than at the within-region level, where other considerations apply.

The general results of the entropy index analysis are given in Table 4.3. For the number of sub-regions in this study (62), the theoretically possible range of $I(y)$ is from 4.1271 (maximum inequality: all manufacturing employment concentrated in one sub-region) to 0.0000 (maximum equality: each sub-region possesses an identical share of United Kingdom manufacturing employment), measured in natural logarithms.

Table 4.3 Entropy indices of sub-regional manufacturing employment distribution, 1959–71

	1959	1966	1971
Within-region	0.6076	0.5525	0.4949
Between-region	0.2024	0.2027	0.1842
Total index	0.8100	0.7553	0.6791
Total as % of maximum possible inequality	19.6	18.3	16.5

These figures provide striking support for two of the anticipated hypotheses. First, the overall United Kingdom index did fall very significantly (by over 16 per cent of the 1959 value) between 1959 and 1971, indicating an increasingly dispersed, or more evenly spread, sub-regional distribution of manufacturing industry. This occurred even with a 1959 entropy index which was far closer to the maximum dispersion situation than to one of maximum spatial concentration. Second, the annual rate of decline in this overall index was over twice as fast (−2.02 per cent) during the later 1966–71 sub-period as during the earlier 1959–66 sub-period (−0.96 per cent), exactly as expected from the earlier discussion.

However, trends in the two component indices of between-region and within-region inequality reveal that the third hypothesis is far too simplistic an expectation of actual changes on these two geographic scales. Admittedly, on its own, the *between-region component* does provide further striking support for the regional policy/migration hypothesis. While the between-region inequality index declined significantly (−1.83 per cent per annum) during the 1966–71 sub-period, it actually *increased* slightly (+0.02 per cent per annum) during the earlier 1959–66 sub-period of relatively passive regional policy, indicating increased regional *concentration* of manufacturing industry. The different performance of the central and peripheral regions during these two sub-periods is clearly illustrated by Table 44, which records negative and positive changes in regional shares of total United Kingdom manufacturing employment between 1959 and 1966, and 1966 and 1971.

The three traditionally-prosperous regions (South East, West Midlands and East Midlands) all increased their shares of national manufacturing employment between 1959 and 1966, while three of the four traditionally-lagging regions (Northern England, Scotland and Northern Ireland) recorded smaller shares in 1966 than in 1959. Only Wales achieved an increase. Between 1966 and 1971 this pattern was completely reversed. While all four peripheral regions *increased* their percentage shares, those of the two most important prosperous manufacturing regions (the South East and West Midlands) declined significantly, illustrating very strikingly the impact of active regional policy during the later 1960s upon the between-region distribution of manufacturing industry.

Table 4.4 Changes in regional percentage shares of United Kingdom manufacturing employment, 1959–66 and 1966–71

	Percentage of UK manufacturing employment	Change in percentage share	Change in percentage share
	1959	1959–66	1966–71
South East	28.7	+ (0.3)	− (0.7)
West Midlands	13.3	+ (0.6)	− (0.4)
East Anglia	1.7	+ (0.4)	+ (0.3)
East Midlands	6.5	+ (0.4)	+ (0.3)
South West	4.3	+ (0.2)	+ (0.4)
Yorkshire–Humberside	10.1	− (0.3)	− (0.2)
North West	15.9	− (0.9)	− (0.6)
North	5.5	− (0.4)	+ (0.4)
Wales	3.3	+ (0.3)	+ (0.3)
Scotland	8.6	− (0.5)	+ (0.1)
N. Ireland	2.1	− (0.1)	+ (0.1)

However, trends in the *within-region component* (Table 4.3) suggest that the simple expectation that recent sub-regional changes are totally dominated by broad inter-regional trends and regional policy is wide of the mark. Not only does the within-region inequality component account for nearly three-quarters of the overall United Kingdom index at all three dates; but the decline in this overall index was primarily due to declining *within-region* inequality, both over the whole 1959–71 period, and in each of the sub-periods. Of course, two regions – the North West and South West – contain both assisted (Development) areas and non-assisted areas: and declining within-region inequality in these two regions may thus be a reflection between assisted and non-assisted sub-regions. This point is supported by the fact that the average annual rate of decline in the South West's individual within-region inequality index shot up from −0.7 per cent during the 1959–66 sub-period to −2.8 per cent during the later sub-period of active regional policy. This latter value was actually the highest rate of within-region inequality index decline recorded by any region between 1966 and 1971. A less striking but similar trend was recorded by the North West (−0.1 per cent to −1.4 per cent). Changes in the within-region component thus do partly reflect the operation of supposedly 'regional' policy.

But in general the decline in the within-region component is too great and too consistent to be satisfactorily explained in this way. Every single region recorded a fall in its individual within-region inequality index not only over the 1959–71 period, but also (with only two exceptions) during each sub-period. This very important finding suggests that powerful intra-regional forces are of greater importance than broad between-region policy, significant though that is, in the steady convergence of UK sub-regional manufacturing activity levels in recent years. While within-region trends may well also reflect industrial migration, factors such as changing intra-regional patterns of land and building costs, availability of adequate premises and labour, transport accessibility, perceived residential amenity and government land-use planning are clearly producing a powerful redistribution of manufacturing activity from traditional major industrial areas to hitherto less industrialized sub-regions in every single region of the United Kingdom (Keeble, 1974b).

The industrial migration component in sub-regional manufacturing change

More direct estimation of the significance of migration as a component in sub-regional change has recently become possible for the first time, following the adoption by the Department of Industry in 1966 of the same sub-regional framework for recording industrial migration as that used by the Department of Employment for recording change in manufacturing employment. Although obtained in different ways, 1971 employment in firms migrant between 1966 and 1971 and manufacturing employment change 1966–71 can be compared for each sub-region to provide a rough but direct estimate of the relationship between the two.

Simple mapping of migrant industry (branches and transfers, excluding moves from abroad) between 1966 and 1971 – measured by the employment created in the destination sub-region by the latter date (Fig 4.1) – reveals that the main movement flows fit the 'dual population hypothesis' (Keeble, 1971; 1972b). This hypothesis differentiates between short-distance 'overspill' movement from major industrial conurbations, generally within the prosperous central regions of the United Kingdom, and long-distance flows to the peripheral areas of higher unemployment. The former is further differentiated from the latter by a much higher proportion of transfers as opposed to branches, and by a different and more growth-oriented industrial structure. Of total movement between 1966 and 1971, some 33 per cent, measured by employment created, falls clearly into the former intra-regional category, while 52 per cent involved long-distance between-region flows to the periphery. The most important destination sub-regions in each category (gross employment gain 6000 jobs or more) were the Outer Metropolitan Area and Solent sub-regions of South East England, followed by Northern Ireland, Tyneside, Merseyside and the South Wales Valleys sub-regions. By contrast, moves from abroad were far more concentrated in the peripheral regions (81 per cent of employment created), notably Northern Ireland and the Edinburgh sub-region, than in the central regions around London and Birmingham (8 per cent). The latter would seem to indicate a deliberate government policy of channelling new, in-coming foreign firms to the assisted areas, and is in marked contrast to the 'laissez-faire' trend of location of such industry around London in the 1920s and 1930s (Keeble, 1972b).

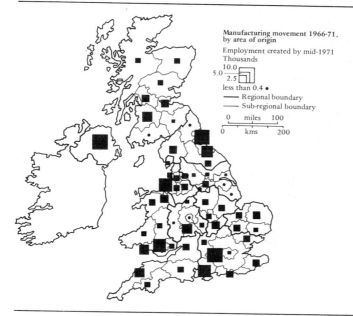

Fig. 4.1   Manufacturing movement 1966–71 by area of destination.

The map of migration by destination sub-region is, however, only part of recent industrial migration trends. Of equal importance is the map of employment losses sustained by origin sub-regions (Fig 4.2), both actual through transfers and implicit through growth lost in emigrant branches. A single sub-region dominates, Greater London, firms from which provided over 50 000 jobs in branches and transfers set up in other sub-regions between 1966 and 1971, or 35 per cent of the employment created by all migrant United Kingdom firms. The only other important individual origins were the Outer Metropolitan Area (21 000 jobs, or 14 per cent) and the West Midlands Conurbation (13 000 jobs, or 9 per cent). In terms of 'real' losses through complete transfers alone, London's dominance as an origin was even more striking, with 54 per cent (27 000 jobs) of all employment lost in this way. The West Midlands Conurbation (13 per cent) and the Outer Metropolitan Area (12 per cent) were second and third respectively.

Such estimates of employment gains and losses through migration permit calculation for each sub-region of a *net* migrant employment change value, 1966–71. This net figure was calculated by subtracting losses as a result of transfer movement from gains from both transfer and branch factory establishment (the latter including moves from abroad). Apparent losses through branch factory emigration were ignored, on the grounds that these represent growth foregone, rather than an actual decline in existing manufacturing employment. In fact many firms establishing branches do live off part of the production already carried out at the main parent plant to the new branch, leading to some decline in total employment in the original location. To the extent that this occurs, the transfer figures used here do underestimate the full impact of industrial emigration upon origin sub-regions. But the conclusions on the importance of emigration as a

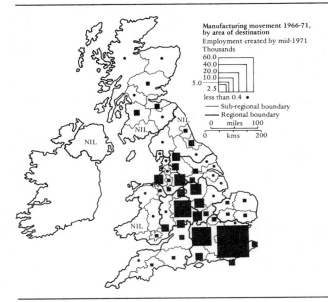

Fig. 4.2   Manufacturing movement 1966–1971 by area of origin.

component of change in industrially-declining sub-regions reached are unlikely to be substantially affected.

Given the geographical coincidence of sub-regions used for recording manufacturing movement *and* manufacturing employment change 1966–71, the net migrant industry employment figure in turn permitted calculation of the importance of migration as a component in total manufacturing change in each sub-region. It also facilitated identification of the performance of 'indigenous' industry between 1966 and 1971: change in the latter was measured by the residual left when net migrant employment was subtracted from total manufacturing employment change. This 'indigenous' industry component in many cases probably includes employment growth in firms immigrant *before* 1966–71. Were a longer time period to have been considered, migration would thus almost certainly have been shown to be even more important for overall manufacturing growth in many areas than is suggested by the evidence for 1966–71. Some results from this simple components of change exercise are presented in Tables 4.5 and 4.6.

Three main findings are worth stressing. First, only a very few (7) sub-regions experienced static or declining manufacturing employment as a consequence of net industrial migration. By far the most important were Greater London and the West Midlands. The great majority of sub-regions (55) were thus net beneficiaries from manufacturing migration. This contrasts strikingly with the pattern of change in 'indigenous' manufacturing employment, where a majority (36) of sub-regions recorded net decline, not growth. Such contrast alone suggests the importance of migration for the maintenance, if not expansion, of manufacturing employment opportunities in many areas. Yet it should be noted that net migration losses were only a very small component of overall manufacturing change in the new sub-regions noted above where migration did lead to a loss of employment. In London and the West Midlands Conurbation, massive decline in

Table 4.5 Employment change in migrant and 'indigenous' industry, 1966–71: central and peripheral sub-regions

	Manufacturing employment change, 1966–71			
	Total sub-regions	Percentage of sub-regions recording net growth in total manuf. industry	Percentage of sub-regions recording net growth in 'indigenous' industry	Percentage of sub-regions in which growth of migrant industry outweighed change in 'indigenous' industry
Peripheral sub-regions	26	65	46	42
Central sub-regions	22	50	45	9
Remainder of UK	14	29	21	7
All United Kingdom	62	52	40	23
Results of χ^2 test, observed & expected frequencies		No significant diff. at 5% level	No significant diff. at 5% level	*Diff. sign* at 2.5% level

Table 4.6 Employment change in migrant and 'indigenous' industry, 1966–71: major and minor sub-regions

	Manufacturing employment change, 1966–71			
	Total sub-regions	Percentage of sub-regions recording net growth in total manuf. industry	Percentage of sub-regions recording net growth in 'indigenous' industry	Percentage of sub-regions in which growth of migrant industry outweighed change in 'indigenous' industry
Major industrial sub-regions (more than 100 000 employees)	21	14	5	10
Medium industrial sub-regions (40 000–100 000 employees)	21	52	38	24
Minor industrial sub-regions (less than 40 000 employees)	20	90	80	35
All United Kingdom	62	52	40	23
Results of χ^2 test, observed & expected frequencies		*Diff. sign.* at 0.5% level	*Diff. sign.* at 0.5% level	No sign. diff. at 5% level

'indigenous' industry (−221 000 jobs and −95 000 jobs respectively) far outweighed the net employment loss from manufacturing migration (−26 000 jobs and −6 000 jobs respectively). On *a priori* grounds, therefore, migration would seem likely to provide a much better explanation of the spatial pattern of manufacturing growth than of that of manufacturing decline.

Second, very clearly, the relative importance of migration as a component in overall manufacturing change was much greater in the peripheral regions than in the rest of the country, despite the fairly substantial volume of movement to centrally-located sub-regions around London and Birmingham. As Table 4.5 shows (column 4), over 40 per cent of all peripheral sub-regions recorded employment gains through migration which were greater in absolute terms than growth or decline of 'indigenous' industry. Indeed, in five of the ten sub-regions involved, overall manufacturing employment would have declined between 1966 and 1971 without the arrival of the migrant plants. In contrast, over 90 per cent (20) of the sub-regions defined as centrally-located, employment changes due to migration were outweighed by changes due to the growth or decline of 'indigenous' industry. In a majority (11) of these sub-regions the most substantial impact of 'indigenous' industrial change manifested itself as a decline. Interestingly enough, these declining sub-regions were nearly all spatially clustered along the central London–Midlands axis. The nine central sub-regions in which 'indigenous' industry expanded more considerably than did immigrant industry were, in contrast, nearly all peripheral to this principal axis. But generally migration was much less important for manufacturing employment change in this group of 22 central sub-regions than was 'indigenous' industry. The difference in the relative importance of migrant and 'indigenous' industry between the central, peripheral and remaining sub-regions revealed by Table 4.5 is significant at the 2.5 per cent probability level, in terms of a χ^2 test on observed and expected frequencies (the latter based on simple proportional allocation to each of the three categories of the total number of observed cases).

This difference suggests that average national-scale estimates of the relative roles in manufacturing growth of new migrant plants, and existing plants, may be misleading if applied to particular parts of a country. For example, Kuklinski (United Nations Economic Committee for Europe, 1967) suggests that 'probably 60–80 per cent of investment in manufacturing industry in developed countries is allocated to the expansion of existing plants and only something under 40 per cent to the construction of new ones'. If it can be assumed, and it is a very arguable assumption, that this estimate is also applicable to relative employment growth in migrant and 'indigenous' plants in those sub-regions which recorded growth in both these categories over the 1966–71 period, then the figures on which Table 4.5 is based show that Kuklinski's proportions are borne out of recent experience at the average national level. Thus, over the 1966–71 period, the contribution of new migrant industry to total manufacturing employment growth in the 21 central and peripheral sub-regions which did record growth in both migrant and 'indigenous' industry was 39 per cent with 'indigenous' manufacturing growth accounting for 61 per cent. However, if the peripheral and central sub-regions are considered separately, significant deviations from this average national breakdown do emerge. Thus the contribution of migrant industry to total manufacturing employment growth in the 10 central sub-regions included in the 21 sub-region sample was in fact only 32 per cent, compared with 68 per cent by 'indigenous' industry. In contrast, migrant industry generated no less than 53 per cent of net manufacturing employment growth in the 11 peripheral sub-regions, 'indigenous' industry only 47 per cent. These figures, which are of intrinsic interest in the light of such average estimates as Kuklinski's, again illustrate the much greater importance of migrant industry as a component in recent peripheral sub-region industrial growth than in that in more centrally-located areas.

The third important set of findings concerns the marked contrast in growth per-

Moore, B. and Rhodes, J. (1974) 'The effects of regional economic policy in the United Kingdom', in: M. E. Sant, ed., *Regional Policy and Planning for Europe*, Saxon House, Farnborough.

Theil, H. (1967) *Economics and Information Theory*, North-Holland, Amsterdam, 488 pp.

Turner, D. M. (1974) 'Location decisions and industrial development certificate policy in the UK', Ch. 15 in: F. E. I. Hamilton, ed., *Spatial Perspectives on Industrial Organization & Decision-Making*, Wiley, London, pp. 393–410.

United Nations Economic Commission for Europe (1967) *Criteria for Industrial Location*, Geneva,

Chapter 5

Regional policy and industrial complexes: reflections on British experience

Kenneth Warren

The concept of the economic region and of industrial regions has long been established in geography. Unfortunately both were frequently viewed as formal rather than functional entities, and described rather than analysed. Since 1950 economic geographers in the West have adopted the more dynamically-focused concepts of the industrial complex and the growth pole (or zone) from the regional scientist or regional economist. In their own right, they have made an important contribution through the analysis of industrial interlinkages. Simultaneously socialist academics and planners have been elaborating ideas on territorial production complexes. Notwithstanding major variations in political conditions, in scale or area involved, in stage of development, in resource endowment – true industrial complexes exist both in the West and in the East. Yet because of their often uncoordinated development, they pose uniquely difficult planning problems. Their dynamism exhibits one of the strengths of capitalism; their serious economic, social and administrative difficulties undoubtedly point up some long-established, if not necessarily inherent, deficiencies.

Planning under capitalism

Socialist writers have sometimes suggested that true territorial production complexes may not exist in an unplanned, capitalist society. Agafanov and Lavrov (1966), for instance, attempt to puzzle out whether the Ruhr is or is not a true complex. The difficulty partly arises from semantic problems. Yet in non-socialist economies market forces and the perception of businessmen have together built up and allowed steady evolution of areas, for up to 200 years, into true spatial industrial complexes. However different the processes of formation, these complexes are very much like territorial production complexes in the socialist economies. One of the earliest to emerge – over two centuries ago, and from an original coal and iron base – has formed the present engineering complex of the English West Midlands. At a higher geographic scale, the industrial belt between Lake Erie and the Ohio river must be viewed as a series of inter-linked territorial production complexes.

Nevertheless one must admit that, under capitalism, adjustments in such regions to changing environments have not been automatic, immediate or perfect. The process, form and speed of change forced upon the complex is affected by a variety of factors: alterations in the structure of industry within the national economy, involving the growth of new and the decline of old manufacturing lines; technological and organizational change within individual industries; and the

An assessment of UK regional industrial policy

The British government made its first, hesitant interference in industrial location in the mid 1930s, but such intervention was carried further by the needs of wartime Britain. By 1945 the basic principles – accepted by all subsequent governments – had been formulated: action must raise the level of economic activity and thus of employment, population and personal income in all regions to the levels comparable of the more favoured areas.

Industrial location controls lie at the heart of British development-area policies and have evolved, becoming more and more complex, yet they too were established twenty-five years ago. They embody both negative and positive powers. Negative powers – highly distinctive of British regional policy – operate through the necessity for a firm to obtain a government Industrial Development Certificate (I.D.C.) before permitting it to build or make major extension to a factory in any area. Positive powers comprise the more usual incentives, grants, loans and concessions. In a sizeable and increasing national economic sector government has direct impact on location and development decisions insofar as it effectively – though by no means simply, as recent experience with the British Steel Corporation (Heal, 1974) shows – exercises controls over the policies of nationalized industries. Its power over the decisions of nominally private concerns is naturally much less, but is nonetheless substantial and growing. British industrial location policy as shaped by regional development thinking is humane if unadventurous. Issue is taken here not with the principle, but with the practice, of this policy: intervention in location has been sectoral and piecemeal rather than comprehensive and has undervalued the development role of infrastructure.

In part, regional policy has been undeniably successful. Much new industry has been steered to the development areas, but, even after thirty years the number of new jobs created has been too small to remove regional differences in unemployment. Unemployment levels in the development areas are twice the national average, being in May 1975 3.4 per cent (West Midlands) and 2.4 per cent (South East) but 4.6 per cent (Scotland), 5.0 per cent (Wales) and 5.4 per cent (Northern England). Between 1960 and 1972 regional policies are credited with creating 80 000 new jobs in Wales, about 8 per cent of total employment there: to remove Welsh unemployment it needed to be three times as great, yet policy was more effective in creating jobs in Wales than anywhere else in the UK (Moore and Rhodes, 1975). British interregional differences in income or in opportunities are smaller than in, say, France, but several indices confirm that peripheral regions are still 'deprived' as compared with the axial belt.

The regional orientation of development planning and decision-taking in heavy industry has been extremely cautious both by nationalized and by private industry. The cumulative effects of this are international uncompetitiveness. Old shipyards have been modernized but no new yards constructed. Failure to build new steelworks or to choose the best locations for expansion has caused the present dilemma facing the British Steel Corporation and the government. Much new industry steered to the Development Areas is light and, providing jobs for women, has been welcome for raising low female activity rates but workers displaced in the decline or rationalization of coal, steel, locomotive, shipbuilding and heavy engineering are overwhelmingly male. Many industrial plants built in the peripheral regions have been branches of firms already operating in the axial belt, causing rapid turnover as branches are closed in time of recession. Attempts have

been quite inadequate to link new industries both in specialization and in space
too little focus being given to the development impact of big public works. In
short, British planning has neglected both industrial-complex and regionally
oriented infrastructure planning despite subservience of peripheral to axial
regions.

Government planners have been content to provide new employment in
problem region without considering sufficiently where the interlinkages of the firm
lie. Within each Development Area activities have been too scattered
perpetuating old urban patterns appropriate enough in an age of colliery employment or of small-scale shipbuilding or textile mill operation but, under present circumstances, inconvenient for the more complex interrelationships of modern
manufacturing, and costly in terms of service and infrastructure provision. The
most impressive example of industrial complex building also shows the limitation
of its practice in Britain: the already diverse, but predominantly heavy, metal
fabricating and engineering economy of mid-Scotland.

A government decision taken late in 1958 ensured that high grade strip-mill
sheet steel production, formerly confined to South Wales and to the Dee–Mersey
areas, should be diffused to Scotland. Then the automobile industry was highly
localized in the English West Midlands and South East. In return for governmen
approval for major extensions to their existing plants, several vehicle firms wer
persuaded also to make large-scale investments in new plants in peripheral areas
Biggest development occurred on Merseyside, smaller projects went to South
Wales though that was by far the biggest sheet-steel making area. Two firms bui
new plants of substantial size in central Scotland. Neither South Wales nor mi
Scotland were ideal for motor complex development and in neither did gove
ment intervention proceed far enough to bring in component trades on a sc
commensurate with their automobile expansion. One result of such half-hear
industrial complex planning was a large increase in interregional movements
multitudes of components, partly by rail and partly by road. These moveme
were increased by the decision by firms to transfer to Merseyside and to Scotl
whole special sectors of their United Kingdom operations so that the flows
material should be two-way and not just outwards to the Development A
plants. Even so, large public subsidies – though providing large new emplo
ment – resulted in substantial social costs and also increased industrial product
costs, contributing to decreased competitiveness of the British motor trade
tighter, more thorough-going intervention might have yielded greater benefit to
regions: no intervention at all might have been better for the buoyancy of
whole national economy.

There was failure within the regions to apply the idea of a localized produc
complex, at any rate in mid-Scotland. There the largest vehicle assembly plant
press shop is at Linwood (southwest of Glasgow), where it was grafted on
plant established for railway wagon-making. A new commercial vehicle and t
tor plant was built at Bathgate 30 miles (48 km) to the east to help revivify an
oil-shale mining area. The hot and cold strip mills were located in between
about 10 miles (15 km) apart), the hot mill being at a new integrated works wh
while wholly dependent on imported iron ore, had been placed inland to mini
distress in a traditional iron and steel district. In short, on the regional and
national scales, a wholly praiseworthy social concern was allowed to confr
economic logic. Perpetuation of economic life in an old area which had
threatened with abandonment encourages extensive urban renewal. This

anyone who knows the older British industrial communities will agree, is in itself highly desirable, but it compounds the difficulties at the next round of decision-taking about industrial location.

These difficulties or deficiencies are inevitable in an old industrial country with a mixed economy and with substantial, but not overriding, government intervention. Yet the problem should at least have been squarely faced: situations and prospects should have been more carefully examined and the costs of following various solutions including sub-optimal, socially-oriented policies more fully assessed.

Infrastructure investment represents an important aspect of British planning of obvious, if less immediate, impact on the Development Areas. New Town construction from 1947 onwards was preoccupied with solving London's overspill problems. The opportunity to use the direct investment and the dispersed workforce to inject new life into peripheral regions was lost even though government was then totally committed to a regional development policy. Over £1000 million spent on Concorde with its Bristol base and largely southern British associated firms, large spending at existing London airports, the possibilities of the (now deferred) third London airport and Channel Tunnel are other cases of big direct or infrastructure spending in the prosperous axial belt.

The significance of transport development policy is even greater. Despite various bold railway reconstruction schemes, Britain has favoured freight movement by road throughout the entire automobile age, so encouraging dispersal and probably maintaining smaller-scale operation than might have been fostered by a railway-orientated transport programme. Britain was late into the motorway era, yet between 1959 and 1973 built 1748 km (1086 miles) of motorway. Rather than use this to integrate the internal economies of the peripheral areas and then subsequently build motorways outwards towards the more dynamic areas of the South East and Midlands, the opposite policy was followed, so gradually extending the sphere of domination of already locationally-favoured manufacturing and service firms. The true cost of this policy to the peripheral regions is probably incapable of measurement, yet undoubtedly detrimental. Development Area policy and motorway construction strategy were in conflict, the regional growth effectiveness of Development Area spending being partially cancelled out by the new economic orientation that the motorways encouraged.

Conclusions

An industrial location policy as the central factor in a regional policy is essential in the old industrial economy of Britain. Yet all British governments have failed to realize that in a mixed economy, where decision-taking about industrial development and expansion is widely diffused, infrastructure spending – no less than direct action – can affect location decisions. Similarly, increased internal regional integration, with industrial complex planning as the core, has been neglected. Though small, Britain comprises a number of effective economic regions operating as concentrations within nationwide flows of materials, products, people and ideas. To recognize and plan for this would bring the impersonal wide sweep of economic planning into line with the realities of social geography. The economist and the politician are all too often preoccupied with national ills or ambitions, the professional planners with local horizons to the neglect of a wider regional amework. A more general conclusion is that in the replanning of an old industrial, mixed-enterprise economy – no less in a centrally-planned socialist one – the role of the geographer is more vital than has yet been recognized.

References

Agafanov, N. T. and Lavrov, S. B. (1966) 'On the fundamental differences between capitalist and socialist regional territorial production complexes', *Soviet Geography Review and Translation*, **7** (7), pp. 56–65.

Heal, D. W. (1974) 'Ownership, control and location decisions: the case of the British steel industry since 1945', Ch. 10 in: F. E. Ian Hamilton, ed., *Spatial Perspectives on Industrial Organization and Decision-Making*, Wiley, London, pp. 265–85.

Moore, B. and Rhodes, J. (1975) *Regional Policy and the Economy of Wales*, Welsh Office, Cardiff.

Chapter 6

Complex territorial changes in old industrial areas of the German Democratic Republic

Horst Kohl

Industry in the German Democratic Republic (GDR) has expanded rapidly in recent years. From 1950 to 1970 production increased five-fold (an index of 537 in 1970 cf. 1950 = 100), while employment grew by only 35 per cent. Increased output was thus achieved above all by mechanization and automation, so raising productivity. This explanation is essential in considering the location of industry since employment changes are generally a poor index of spatial shifts in productive capacity. Yet the population variable is a very crucial factor in planning industrial location in the GDR because, directly or indirectly, there is a scarcity of labour.

The population variable

Such national scarcity results because, first, population declined in the GDR from 18.4 million inhabitants in 1950 to only 17.1 million in 1970; simultaneously second, a rapidly ageing population reduced the working population as a proportion of the total population from 64.1 per cent to 57.8 per cent (the share of old-age pensioners grew considerably, from 13.8 per cent to 19.5 per cent). Nevertheless, employment was increased from 7.2 million (1950) to 7.8 million (1970), mainly by employing more women who, in 1970, made up 48.3 per cent of the labour force.

Regional population trends, however, are quite divergent. In the more agricultural north, it has increased substantially. Only recently has the rate of increase tailed off towards the national average, natural increase in the district of Rostock (Fig. 6.1), for example, decreasing from 9 per 1000 in 1965 to 4 per 1000 in 1970; in neighbouring Schwerin comparable figures were 7 and 2 per 1000. This will yield some increase in labour supply in the near future, which new industry can absorb or which can migrate to other regions, but supply will decline in the long run. By contrast, most other regions, which are strongly industrialized, demonstrate either very small natural population increases or even decreases. In major urban agglomerations and cities population is decreasing slowly and interregional mobility of labour cannot provide sufficient compensation for this trend. Some rural areas still often exhibit natural increases. In the central and southern GDR, therefore, the labour force situation demands planning to shift workers from one occupation to another after rationalization and automation in their former places of employment. Thus the contrast between the north and most other parts of the country is inversely correlated with the intensity of industrial development.

Fig. 6.1   The Bezirke and major cities in the German Democratic Republic.

Industrial structure and location policy

An essential question for regional planning is whether industries should construct new capacities in areas with potential future labour reserves, that is in the north, or should the labour of the north be ordered to go to central and southern areas where industrial expansion is easier? Or is some combination of these strategies desirable? There is no single answer to this national and regional industrial question.

Spatial planning in the GDR previously aimed at reducing inherited disproportions in economic structure: sharp regional contrasts in levels of industrialization, excessive urban and regional industrial specialization and inadequate spatial balance between the demand for, and the supply of, labour. The solution was to reorganize the older industries in the south and to construct new plants in the same areas for complementary purposes. For example, a major sulphuric acid plant was constructed at Coswig on the northern fringe of the major Halle chemicals agglomeration. The area did not possess this type of plant though local demand for its products was very high and favourable raw-materials supplies exist nearby. Most labour came from the north to work in the expanded and modernized chemicals and engineering industries. In the north, only specific new industries were developed and older plants modernized. More recently, since 1966, industrialization in the north has been intensified, so diminishing labour migration to other regions.

Thus, today two quite different industrial structures exist. Central and southern urban–industrial agglomerations (Berlin, Halle-Leipzig, Dresden and Karl Marx Stadt-Zwickau) cover 15 per cent of the area of the GDR but concentrate almost 50 per cent of its industrial workers (Table 6.1). These areas have favourable preconditions for further industrial expansion production except for labour scarcities.

Table 6.1 Employment of production workers in industry in the area of the German Democratic Republic in 1939, 1956 and 1966

	1939	1956	1966
Bezirke	Thousands Percentage	Thousands Percentage	Thousands Percentage
Berlin†	392.2	256.1	234.8
Rostock	76.3	105.2	105.5
Schwerin	51.9	62.7	57.6
Neubrandenburg	48.8	48.5	48.1
Potsdam	207.9	170.0	159.3
Frankfurt	108.2	80.2	85.6
Cottbus	171.9	171.9	186.5
Magdeburg	238.7	214.5	221.9
Halle	291.6	460.3	446.5
Erfurt	270.3	269.8	277.3
Gera	177.1	189.1	161.3
Suhl	148.6	149.8	146.8
Dresden	506.9	493.9	460.0
Leipzig	392.8	369.4	353.3
Karl-Marx-Stadt‡	756.4	634.6	558.7
Total	3778.6	3475.9	3513.2

Source: Based on figures from tables in: H. Kohl, G. Jacob, H. J. Kramm, W. Roubitschek and G. Schmidt-Renner (1969) *Ökonomische Geographie der Deutschen Demokratischen Republik*, VEB Hermann Haack, Gotha/Leipzig, pp. 42, 50, 52.

† These figures refer to (East) Berlin, capital of the GDR.
‡ Prior to 1953 Karl-Marx-Stadt was known as Chemnitz.

Their future growth demands automation and rationalization of industrial units and their inter-relationships rather than creation of more jobs. This means that, spatially, industry in the central and southern districts will be relatively inert. For example, chemical industries now use oil as a raw material instead of lignite and this has demanded the development of basic petrochemicals output. Thus the Leuna II Works was created as a petrochemical nucleus right in the heart of the existing chemicals industrial area. The workers required in this important plant came from other local chemical works where conversion from lignite to oil had made their employment unnecessary. The Leuna II Works now process piped petroleum and pumps its basic petrochemical products to neighbouring chemical industries for subsequent processing.

Divergent trends in employment are observable in and around the major industrial agglomerations. Manufacturing jobs are declining slowly in larger cities and currently vary as a proportion of total employment from 39 per cent in Berlin to 57 per cent in Karl-Marx-Stadt. The hinterlands of the major centres show a continual increase in manufacturing employment which varies from 40 per cent of all jobs in Berlin *bezirke* to 63 per cent in Halle-Leipzig *bezirke*. Thus while interregional changes are very small, intra-regional plant movement from major cities is significant.

Industry in older centres developed under conditions of capitalist profit in the past without integrated planning. Many factories became cramped in old town quarters and often unhealthy mixtures of industry and residential areas emerged. Socialist territorial planning is bent on renewal of such areas. This process demands long-term action because the problems of conversion are so great and the costs very high. Conversion is proceeding as a process of spatial rationalization. The major factories suitable for the planned specialization of a given area are modernized for highly efficient industrial production; others are closed or are relocated to new sites. To some extent suitable existing industrial plants can be rationalized by reallocating manufacturing stages and related functions among them to create integrated complexes of depots for raw materials or spare-parts, repair capacities and infrastructure facilities providing energy, heat, water and transport as well as vertically-linked processing. Unfavourably situated housing is replaced by better dwellings elsewhere. Such complex conversion is under way at present in Berlin-Schöneweide for electrical engineering and at Leipzig-Plagwitz for mechanical engineering industries.

Rostock, Schwerin and Neubrandenburg districts and northern Magdeburg, Potsdam and Frankfurt-am-Oder were once dominantly agrarian provinces. Industrialization began in the 1950s here with the construction of major shipbuilding yards, influencing all larger ports and many towns in the hinterland where marine components industries were located. Expansion of food-processing intensified the linkages of towns with their agrarian surroundings. Further industrial development has been encouraged (like steel at Eisenhuttenstadt) by adequate regional labour supplies. Often industries have been constructed together in defined zones, like industrial estates, and are partially integrated. These may be called 'investment complexes' such as at Schwerin-Süd, Neubrandenburg-Ost and Greifswald. The prerequisite for the development of new 'propulsive industries' is the new energy base of the north: first, the nuclear power station east of Greifswald, and second, the oil refining and petrochemicals complex at Schwedt at the western end of the 'Friendship' pipeline which brings oil from the Volga fields in the USSR.

Complex spatial development

Persistent increases in industrial production have created substantial territorial problems with growing economic demands for land. In highly industrialized countries the location of industry is a decisive prerequisite for territorial order so that industrial dynamics exercise the utmost impact on the form and functioning of a region. In socialist countries, public ownership of the means of production provides the possibility and creates the necessity for planned location of industries in the interest of the people. This sweeping statement, instantly formulable, is, however, by no means easily applicable in territorial planning because of the multiplicity of regional economic variables to be considered. This has led to broad discussion in the USSR of the aims of 'territorial production complexes' (Kolossovsky) and to applied studies for regional economic modelling.

Complex territorial questions are posed, of course, in different ways according to development levels of the areas in question. Those economic regions that were highly industrialized already in the past (Berlin and Halle-Leipzig district, or Moscow and the Donbass in the USSR) expose different problems of territorial development as compared with new investment complexes in the sparsely-industrialized northern GDR or in Siberia. The former areas have developed under changing social conditions and show increasing congestion. The latter complexes, including cities, have developed essentially according to interpretations of the territorial planning concepts. Highly industrialized areas, evolving over long periods in 'historical layers and strata', raise several questions for spatial planning.

Territorial specialization in industry

The specializations of industrial regions as an expression of the spatial division of labour occurred spontaneously under capitalism. In the GDR, this process resulted in a marked contrast between the agricultural north and the highly industrialized south with attendant differences in working and living conditions. Systematic specialization of industrial areas in socialist countries is secured through long-term optimization in production and services, paralleled by international improvement of working and living conditions everywhere. Specialization proceeds both in the higher-order, i.e. more advanced integrated industrial regions (or in Comecon) and emerging in lower-order, less advanced and structurally simpler industrial areas. Accordingly, systematic planned specialization takes account of the spatial structures of the whole and of the integral parts of various regional hierarchies.

The potentialities inherent in population, production, infra-structure and resources necessarily play a substantive role in the process of specialization. This means for old industrial areas that the consequences of earlier specialization which manifest themselves in workers' skills, basic fixed capital in production and infrastructure, the degree of exploitation of natural resources, had decisive impact in shaping specializations both to be continued and to be initiated. This impact correlates with the level of development of the industrial area in general and with its degree of specialization in particular. Thus those areas having a high concentration of industry, or a high rate of industrialization with noticeable specialized production are relatively constrained in taking up new specialisms. Economically, this finding in the GDR is reflected in the demand presented also by Kretschmer (1974) that '... the location of already existing production facilities should be chosen as the place for investments in expanded capacity with a view to utilizing the experience gained by workers during production and to utilizing production facilities and auxiliary plants to a higher degree'.

While in the 1950s and 1960s the north GDR experienced introduction of fairly wide range of specialized industrial production (shipbuilding, mechanical engineering and foodstuffs) the already congested south (Halle, Leipzig, Dresden, Karl-Marx-Stadt and Gera) did not change essentially the spectrum of its major industries. Specialized industries developed in new areas depended upon the availability of very large capital investments in several industries, whereas new specialized industries could be introduced in old areas by investing small funds in the use of existing sites. Herein lies one of the essential causes of the continuity of location despite a *change of production*. Therefore, Mohs (1972) justifiably points to the high regional capacity for scientific and technical progress both in the dynamic development of structurally-important industries and in the dynamics of territorial changes in structure.

The costs incurred in changing facilities for specialized production toward achieving optimal territorial structures while using existing industrial equipment depends upon capital intensity. If in GDR industry the average fixed assets equals 80 000 Marks (1970) per worker employed in the energy, fuel, chemical and metallurgical industries, it is rather difficult, often impossible, to make fundamental changes in the facilities. Such changes will be effected in the event of depleted resources or of radical changes in technologies. In contrast, in those GDR industries where the average fixed assets lie below 40 000 Marks (1970) per worker employed (engineering, electrical and electronics, instrument manufacture, light industry and textiles) changes in the profile of production are more feasible.

Even in the highly industrialized south this contrast is strikingly apparent. The production profiles of districts dominated by capital-intensive industries were changed only slightly, e.g. in Halle district, where energy, fuel, chemical and metallurgical industries accounted for 58.8 per cent of gross industrial production (1971). The mix of districts with large industries having lower capital intensity was changed more noticeably, e.g. Karl-Marx-Stadt, where mechanical and electrical engineering, electronics, instrument manufacture, light industries and textiles, accounted for 79.4 per cent of gross industrial production (1971). In this district premises of the formerly large textile industry were partially reconverted for new engineering and electronics industries.

Specialization and complex territorial development

Specialized production constitutes the essence of manufacturing in heavily industrialised areas. If one should succeed in adapting industries adequately to establish optimum harmony between industry as a whole and other elements of the region, then even the conversion of old industrial areas could be called 'complex territorial development'. The major negative legacy of capitalist development is that old industrial locations frequently developed individual reference networks without paying heed to any regional considerations: side-by-side plant siting often existed without many linkages so generating excess demand for land, labour, water and transport.

To improve such areas concepts of development are required both for individual areas and a master plan for the entire national spatial system. Economic reality will constitute the starting platform from which it will be possible to optimize the development of the area with regard to the growth of national income and the improvements of living conditions. Optimization is difficult in the old industrial areas because of the multiplicity of existing and mutually-interacting elements. Of course, the aim of achieving an economically-rational combination of industrial locations plays an important role in the complex-territorial development of an area. Specialized industries have to be substituted one for another in particular premises, a process of 're-profiling' accomplished through centralized manufacture of machinery.

The hierarchy of complex territorial developments

Modern Siberian territorial production complexes (T.P.C.) have become known specifically as examples which demonstrate application of Kolossovsky's T.P.C. concept. The specific profiles of production in these complexes and their gigantic dimensions make it impossible to apply them automatically to other areas like the GDR. If, however, the essence of the theory of territorial production complexes is extracted it can serve as a guideline for a general orientation of development in most different areas, irrespective of size, state of development, structure and degree of congestion. The 'territorial production complex' in its most generalized form constitutes an economic area marked by outstanding specialized and complementary production, proportionately allocated, and shaped or developed systematically in the interest of society. As such it can guide conversion of old industrial centres. This has for long been experienced in the GDR, as shown by the (new) investment and (old) rationalization complexes. Old and other industrial areas show a great range of diversity with regard to size, level, structure and congestion. Thus the relevance of each level of complex territorial development to these old centres should be carefully studied.

In this context there is a need for delimiting the areas objectively to ensure the complex territorial development. The problem of economic regionalization can be dealt with in a vertical and horizontal manner. *Vertical regionalization*, i.e. the hierarchy of industrial areas according to size, proceeds from the notion that increasing spatial dimensions have to match progressive concentration and specialization processes. This would mean that even smaller countries in their entirety, or even parts of them combined with frontier areas in other Comecon countries can be categorized as higher-order economic entities. Even if a higher degree of complexity is achievable only within relatively larger areas because of the effects of industry, the areas of lower order should not be neglected because of their reduced possibilities to form complexes. This chain of hierarchically-nested economic areas ends with the individual industrial site or estate and its environments.

Horizontal economic regionalization, i.e. the subdivision of space into standard areas of dimensions, is made specifically difficult in the old industrial areas. Historically, manifold overlapping linkages and sales relations in many locations, and variously expanded and superimposed infrastructural levels, input and output, have created, as a rule, very complex spatial–functional relations. Thus the limits of areas will be formed by boundary belts which every planning operation has to take into account because a single boundary, even if drawn according to important regional economic factors, will in reality remain abstract. Yet such a single boundary provides a useful long-term planning framework to advance integrated regional development by employing standard measures, such as new investments, re-profiling of factories and improvement of infrastructure. Regional boundaries, though, must be altered through time to adapt to changing spatial reality.

Economic dynamics which become strkingly evident in the problems of regionalization, however, constitute only one factor for defining areas. Another closely related factor is the political attitude adopted and the efficiency shown by man in this process. Democratic cooperation, based necessarily on the experience gained by the competence of local councils, demands relative stability in the politico-administrative areas which in the GDR also constitute entities for planning. Therefore, an adjustment of boundaries to the changing spatial reality cannot be continuously effected. Such adjustment should be only periodic.

References

Kehrer, G. (1974) 'Berlin, die Hauptstadt der Deutschen Demokratischen Republik', in: H. Kohl, ed., *Bezirke den Deutsche Demokratischen Republik*, Gotha/Leipzig.

Kohl, H. and Zimm, A. (1973) 'Die Ballungsproblematik der DDR in theoretischer Sicht', *Wissenschaftliche Zeitschrift der Humboldt-Universitat zu Berlin*, Math-Nat., H/1.

Kolosovsky, N. N. (1958) 'Proizvodstvenna-territorial'nye sochetanye (kompleks) r. Sovetskoi ekonomicheskoi geografii', in *Osnovi Ekonomicheskogo Raionirovaniya*, Gospolitizdat, Moscow, 200 pp.

Kretschmer, K. (1974) 'Inhaltliche Aufgaben der langfristigen Planung der Standortverteilung der Industrie in der DDR bis 1990', *Informationen der Forschungleitstelle fur Territorialplanung*, 11, p. 6.

Mohs, G. (1972) 'Struckturentwicklung und Planung von Ballungsgebieten, als Problem und Aufgabe der territorialen Strukturforsch-ng', *Petermanns Geographische Mitteilungen*, 1, pp. 3/4.

Chapter 7

A long-term regional distribution model for Hungarian industry

Gyula Bora

The use of computers is vigorously influencing national planning and within it also regional planning. Already mathematical modelling of the pre-plan decision phase has already achieved substantial results in Hungarian national economic planning. However, a start has only just been made with regional planning. Our proposed research thus aims at evolving a model system permitting the integration of the effects of space and other factors in the preparation of regional plans. Recently, the plan for the development of the Hungarian national settlement network up to the year 2000 and the principles of regional policy were laid down by the government. Currently work on preparing the developmental principles for, and the plan of, the Hungarian economy till 1985 is in progress, including a long-term regional developmental plan. This latter takes into account the structure of settlements and labour resources and aims at a more rational spatial structure which may result in a more effective territorial distribution of industry.

Rapid industrial growth (a 240 per cent increase in employment) has permitted, and industrialization policy has brought about, essential changes in the spatial distribution of Hungarian industry since 1950 (Table 7.1). The most outstanding result is the radical decrease in the proportion of industrial labour employed by industry in Budapest from 55 to 36 per cent between 1950 and 1970. Yet, despite considerable industrialization in the provinces, some areas remained industrially backward (Table 7.1) and still with a labour surplus.

Data presented in Table 7.1 indeed indicate the following postwar trends. First, the industrial growth of the city of Budapest has been partially decentralized into the suburban zone of Pest county where there was little prewar industry. Second, there has generally been far more rapid expansion of highly-capitalized industries outside Budapest in both developed northern and the more industrialized as well as the less industrialized Transdanubian counties where industries tend to process and manufacture minerals and metals. On the other hand the Alföld industries are labour-intensive and reflect the predominance of food-processing and light industries. Third, industry generally has grown faster in the less developed than in the more developed counties, but this has still not eliminated the dominance of Hungarian industry by the Budapest region and the northern and northwest Transdanubian areas which accounted in 1970 for 78.6 per cent of jobs and 82.3 per cent of invested capital (Fig. 7.1).

To reinforce the locational principles of the fifteen-year regional plan, a model involving six alternatives was prepared in 1970. The model attempts to optimize the spatial distribution of industry in 1985. Calculations were made by a research team of the Committee of the National Planning Bureau comprising I. Bartke, I. Iles and G. Bora. Data and research preliminaries were undertaken by the Depart-

Table 7.1 Some features of the spatial distribution and change in Hungarian industry, 1949–70

Counties	Index of increased industrial employment 1949–70 (1949 = 100)	Percentage of Hungarian industry, 1970		Intensity of industrial development per 1000 population, 1970	
		Employment	Fixed assets	Employment (persons)	Fixed assets (million forints)
Capital Area		43.5	35.4	246	30.2
Budapest city	188	36.0	39.5	312	37.4
Pest County	731	7.5	5.9	96	13.8
Northern counties		13.1	18.8	146	33.6
Borsod-Abaúj-Zemplén	193	8.2	13.8	162	43.1
Heves	620	2.6	3.1	112	22.0
Nógrád	123	2.3	1.9	140	19.5
Industrially-developed transdanubia		20.0	28.1	156	35.4
Baranya	265	3.8	5.7	136	33.3
Fejér	547	3.2	5.9	123	36.2
Győr-Sopron	194	4.6	3.6	172	21.9
Komárom	172	4.4	6.8	222	54.7
Veszprem	334	4.0	6.1	143	35.8
Industrially-underdeveloped western transdanubia		7.1	6.4	85	13.3
Somogy	538	1.7	1.6	65	10.8
Tolna	496	1.5	0.8	78	7.3
Vas	308	2.2	1.3	114	11.9
Zala	331	1.7	2.7	89	24.3
Southern and eastern Alföld counties		16.3	11.3	79	9.2
Bács-Kiskun	558	3.2	1.4	80	6.0
Békés	277	2.6	1.9	82	10.2
Csongrad	392	3.8	2.2	129	12.2
Hajdu-Bihar	250	2.6	2.2	71	10.1
Szabolcs-Szatmár	432	1.5	1.2	38	5.2
Szolnok	388	2.6	2.4	86	12.9
Hungary	240	100	100	149	23.6

Source: Körödi, J. and Mártón, G. (1972) *A Magyar Ipar Területi Kérdései,* Kossuth Könyvkiado, Budapest

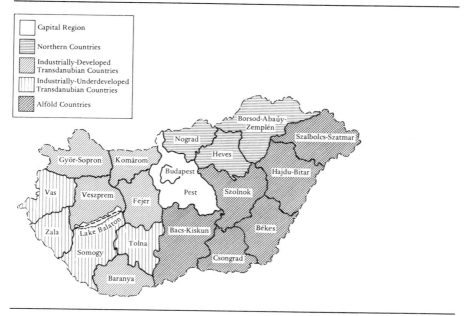

Fig. 7.1   The Counties of Hungary categorized according to their development level.

ment of Economic Geography and Regional Science at the Karl Marx University of Economics, while programming was executed at the *Infelor* Computer Centre of the Central Statistical Office.

The method of calculation

The so-called 'transport model' with capacity constraints was used. Since the calculations were made in parallel with the projecting of long-term plans for different industrial branches, the projections of industrial labour in the different branches for 1985 depended on the information embodied in the long-term national plan. Under such conditions, the model can be defined as: given m industrial branch, the country's total industrial labour will increase by $l_1, l_2 \ldots l$ and given n settlement in which the increase of industrial labour will be equal to t_1, $t_2 \ldots t$. Accordingly, the sum of increments by branches and settlements must be equal to one another. Thus,

$$\sum_{i=1}^{m} l_i \qquad \sum_{j=1}^{n} t_j$$

The allocation of the surplus of industrial labour among the settlements should be of such magnitude and of such structure as to correspond to the industrial situation of the settlements with minimum costs of investments and operations.

Matrix c_{ij} contains the coefficients of developmental costs. If the number of industrial workers to be settled in settlement j of branch i is denoted by x_{ij}, the total costs of investments and operations can be described by the following function:

$$\sum_{i=1}^{m} \sum_{i=1}^{n} c_{ij}\ x_{ij}$$

We seek to minimize this function under the conditions:

$$x_{ij} = 0$$

$$\sum_{\substack{m \\ i=1}} X_{ij} = t_j$$

$$\sum_{j=1}^{n} X_{ij} = l_i$$

Our model raises two problems: first, how to determine numerically the costs of industrialization by branches and settlements (c_{ij}), and second, how to set out the constraints of each settlements (t_j). The model matrix was 61 × 112, that is, increment of labour in 61 industrial branches was to be distributed among 112 settlements decided by the so-called Long-Term Plan for Settlement Network which scheduled the development of 112 towns by the year 2000 as against 75 existing towns.

Calculations were based on the spatial distribution of socialist industry in 1968 defined as State and cooperative industry. The changes to be made in industry were considered up to 1985 including the closing down of some enterprises (a number of plants will be removed from Budapest), and large-scale automation facilitating the freeing and hence relocation of part of the total industrial labour of 1968. As this portion was estimated at 20 per cent of the industrial workforce in 1968, the number of workers that would be spatially distributable was determined by adding 20 per cent of redistributable labour to the increment of 1968 to 1985. This yielded a total of 678 000 industrial jobs to be allocated among the settlements.

The result of the programme clearly depended upon how successfully the elements of matrix c_{ij} were estimated. Therefore, a method for this was elaborated using technical coefficients. The 112 settlements were arranged according to 11 location factors: labour force, skills, transport facilities, energy and raw material resources, technical linkages, markets, water supply, infrastructural requirements, research background and industrial traditions. Each town was ranked by and each branch of industry was ranked according to their relative requirements of these location factors by 11 numbers ranging from 1 to 5. Settlements were also ranked by a point scale by industrial branches (matrix of costs) so that the vectors of 11 factors of the industrial branches were subtracted from the vectors of 11 factors of the towns. Negative differences indicated the unsuitability of the locational attributes of a given settlement for a given branch of industry. The matrix of costs was obtained by summing the vectors by industrial branches and settlements. Thus, the technical coefficients identify relative excess costs of location. The minimization of these excess costs formed the optimum criterion in programming.

The conditions of the six alternatives were the following:

Alternative A is a concentrated pattern of industrial growth in 35 significant settlements (19 county seats and 16 preferential settlements) allowing only minimal (23 000) growth of industrial employment in Budapest.

Alternative B is a decentralized variation on 'A'. Growth in Budapest is similar to that in 'A', but in the provinces the growth in jobs was allocated among 111 settlements. Industrial labour constraints in rural settlements were applied according to the requirements of the Long-Term Plan for the Settlement Network.

Alternative C is a concentrated alternative allowing greater employment growth in Budapest (about 50 000). The remainder of provincial growth is distributed as in 'A'.

Alternative D permits the highest employment growth specified by the programme for 109 settlements. For Budapest, Miskolc and Debrecen, however, it specifies an increase between the maximum and minimum values. This alternative incorporates more economic efficiency in the selection of settlements as growth centres for employment.

Alternative E projects a large decrease (120 000) in industrial jobs in Budapest. National growth in industrial employment, including decentralization from Budapest, was allocated among 35 rural settlements in a concentrated fashion in proportion to their expected labour resources and the resources of their hinterland, creating a network of new towns.

Alternative F is a strongly decentralized pattern and calls for a smaller (23 000) decrease in industrial jobs in Budapest. The growth in employment was allocated in a decentralized fashion among 111 settlements in proportion to their expected potential labour resources.

For each alternative the following calculations were made: (1) the spatial distribution of industry in 1985, 65 industrial branches being aggregated into eight groups; (2) the structure of industry by counties in 1985 calculated for the 8 groups of industry; (3) the proportion of female labour in industrial employment by counties in 1985; and (4) the distribution of industrial labour in 1985 by settlement categories. These categories were: Budapest, the five main provincial cities (Miskolc, Debrecen, Szeged, Pecs, Győr), four different urban-type settlements to be urbanized before the year 2000, and non-urban settlements. For the calculations counties were grouped into three categories according to their development level: first, *Budapest and Pest County* (the Budapest agglomeration), the most industrialized area; second *industrially-developed counties* such as areas with mineral resources and substantial industrialization (chiefly the central part of Transdanubia and northern Hungary); and third *industrially backward counties*, the formerly agricultural areas where industrialization only started in the last 25 years and where further industrial development is required (chiefly the Great Plain and South-West Transdanubia).

The results

A number of important conclusions emerge regarding the long-term location of industry. Optimal industrial structure by settlements and the rationality of regional proportions and concentrations can be deduced by comparing the six alternatives. Yet the model only partly involved national economic efficiency. It has been assumed that during the long-term plan period regional concentration may take place independently of development. Employment of transferable industry in the non-preferred, mostly rural settlements was also reallocated among the preferred settlements. For this and other reasons (e.g. the decline of coal-mining), industrial labour in non-urban settlements is decreasing.

The programme permitted classification of the alternatives according to efficiency. From this viewpoint, the alternatives with concentrated patterns are the most desirable, especially those requiring further increases in industrial employment in Budapest. Alternatives C and D thus proved to be the most efficient. Undesirable on grounds of inefficiency are those alternatives which presume a large-scale decrease in the industrial labour force of Budapest, or require long-term dispersed location of industry. Thus, the final draft of the long-term plan must necessarily pay attention to the proportion between Budapest and the provinces to satisfy the efficiency criterion.

Furthermore, the six alternatives point out expected changes in regional proportions resulting from different principles. They also show to what extent would the more rational and efficient location policy be able to change the actual regional inequalities during fifteen years. The results indicate the following tendencies: First, fundamental regional inequalities can be reduced further by improving relationships between Budapest and the provinces. Second, the importance of the industrially-backward counties in the nation's total industry activity can be increased further. Depending on alternatives, an increase of 180 000 to 250 000 industrial jobs in fifteen years could be achieved, which would mean the large-scale industrialization of backward counties. Third, the regional importance of industrially-developed counties are little modified by the alternatives since only a small proportional increase is to be expected in this category as a whole. It calls for a substantial industrialization only in the developed counties where coal-mining employment will decrease significantly, and where redirection of labour into other occupations and industries requires large investments.

A further important result of the programme is data on the changes expected in industrial structure by counties. Considering all the alternatives, *no essential change is expected in the industrial structure of Budapest and Pest County*, though increased machinery production will substitute decreased light industry in Budapest city. Because of relative decline in coal-mining, important structural changes in industrially-developed counties must involve also a relative decline in heavy industries (metallurgy, energy production) and a shift towards manufacturing primarily through expansion of engineering. All programmes show, however, significant increase in the scale of light industry because industrially-developed counties still have a considerable surplus of female labour whose employment hitherto was hindered by the dominance of heavy industry. But the most dynamic industry in Hungary will be chemicals, though its proportional increase is not significant in the six alternatives because its great intensity generates only small increases in employment.

The industrially-backward counties will experience more limited structural

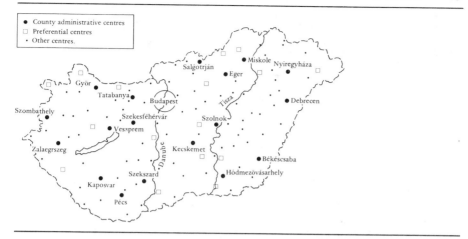

Fig. 7.2 The County, Preferred and other centres considered for allocation of industrial jobs in Hungary.

change than the industrially-developed ones, because neither coal-mining nor other heavy industries were very significant. In 1968 their structure comprises only three main groups of manufacturing: engineering, consumer goods and foods. The relative exp:nsion of the machine industry indicated by the programme was smaller than was expected, so that changes are predicted to occur mostly (in all alternatives) in the greater growth of light manufacturing while substantial relative decline will be recorded in the food industry. Machinery industries received lower priority as a result of technical constraints imposed by the programme, i.e. it makes high demands on skilled labour and production linkages which are not at all suitable everywhere. It is noteworthy that the importance of the chemical industry is perceptibly increasing in the majority of counties, mainly on account of its great demand for water which is readily available in a number of industrially-backward areas along the rivers Danube and Tisza.

Great differences are evident between the concentrated and decentralized alternatives regarding changes in the spatial distribution of industry among urban categories. Yet the major town categories were preferred by the programme for industrial growth, i.e. the towns with more than 30 000 inhabitants. To sum up, the tendencies in the spatial distribution and structural change of industry by counties, revealed by the programme, correspond fundamentally to the regional principles of the Hungarian government, so permitting design of a rational long-term plan of industrial location.

Chapter 8

Spatial industrial changes in Poland since 1945

Ryszard Wilczewski, Teofil Lijewski and Bronisław Kortus

During the post-war period from 1946 to 1972 industrialization has been the major factor in economic growth and structural change in Poland, as in other Eastern European countries. Intense and continued investment activity achieved a high average annual growth rate of 9.3 per cent in value-added in industry. Gross value-added in manufacturing, calculated at 1971 prices, rose from only 75 billion złotys in 1950 to 528 billion złotys in 1972 (G.U.S., 1973). Simultaneously, the contribution of industry to Polish national income increased (at 1971 prices) from 33 per cent in 1950 to 51 per cent in 1972. The main growth factors were a high rate of increase in industrial employment combined with higher productivity. Employment in industry rose from only 1.4 million persons in 1946 to 4.6 million in 1972, an increase per 1000 population from 60 to 137 in the same period. Such growth caused revolutionary changes in social structure, increasing the percentage of population living in towns from 34 in 1946 to 53 in 1972, and converting initial agricultural labour surpluses into growing shortages of farm labour in many areas.

Even in the most industrialized countries the index of industrial employment rarely exceeds 160–190 persons per 1000 inhabitants. Currently it is 111 in France, 131 in the USSR, 149 in the German Federal Republic, 165 in the UK and 190 in Czechoslovakia. Poland is thus very near to the admissible limit regarding the role of industrial employment in the occupational structure of the population. Indeed this is all the more so since productivity is still significantly below that in more developed countries. Though productivity has been increased, roughly job-creation has been a more significant factor (and goal) of growth in Poland (Table 8.1).

The crucial issue now, therefore, is to expand production largely, if not solely, by raising labour productivity. Investment policy needs to be altered to decrease the rate of new job creation and to intensify labour-saving innovations through general modernization and progressive automation. Hitherto, the strategy of extensive industrialization, based on massive increases in employment, have brought about qualitative industrial 'saturation' in all regions of Poland, facilitating substantial levelling of interregional economic differentials. New policies for modernizing fixed assets, however, can result in increased growth in more industrialized areas and this certainly decreases the scope for future changes in the location of industry. Realistic estimates of the prospects for such spatial shifts become easier through an examination of the locational changes which were achieved during the phase of extensive industrial development that was completed in the early 1970s.

Table 8.1 Labour productivity and its contribution to increased industrial production between 1961 and 1972 in selected countries

Country	Average annual increase in labour productivity (percent)	Contribution of increased labour productivity to increased industrial production (percent)		
		1961–5	1966–70	1971–2
Poland	5.1	66	63	63
Soviet Union	5.2	59	70	82
Czechoslovakia	4.4	66	82	74
Hungary	4.7	66	67	100†
German Federal Republic	5.3	73	95	48
France	5.1	72	95	81
Italy	3.9	74	63	100†
Sweden	5.9	98	100†	100†
Japan	9.5	70	88	97

Source: Rocznik Statystyczny Międzynarodowy, Warsaw, 1973, p. 122.
† In cases where industrial employment decreased, it is accepted that increased industrial production results entirely from higher labour productivity.

Quantitative analysis: application of the shift-share technique

These locational shifts can be readily investigated using shift-share analysis (Fuchs, 1962; Perloff, 1960). The method measures differences in the rates of increment in a given variable between regions by means of calculating relative 'net gains' or 'net losses' of a given region as compared with nation-wide trends in that variable (see Appendix, p. 97). Estimates were also made of the changed shares of individual regions in general employment and in fixed industrial assets. Spatial changes are examined by periods. These correspond with the main phases of post-war industrial development in Poland: first, the immediate post-war years, 1946–9, were devoted to reconstruction and reorganization of pre-war industry; such policy could not make radical changes in the geographic distribution of industry. Second, new industrialization commenced in 1950 with a high rate of investment in new projects, mainly in the heavy industries. Employment increased rapidly and lay at the root of significant locational shifts until 1960. Third, between 1960 and 1972 policy had to take account of the approaching industrial employment saturation and hence to begin to restrict emphasis upon job-creation.

The analysis was carried out in two stages. The first stage calculates the extent of net spatial shifts in industrial employment and fixed assets during the period 1951–72. Data were drawn from statistics for the seventeen voivodships into which Poland was then divided (Fig. 8.1). The second stage examines the relative changes in the importance of varied groups of geographic areas in the overall spatial distribution of Polish industrial employment and fixed assets in the same period. These areas are: (1) the 17 voivodships grouped into 7 macro-regions (Fig. 8.1), (2) selected voivodships and (3) 15 old and 5 new industrial districts and the rest of Poland (Fig. 8.2).

Tables 8.2 and 8.3 clearly demonstrate that the greatest shifts in both employment and fixed capital were achieved during the period of basic industrialization, i.e. between 1951 and 1960. The rate and extent of spatial changes decreased significantly during the following period 1961–72. This decrease in the net

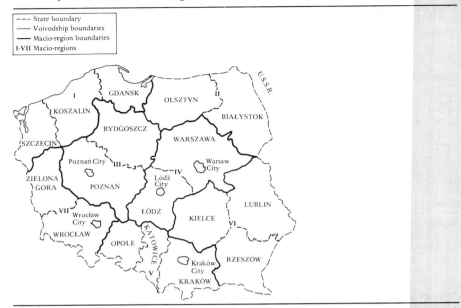

Fig. 8.1 The vovoidships and macro-economic regions of Poland till 1975 (macro–economic regions: I – Seacoast;   II – North-East;   III – Middle West;   IV – Central;   V – South;   VI – South-East;   VII – South-West).

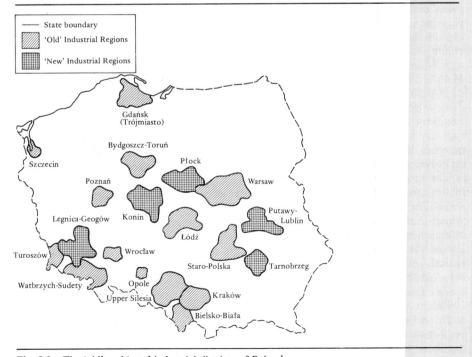

Fig. 8.2 The 'old' and 'new' industrial districts of Poland.

Table 8.2 Total net shifts in industrial employment

Geographic areas		Shifts		
		1951–60	1961–72	1951–72
Macroregions	Industrial employment (000s)	265.4	223.2	609.4
	Percentage Shift	27.3	15.2	25.3
Percentage shares of the macroregions in overall shifts:				
Seacoast		+21.5	+25.5	+23.1
North-East		+15.1	+12.3	+14.1
Middle-West		+30.6	+ 8.3	+22.6
Central		−15.5	−19.2	−17.0
South		−65.9	−80.9	−71.7
South-East		+32.8	+52.5	+40.2
South-West		−18.5	+ 1.3	−11.3
Voivodships	Industrial employment (000s)	412.9	224.9	850.2
	Percentage shift	42.5	17.0	35.3
Percentage share of some voivodships in the overall shifts:				
Katowice		−56.5	−72.0	−61.0
Łódz with Łódź City		−30.2	−23.8	−28.3
Warszawa with Warsaw City		+20.2	+ 6.3	+16.2
Rzeszów		+ 9.1	+23.5	+13.3
Poznan with Poznań City		+12.6	+ 5.4	+10.6
Kraków with Kraków City		+14.1	+ 0.2	+10.1
Białystok		+ 5.5	+ 6.5	+ 5.8
Lublin		+ 6.3	+11.3	+ 7.8
Industrial districts				
Poland total	Industrial employment (000s)	216	311	—
	Percentage shift	11.6	16.2	—
Percentage share in overall shifts				
Old industrial districts		−100.0	−100.0	—
New industrial districts		+ 14.4	+ 18.6	—
Rest of the country		+ 85.6	+ 81.4	—

Sources: *Rocznik Statystyczny Przemysłu 1971*, G.U.S., Warsaw, 1971.
    Rocznik Statystyczny Przemysłu 1973, G.U.S., Warsaw, 1973.

marginal shifts in employment and investment location is closely related to trends in Polish industrial investment planning, notably the relative (but not absolute) reduction in the contribution to growth of new projects and the parallel increase in the importance of extensions and modernization of existing factories and mines. Net overall shifts in the spatial pattern of industry were only relative. In absolute terms, there was remarkable growth in employment and fixed capital in all industrial regions, the oldest industrial areas of Katowice and Łodź included. But Tables 8.2 and 8.3 also indicate clearly that the spatial pattern of employment growth contributed more to spatial shifts during the 1950s than during the 1960s when shifts in both jobs and fixed capital are more in line. Better utilization of spare capacity in older industrial plants added to this trend, especially in the early 1950s.

The contributions of particular voivodships to overall shifts express the spatial tendencies of changes in industrial distribution much more clearly than do the shares of the macro-regions. The key areas from which industry shifts to other

Table 8.3 Total net shifts in fixed assets

Geographical areas		Shifts	
		1951–60†	1961–72‡
Macroregions	milliard zlotys	27.5	104.5
	Percentage	16.5	17.4
Share of the macroregions in overall percentage shifts:			
Seacoast		−12.3	+ 5.1
North-East		+ 3.4	+ 4.1
Middle-West		+ 1.9	+25.9
Central		+32.1	+25.8
South		−38.5	−79.0
South-East		+62.2	+39.2
South-West		−49.2	−21.0
Voivodships	milliard zlotys	41.3	118.5
	Percentage	24.9	19.8
Share of some voivodships percentage in overall shifts:			
Katowice		−48.8	−67.8
Łódź		− 6.5	− 4.1
Wrocław		−24.6	−15.1
Warszawa (with Warsaw City)		+27.9	+26.8
Rzeszów		+17.5	+16.7
Poznan (with Poznań City)		− 1.9	+15.7
Kraków (with Kraków City)		+23.4	+ 7.7
Białystok		+ 3.9	+ 1.8
Lublin		+12.9	+

Sources: *Rocznik Statystyczny Inwestycji i Środków Trwałych 1970*; G.U.S., Warsaw, 1970;
Rocznik Statystyczny 1973, G.U.S., Warsaw, 1973.

† in 1960 prices.
‡ in 1971 prices.

regions are the voivodships of Katowice and Łódź. Misztal (1970) shows that these two voivodships boasted 402 000 industrial workers between 1907 and 1910, or 34 per cent of all employment on present Polish territory. Since then, and most particularly since 1946, that percentage has decreased relatively while actual employment has increased significantly. Industry in Katowice and Łódź employed 1.3 million people in 1972, or 29 per cent of total industrial employment.

The negative shift demonstrated by Katowice voivodship was greater in the 1961–72 period than in the preceding decade; deglomeration from this area accelerated with time. Overall, its negative shift was equally matched with Łódź voivodship in the postwar period. Table 8.4 shows, however, that 'net gains' were distributed throughout the remainder of Poland, although there is a substantial degree of inverse correlation between the level of industrialization in 1960 (i.e. the number of industrially-employed persons per 100 population) and the extent of net gains between 1951 and 1972. The highest relative rates of growth in industrial employment were achieved in the least industrialized voivodships, particularly Białystok, Rzeszów, Olsztyn, Lublin and Koszalin. Yet it should be remembered that industrial centres in such voivodships are limited in scale and leave large tracts unindustrialized. Thus an above-average increment in the index of industrialization does not necessarily imply the improved position of previously

Table 8.4   Inter-voivodship shifts and expected increment of employment†

Voivedships	Industrially employed persons per 1000 inhabitants in 1960	Percentage shift 1951–72
Białystok	42.0	265
Lublin	42.4	167
Olsztyn	45.9	202
Koszalin	49.7	161
Rzeszów	62.6	231
Kielce	73.2	38
Szczecin	75.7	123
Warsaw	81.7	87
Poznan	87.3	72
Bydgoszcz	87.8	50
Zielona Góra	95.6	30
Gdansk	97.0	98
Kraków	103.4	55
Wrocław	138.0	32
Opole	118.7	− 5
Łódź	142.9	−68
Katowice	220.9	−69

Source: *Rocznik Statystyczny 1973*, G.U.S., Warsaw, 1973.

† Mathematical formulation: $Yw - Hw/Hw - Xw$. 100; designations see Appendix.

underdeveloped parts of the voivodships. Yet generally the development of underdeveloped regions resulted more from their real industrialization than from spatial proximity to existing industrial regions.

Table 8.5 presents data relating to the broad postwar changes apparent in the industrial regions relative to the rest of Poland. The twenty industrial regions defined embrace 17 per cent of Polish territory, yet in 1972 they localized 43 per cent of the total population and generated 60 per cent of industrial activity. The most important group comprises the fifteen old industrial districts, the relative position of which weakened to a limited extent between 1949 and 1972 (Table 8.5). This group comprises the regions of Szczecin, Gdańsk, Bydgoszcz-Toruń, Poznań, Warsaw, Łódź, Staropolska, Turoszów, Wałbrzych, Wrocław, Opole, Upper Silesia, Bielsko-Biała and Kraków. Combined, these old districts employed 56 per cent of Polish industrial labour and accounted for 52 per cent of Polish industrial capital in 1972 as against 66 per cent and 59 per cent respectively in 1949. Only five significant new industrial regions have been established since 1950: Konin, Płock, Legnica-Głogów, Puławy and Tarnobrzeg. They embrace a large area, 13 000 sq km, but in 1972 were still in a stage of crystallization and even currently account for only 5.5 per cent of gross industrial capital and 3.8 per cent of industrial employment.

The ratio of the proportions of invested capital to employment speaks well of the level of technology in the new districts. Nevertheless, employment per 1000 inhabitants there only slightly exceeds the average for the remainder of Poland. Why, then, have they been classified as industrial districts along with the older areas where the index of industrial employment per 1000 inhabitants is significantly higher? Basically the answer lies in their typically high concentration of investment and associated key role in Polish economic development. Such districts have become important through the exploitation and processing of local or highly-

Table 8.5 Changes in the industrial districts of Poland, 1949–72

	Employment on 31.XII†													Investments/current prices/					
	Area in thous	In thous. of persons			structure			In persons per 1000 inhabitants			per 1 km²			% of the total			per 1 inhabitant thous. zl.		
	km²	1949	1960	1972	1948	1960	1972	1949	1960	1972	1949	1960	1972	1961–5 average	1970	1972	1961–5 average	1970	1972
	2	3	4	5	6	7	8	9	10	11	12	13	14	15	16	17	18	19	20
Poland	312.7	2050	3300	5209	100.0	100.0	100.0	83	110	157	6.6	10.6	16.7	100.0	100.0	100.0	1.7	2.4	4.0
Industrial districts	53.8	1355	2129	3108	66.0	64.5	59.7	160	176	218	—	39.6	57.7	70.5	61.2	59.5	2.9	3.5	5.5
Old districts	40.4	1355	2043	2914	66.0	61.9	55.9	160	185	225	33.5	50.6	72.1	58.5	48.8	51.1	2.7	3.1	5.2
New districts	13.4	—	86	194	—	2.6	3.8	—	80	147	—	6.4	14.5	11.7	12.4	8.4	5.5	7.8	8.4
Remaining area of the country	258.9	695	1171	2101	34.0	35.5	40.3	43	66	111	2.7	4.5	8.1	29.5	38.8	40.5	0.8	1.7	2.8

† With trainees, and auxiliary plants in other branches of economy. It increases employment by about 14% in comparance to figures used in other parts of the paper.

Rocznik Statystyczny Przemysłu 1973, p. 557; Rocznik Statystyczny Przomysłu 1971, p. 459;
Rocznik Statystyki Powiatów 1973, pp. 26, 110; Rozwój Gospodarczy Powiatów 1950–65. G.U.S., Warsaw, 1967;
Statystyka Układów Regionalnych, G.U.S., 1972, pp. 91 i 107.

accessible mineral resources: lignite (Konin), copper (Legnica-Głogów), sulphur (Tarnobrzeg), oil (Płock) and natural gas (Puławy).

Interregional differences in levels of industrialization have diminished only very gradually since 1945. Trends in the coefficient of localization show this. Between 1949 and 1972 the coefficient decreased from 0.45 to 0.29 at the voivodship level and from 0.53 to 0.43 at the industrial-district level. The fundamental force behind the achievement of diminishing interregional differentials was undoubtedly the high rate of industrial growth in Poland as a whole. As a result the absolute level of industrialization in the remainder of Poland – that is outside the twenty industrial districts – was one-third higher in 1972 than the average for the whole of Poland in 1949, as measured in industrial employees per 1000 inhabitants. By contrast, the figure for the old districts in 1949 was 3.7 times higher than elsewhere in Poland, but by 1972 it was only twice as great. Yet the absolute difference remained almost unchanged, being equal to 117 persons in 1949, 119 persons in 1960 and 114 persons in 1972. A similar, but weaker, tendency is apparent in the changes in industrial employment per square kilometer although industrial growth and its localization generally led to a continued rise in the gap between the industrial districts and the rest of Poland: from thirty-one employees per square kilometer in 1949, through forty-six employees in 1960 to sixty-four employees per square kilometre in 1972.

Overall, the rate of levelling in differences was so slow and its acceleration so negligible between 1961 and 1972 that one should take heed of the fully reliable calculations made in Kuklinski and Najgrakowski (1964). These indicate that if the rates of population growth and industrialization of the period 1946–60 are sustained, then economic differences between industrialized and non-industrialized areas will disappear after 365 years – in effect, never. However, actual future trends are unclear, particularly as the substantial deglomeration of industry achieved between 1960 and 1970 gave way to remarkable expansion in the old districts following the policy changes of 1970. Yet it is too early to quantify any answer to the question as to what extent the decrease in interregional differences during the period 1960 to 1972 was the logical outcome of industrial development processes and to what extent was it a result of specific deglomeration policy between 1965 and 1970. The latter set artificial and economically very costly limits to the development of industry in the old industrial districts, especially the largest agglomerations. Removal of these limits is clearly reflected in the sharp rise in the proportion of industrial capital invested in the six largest old urban–industrial aggomerations of Warsaw, Kraków, Lódź and Poznań and in Katowice voivodship. In 1965 these agglomerations localized 37 per cent of Poland's invested capital. By 1970 this had fallen to 32.6 per cent but by 1972 it was up again to 35.3 per cent. Had deglomeration policies not been applied between 1965 and 1970 then the rate of decrease in interregional divergences would have been much slower than it was in reality.

One of the dangers built into the long-term planning of the development of the national economy is thinking based on extrapolation into the future not only of the rates and proportions from previous periods, but also the existing lines of thinking which perpetuate regional trends. A major purpose of regional policy is to achieve better distribution of national income among the regions of a country. As Klaassen (1972) observes, interregional income differentials are largely caused by differences in economic structure. In most cases the highest incomes per employee are earned in Poland in industry so that diminishing interregional differences was seen to depend upon industrialization. Klaassen rightly stresses, though, that policies towards regional equality can endanger economic growth in a country as a whole.

However, if the purpose of regional policy is to exploit the natural resources of a region so as to optimize national economic growth and if at the same time the aim is to level spatial differences in living standards — which does *not*, in a planned socialist economy, require generation of the same per capita income in all regions — then traditional thinking on this problem is altered. It means that industrial location policy is directed at satisfying the superior interests of the entire State, namely of maximizing national income among other goals, and that the process of achievement of interregional equalization is less important even if it may slow down or even stop. This view takes on new meaning today when it is accepted in Poland that the acceleration of economic growth and urbanization in less developed areas does not rest inevitably upon the location there of industrial plants. The proper and potential roles of agriculture, tourism and other activities should be given due consideration (Kuklinski, 1967).

Types of industrial migration

Intensive industrialization created opportunities for substantial industrial migration in Poland after 1945. The following have been the major reasons for migration: (1) Heavy destruction of fixed assets in the Second World War was not evenly distributed, older and more important industrial regions (Upper Silesia, Łódź, the Sudety area) suffering the least, whilst smaller centres of modern industries in Warsaw, south-eastern Poland and lower Silesia were very badly destroyed and some plants could not be rebuilt. (2) The new discovery of resources of copper (between Lubin and Głogów in north-west Silesia), sulphur (around Tarnobrzeg in south-east Poland), brown coal (at Turoszów in western Silesia and around Konin in central Poland) and natural gas (in south-eastern and central Poland) has stimulated construction of raw-material and energy-using manufacturing industries in many new locations. (3) Changes in the regional distribution of demand encouraged spatial shifts in other mineral-based industries such as cement, lime, brick-making and the prefabricated concrete industry, as well as in an expanding light and consumer-goods manufacturing sector. (4) Policies by the postwar socialist government have attempted to equalize the economic levels of all regions to eliminate legacies of historically-sharp regional differentiation so that many investments were located in backward regions for social reasons. (5) A related factor is the Polish situation in agriculture where 85 per cent of the farm land is privately owned and fragmentation results in high rates of underemployment. Thus, the State has constructed some industries in overpopulated agrarian districts to provide jobs locally and to reduce extension of long-distance commuting to towns where housing is scarce. (6) Increased scale and vertical-integration economies have led to greater concentration of production in larger plants. (7) To contend with this trend a policy of deglomeration was applied in the 1960s to the largest agglomerations, Upper Silesia and Warsaw, but it was abandoned in 1970. (8) Expansion of water-using industries, especially power plants, and the chemical and paper industries, has led to new groupings alongside larger rivers. (9) The reconstruction of the old central districts of many cities has necessitated removal of old industrial functions to new plants in the suburbs.

Three geographic scales of migration may be generally distinguished in distance moved and in importance of administrative boundaries crossed. *Local* migration occurs from the city to the suburban zone, mostly in the cases of Warsaw, Łódź, Poznán and Kraków. *Regional* migration occurs within an administrative or economic unit (former voivodships or macro-economic regions) and ranges from 50 to 150 km: for example, the building of branch plants in Warsaw voivodship to replace old plants in Warsaw. *National* migration occurs between different regions, shifts exceeding 150 km, and results from new plant construction or development of new resource-using industrial regions – like recent growth in power and chemical industries not in the Silesian coal basins but in central (Konin, Kozienice, Warsaw) and northern Poland (Lower Odra, Ostrołęka), the location of the chemical industry along the Vistula (Machów, Puławy, Płock, Włocławek, Toruń), dispersion of cement production from southern to central and eastern Poland, the northward movement of cellulose and paper industries (Ostrołęka, Świecie, Kwidzyń), and development of food processing in eastern Poland. One more stage should be distinguished: *international migration*, resulting from planned cooperation in COMECON. For example, Poland is constructing plants in the Soviet Union, while simultaneously its copper and sulphur industries are supported by other socialist countries.

Industrial migration does not imply only physical movement of productive capacity from one place to another. It also means: first, *construction of new plants in new places* (virgin site development), typical in less developed regions and in industries which require specific buildings, installations and sites (the power, metallurgical, cement, glass, saw-milling, grain milling and sugar refining industries); second, *extension and modernization of existing plants* at lower cost especially in machinery and engineering industries, shipyards, certain chemical industries, furniture production, textiles, clothing and leather industries, printing and food processing; third, *adaptation of unused buildings or of closed industrial plants to new industrial uses* has been significant in especially in western and northern areas where many war-damaged buildings were left in 1945. Today, when enterprises close, their buildings are used for other lines of production: for example, buildings at closed iron-ore mines near Częstochowa and Kielce have been occupied by machinery industries. Such adaptation often led to some casual migration as re-used buildings were sometimes unfavourably located: over a longer period new factory construction would have been more economic but in the short term it was the only feasible solution when materials and buildings were acutely scarce.

Different industries experience different types, degrees and directions of migration. *Mineral extraction* has been spreading from its pre-war limits, mostly in the Silesian Industrial District and Lower Silesia, in all directions and several new material manufacturing areas have been opened. Once highly concentrated in Upper Silesia, steelmaking has spread to the east (Nowa Huta, Stalowa Wola) and north-east (Częstochowa, Warsaw, Ostrowiec). The huge new Katowice integrated steelworks constructed near Dąbrowa Górnicza will reverse this migratory trend to Upper Silesia. *Copper smelting* around Bolesławiec and Złotoryja in Lower Silesia has shifted to the Legnica–Głogów district. *Engineering* industries (machinery, vehicles, electrical equipment) show the highest rates of industrial growth, and account for 37 per cent of all new industrial jobs in Poland since the Second World War. Yet their migration is insignificant since they have continued to develop mainly in large cities. A northward shift may be detected on the national scale resulting from relative stagnation in these industries in Upper Silesia, whilst northern cities (Gdańsk, Gdynia, Szczecin) have experienced a rapid growth in shipbuilding and central cities (Warsaw, Łódź and Poznań) growth in varied machinery and electrical industries. Construction of branch plants in small towns has contributed to regional deglomeration from large cities. *Chemicals* industries have tended to migrate northwards too, mostly in search of water supply from major rivers and oil and gas feedstock sources and production in coalfields is tending to stagnate. *Timber industries* have developed slowly and show hardly any migration by contrast to the paper industry, which shows distinct migration northwards to use the larger water supplies of the main rivers (Ostrołęka, Kostrzyn, Świecie, Kwidzyń). *Textiles*, traditionally concentrated in Łódź, Bielsko, Sudety, has changed little though cotton industries have developed in north-eastern Poland (Białystock, Zambrów, Łomża) and knitwear has been widely diffused, even into peripheral areas like Stargard Szczecinski (north-west), Biłgoraj and Jarosław (south-east). *Clothing*, generally localized in larger cities, has also tended to deglomerate through the construction of branch plants in smaller towns where female labour is available.

Food processing exhibits diverse trends. Consumer-oriented activities expand in accordance with the distribution of population (bakeries, breweries, beverages, meat packing). Others move to regions with a surplus of marketable agricultural products (slaughterhouses, dairies, poultry and egg processing, grain mills, sugar factories, fruit and vegetable processing). At the national scale food processing is migrating eastwards to where the increase in agricultural production (especially of livestock products) is more significant.

The location of new capacities

The fixed asset value of new industrial capacities built in Poland between 1945 and 1970 exceeds 20 million zlotys (US $1 million). Such plants have consumed most investment as the socialist economic system favours construction of large plants which yield scale economies. Altogether data was collected for 1270 plants constructed, reconstructed or expanded sufficiently that they can be treated as new. Heavy industry, which produces capital goods and supplies energy, dominates the investment structure because of both demand for heavy industrial products in the industrialization process and favourable raw material supply in Poland.

The location of new industrial plants is governed by several general factors, partially contradictory with each other. However, one of these tendencies prevails in the end, according to the kind of plant and to its purpose. Often the choice of location must compromise between a number of factors, the most important being:

(1) *The existing network of industry*, which is manifest in the expansion of existing or the reconstruction of destroyed plants, and the construction of new ones within traditional industrial areas or centres, especially of engineering, chemical and textile industries. Thus among 348 new engineering plants 140, representing 60 per cent of the total fixed assets invested in new engineering plants, have been located adjacent or very near existing old factories. Thus, while the machinery, electrical engineering, vehicle and transport equipment industries are the most dynamic growth industries in Poland, they are characterized by great

immobility, notwithstanding the theoretical freedom of location. Such factors as staff skills, strongly developed inter-factory cooperation and connections with scientific research play a great role in this situation. Similarly inertia in the chemical industry has resulted from concentration of investment in seven large integrated chemical plants including those built by Nazi Germany on Polish soil for military purposes at Kędzierzyn, Blachownia Śląska, Brzeg Dolny and Oświęcim (Auschwitz).

(2) *Material orientation* of new plants prevails among all location tendencies as measured in investment because much Polish industry is material or energy-intensive: 30 per cent of the total value of fixed assets of all new factories and including thermal-power plants, coal- and lignite-processing, copper mills, aluminium, sulphur-processing, steel, cement, zinc and lead mills, oil and natural gas installations.

(3) *Market orientation* relates to factories located as near the planned consumers as possible: the population, other factories or industrial installations, different economic sectors such as agriculture, forestry, transport or construction. The market tendency generally signifies the concentration of factories in or near existing urban agglomerations and industrial centres.

(4) *Labour orientation* is significant when future employment in the factory decides its location: reserves of unskilled labour, especially women, in small non-industrialized towns and in overpopulated agricultural regions, or small reserves of skilled labour which appear when some factories go into liquidation or when vocational schools train more specialist than are required in a given area. The most important labour-oriented industries are (in rank order of fixed asset value): textiles, metal, chemical, machine, timber, electrical engineering, shoe-making and clothing.

(5) *Agglomeration advantages* decide location when factories are sited to derive benefits from joint location with other industries, from existing social infrastructure, and from urban services (professions, design and planning): eighty-eight factories in the electrical engineering and electronics, precision instruments, pharmaceuticals and so-called 'cultural goods' (music, record, film) industries.

(6) Finally, *transport orientation* has decided the location of a few industrial plants in Poland (e.g. the oil refinery in Plock on the 'Friendship' pipeline and some port industries). Though most goods move by rail in Poland, railways influence site, not location. *State defence, political issues* and *international agreements* have decided the location of only a small fraction of new plants.

The majority of these locational orientations tend to concentrate industrial plants in certain centres and regions with especially advantageous conditions for industrialization. Thus of 1270 plants built during the years 1945–70, 715 are localized in twenty regions and five centres – 56 per cent of all new plants but 80 per cent of the total fixed assets and 71 per cent of the jobs in all newly-created plants. Thus, larger, capital-intensive plants are concentrated in such centres and regions as compared with dispersal of smaller factories throughout Poland.

Industrially-developed regions are those poviats (districts) which each localize more than 1 per cent of total national industrial investment. Among the five urban centres and twenty regions two groups can be noticed: raw-materials regions which have been created and partially developed thanks to mineral extraction and processing, mainly in southern Poland; and urban–industrial regions which have emerged around major cities. Kraków and Bydgoszcz can be included in both groups. Only two regions developed away from mineral fields and big towns:

Rzeszów which owes its foundation to inter-war investment located there for reasons of national defence, and Bielsko where engineering developed to 'convert' old traditions in weaving and cloth-making into modern industrial structure. Strong correlation exists between industrialization and urbanization: all cities with more than 100 000 inhabitants in 1970, except only Białystok and Lublin, are situated within industrial regions.

Structural changes in Upper Silesia

The Upper Silesian Industrial Region (Fig. 8.3), the largest mining and manufacturing area in Poland, has an area of 2700 sq km and 2.2 million people: one-third of the labour force was employed in industry in 1970. It forms a complex based on coal according to Chardonnet's (1953) or, according to Kolossovsky's definition (1958), one with a clear dominance of a coal–metallurgical cycle exhibiting multiple technical and production linkages of both a vertical and a horizontal nature on the intra-regional, inter-regional and international scales.

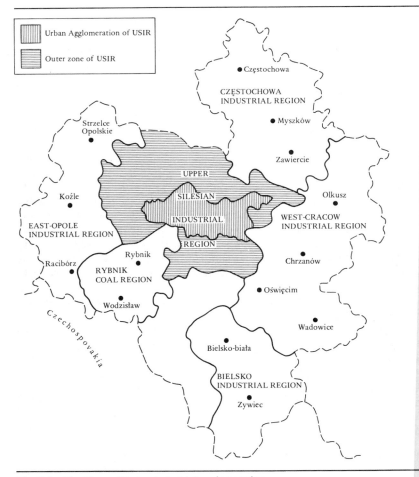

Fig. 8.3   The Upper Silesian industrial agglomeration.

Table 8.6 Evolution of the industrial structure of the Upper Silesian industrial region, 1946–70

Industrial branches	1946	1956	1965	1970	1946–70
Electricity	2.4	1.8	2.0	2.2	−0.2
Fuels	49.7	48.5	43.9	40.6	−9.1
Ferrous metallurgy	18.7	13.7	13.4	14.0	−4.7
Non-ferrous metallurgy	3.8	4.1	3.1	3.5	−0.3
Machinery and electrical engineering	11.4	15.8	19.1	20.8	+9.4
Chemicals	3.6	3.4	3.9	4.2	+0.6
Building materials	3.0	3.3	3.5	3.2	+0.2
Glass and pottery	0.8	1.2	0.9	1.0	+0.2
Timber manufacturing	0.8	1.0	1.1	0.8	—
Paper	0.7	0.5	0.5	0.4	−0.3
Textiles	1.3	1.0	1.3	1.2	−0.1
Clothing	0.5	0.9	1.6	2.1	+1.6
Leather and footwear industry	0.2	0.4	0.7	0.6	+0.4
Foods	1.9	3.5	4.1	4.4	+2.5
Printing	0.9	0.5	0.6	0.6	−0.3
Other branches	0.3	0.4	0.4	0.5	+0.2
Total	100.0	100.0	100.0	100.0	

As in other 'old coalfield' regions of Europe, Upper Silesia has undergone significant structural changes in recent years, but not because of a 'coal crisis'. Expansion of coal output to meet the demands of postwar Polish industrialization has raised production in Upper Silesia from 61 million tons (1950) to 107 million tons (1973). Yet for more than a decade there has been stagnation, though little decline, in mining employment. The most significant problem, however, is structural diversification of a narrow industrial base.

Table 8.6 presents the impact of planned structural change on employment between 1950 and 1970. Trends accorded with contemporary changes in Poland and in other coalfields of the world, but a 'structural crisis' does exist insofar as changes have been slow. Coal-mining, ferrous and non-ferrous metals, mining and metallurgy, still dominate the regional economy, despite their relative decline from employing 72 per cent of Upper Silesian industrial workers (1946) to 58 per cent (1970). The region still retains its 'mono-industrial' structure. Yet the importance of machinery, electrical engineering and chemicals has increased substantially to employ 25 per cent of a very much larger regional industrial workforce, compared to only 15 per cent in 1946.

It is instructive to compare the industrial structure of the Upper Silesian Industrial Region (USIR) with that of the Ruhr region (Table 8.7). Clearly the process of technical and structural modernization has progressed much more rapidly in the Ruhr than in Upper Silesia.

The situation in Upper Silesia largely reflects the divergent development trends among particular branches of industry between the coalfield and other regions of Poland resulting from national industrialization and location policies (Fig. 8.4). Table 8.8 shows that the lag of Upper Silesia was greatest just in the most modern growth industries, i.e. 0.4 in chemicals and 0.6 in the machinery and electrical engineering industries. Neglect of non-ferrous metallurgy is less critically important since it resulted from faster growth in resource-rich Lower Silesia. Lags in industrial structure are accompanied in Upper Silesia by equally retarded socio-

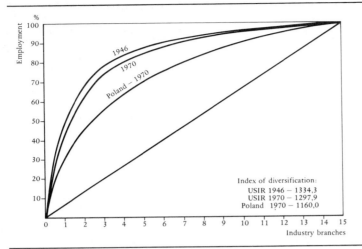

Fig. 8.4   Changes in the industry branch structure of the Upper Silesian industrial region according to Rodgers' index of classification

economic characteristics. Though regional urbanization is the most advanced in Poland (92 per cent of the population live in towns) the occupational structure shows that most people work in socialized industries and construction (68 per cent in 1970), only 30 per cent in services.

Table 8.7 The industrial structures of the Upper Silesian and Ruhr regions

Industries	Percentage of employment		Percentage of the value of production	
	Ruhr (1971)	USIR (1970)	Ruhr (1971)	USIR (1970)
Coal mining	22.0	40.6	11.1	26.3
Metallurgy	23.5	17.5	28.3	30.9
Machinery and electrical engineering	32.2	20.8	30.0	20.3
Chemicals	7.7	4.2	16.2	6.2
Other industries	14.6	16.9	14.4	16.3
Total	100.0	100.0	100.0	100.0

What factors explain these overall features? Why has structural change been so slow? First, localization of much of Poland's raw-materials and fuel resources in Upper Silesia conditioned the development and continued expansion there of coal-mining, coal-processing, ferrous and non-ferrous metallurgy: in 1970, more than 70 per cent of coal, 80 per cent zinc, 90 per cent lead and 40 per cent steel came from this region.

Second, the basic features of present-day Upper Silesia were shaped in the nineteenth-century under political and economic conditions – partition of both Poland and of the region – which inhibited the evolution of an integrated and rational industrial structure. Germany, Russia and Austria, rulers of this territory

Table 8.8 The growth rates of industrial branches in Poland and Upper Silesia 1946–70

	Index of growth (1946 = 100)		Index of retardation	
	USIR	Poland	USIR	: Poland
Electricity	162.4	261.8	0.6	
Fuels	151.5	173.1	0.9	
Ferrous metallurgy	138.0	226.4	0.6	
Non-ferrous metallurgy	172.1	395.7	0.4	
Machinery and electrical engineering	338.9	563.2	0.6	
Chemicals	220.4	546.2	0.4	
Building materials and glass	205.4	312.8	0.7	
Timber and paper	158.1	236.9	0.7	
Textiles and clothing	343.6	256.2	1.3	
Leather and footwear	567.5	642.3	0.9	
Foods	398.8	308.7	1.3	
Other	168.7	313.0	0.5	
Total	185.2	323.9	0.6	

at that time, applied policies preferring raw-material exploitation and simple processing to the development of manufacturing. The mono-industrial character of the region increased during the interwar period under continued political division between Germany and Poland and dominance of foreign capital in the Polish part.

Third, after 1945 Upper Silesia became the chief fuel and capital-goods' base for rebuilding and later newly developing Poland. Investment costs in existing industries were lower there but investment in new industries to exploit regional infrastructural potentials was insufficient.

Fourth, postwar Polish regional policy for limiting industrial expansion in, and encouraging deglomeration from, the Upper Silesian Industrial Region inhibited structural modernization. Preference was given to the development of the coal industry and of activities directly connected with it, and the location of more footloose industries was hampered. One major result of such investment and location policy currently is the small percentage of *new* plants – whether measured in employment, value added or fixed assets – in the region (14 per cent) cf. the Polish average of 35 per cent.

Significant changes in State economic policy since 1970 have favoured modernization throughout Polish industry. Two essential processes operate to modernize industry in Upper Silesia. First, accelerated investment in growth industries – especially machinery, electrical and chemical industries – has begun with greater growth of consumer-oriented production (e.g. car industry), is leading to further diversification. Second, modernization continued in collieries, doubling their productivity between 1946 and 1970. Planners project that by the year 2000 Upper Silesian Industrial Region will produce up to 150 million tons, i.e. an increase of 50 per cent, but employment will be little higher than now. Essential reconstruction in ferrous metallurgy involves construction of the large new steel plant 'Katowice' and conversion or closure of old plants. More sophisticated processes have been introduced into the coke chemicals industry but future growth will be rapid in petrochemicals.

If we apply the terminology used by Bandman (1972) in describing industrial complexes, the *specialized* branches of Upper Silesian industry till now have been coal mining, ferrous and non-ferrous metallurgy and some types of chemicals. *Auxiliary* branches have been machinery, electrical engineering, building materials and some chemicals. Following the structural changes now coming into effect, the range of specialized branches will increase and shape decisively further development of the Upper Silesian Industrial Region. This process is being accompanied by improved technical and higher education and by the development of scientific research. Upper Silesia is now second only to Warsaw in this field. Thus a process of 'emancipation' of higher education and science has taken place analogous to that which has also occurred in other similar European industrial regions, and which enhances the process of regional technical and social modernization. Simultaneously, automation of production processes releases labour and permits greater expansion of services. Yet another field of regional improvement requires greater future action – protection of the human environment – because of longstanding industrial pollution and ageing urban areas. Nevertheless an essential feature of the industrial complex is its 'maturity' which is expressed in the degree and strength of internal linkages. But it is equally important to assess the degree of the modernity or retardation of old industrial regions, for it is only those with modern manufacturing structures which guarantee high rates of economic development and efficiency.

Future trends

Already one can predict with great certainty that between 1975 and 1990 the spatial and structural correlation of industrialization and urbanization with general socio-economic development in Poland will weaken significantly. Thus industrial location in future cannot be taken as the main planning tool of urbanization and spatial development: equally, however, this does not mean that industry will cease to be an important element in planning spatial change. In fact industrial progress will continue, but chiefly through modernizing and expanding production in existing plants. This process will frequently require the construction of new premises, but alongside the old, so increasing industrial concentration. Such a trend, deliberately propelled by planning decisions, is intended to realize the benefits of large scale production: in the past this goal has often taken a secondary place behind social or other goals. Spatial concentration, however, has other benefits, too: it can assist in making effective measures for environmental protection over a larger part of the country.

The high level of economic development which will be achieved by Poland and other East European countries in the thirty-year period to come will free the urbanization process from direct dependence upon the dynamics and location of industrial activity. During the late 1970s it should be possible to make the rapid increase in living and general urban social standards the top policy priority. In spatial terms this radical change in the system of priorities will materialize through the rapid diffusion of urbanization processes, the widespread development of infrastructure and of the service network.

References

Bandman, M. K. (1972) *The Scheme and Composition of Optimization Models for Forming Spatial Production Complexes*, Novisibirsk (in Russian).

Chardonnet, J. (1953) *Les Grands Types de Complexes Industriels* Editions Sivey, Paris.

Fuchs, V. R. (1962) *Change in the Location of Manufacturing in the United States since 1929*, Yale University Press, New Haven.

Glówny Urząd Statystyczny (G.U.S.) (1973) *Dochód Narodowy*, G.U.S., Warsaw, pp. 2, 51.

Gresillon, M. (1973) 'Nordfrankreich: eine Region im Krisenzustand', *Geographische Berichte*, **67(2)**, pp. 71–89.

Klaassen, L. H. (1972) 'Growth poles in economic theory and policy', in: A. R. Kuklinski & R. Petrella, eds., *Growth Poles & Regional Policies*, Mouton, The Hague.

Kolossovsky, N. N. (1958) 'Proizvodstvenna-teritorialniye kompleksy v Sovetskoi ekonomicheskoi geografii', *Osnovy Ekonomicheskogo Rayonirovaniya*, Moscow, 200 pp.

Kortus, B. (1964) 'Donbas and Upper Silesia: a comparative analysis of two industrial regions', *Geographia Polonica*, **2**, pp. 183–92.

Kuklinski, A. R. (1967) 'Przemiany struktury regionalnej w Polsce', in: *Zakłady Przemysłowe w Polsce XIX i XX Wieku*, P.W.E., Warsaw.

Kuklinski, A. R. and Najgrakowski, N. (1964) 'Zróznicowanie przestrzenne poziomów upremysłoweinia i urbanizacji na terenie Polski', *Miasto*, **718**.

Misztal, S. (1970), *Przemiany w Strukturze Przestrzennej Przemysłu na Ziemiach Polskich 1860–1965*, Panstwowe Wydawnictwo Naukowe, Warsaw.

Perloff, H. S. (1960) *Regions, Resources & Economic Growth*, Johns Hopkins Press, Baltimore.

Pounds, N. J. G. (1958) *The Upper Silesian Industrial Region*, Indiana University Press, Bloomington.

Riquet, P. (1972) 'Conversion industrielle et reutilisation de l'espace dans la Ruhr', *Annales de Geographie*, pp. 182–91.

Wrzosek, A. (1964), 'Changes in the spatial structure of industry in Upper Silesia, 1946–1960', *Geographia Polonica*, **2**.

Appendix

The method of calculating net shifts

The shift-share technique is that outlined by V. R. Fuchs. Mathematical formulation of the net shift method is as follows:

X_v the value of the variable in voivodship v in the initial year of the period studies;

Y_v the value of the variable in voivodship v in the terminal year of the period studies;

X.. the total value of the variable in the initial year of the period in the whole country;

Y.. the total value of the variable in the terminal year of the period in the whole country;

$H_w = X_w \dfrac{Y..}{X..}$ = the expected value of the variable in the terminal year of the period in voivodship v;

then:

$Y_v - X_v$ = the actual increment of the variable in voivodship V;

$H_v - X_v$ = the expected increment of the variable in voivodship V;

$Y_v - X_v$ = the inter-voivodship 'gains' or 'loss' of the industry in the voivodship expressed in employment or value of fixed assets;

$$\sum_V \frac{|Y_V - H_V|}{2} =$$ the total net shift on the national scale expressed in absolute figures;

$$\sum_V \frac{|Y_V - H_V|}{2|v.. - X..|} =$$ the total net shift on the national scale expressed in relative figures.

Chapter 9

Mezzogiorno: regional inequalities in industrial growth within an underdeveloped region

Alan Rodgers

The process and character of industrial growth in less developed regions and the consequences of that growth are still imperfectly understood despite a rapidly expanding literature on that topic (Hamilton, 1967; Keeble, 1967). This paper is concerned with the evolving pattern of industrial development in the Mezzogiorno, or southern Italy, represented in Fig. 9.1. The region is a classic area of subnational underdevelopment, the problems of which are replicated widely elsewhere in the developed world. Here a region is treated with long development experience involving large State investments since 1950 to narrow the major socio-economic gap between it and the far more prosperous Northern Italy (Allen & MacLennan, 1970). Attempts have been made to measure the relationship between population migration, the evolving pattern of industrialization and socio-economic development in southern Italy (Rodgers, 1970). Research then required *estimates* of manufacturing employment for 1966, the end period of that analysis. While the assessment proved to be reasonably correct, the 1960s saw significant growth not adequately reflected in the data. Recent publication of detailed employment statistics in the 1971 Census of Industry now makes possible more exact and more meaningful evaluation of the scale and spatial differentiation of industrial change in the Mezzogiorno since 1951. Concern here then is with two questions: first, where had industry grown most rapidly and why? And second, in a reciprocal sense, where have there been lags in industrial development and why? These are evaluated in terms of industrial location concepts and regional development theory.

The data base

Primary sources for this study were statistics published in the Censuses on Industry for 1951, 1961 and 1971 (Istituto Centrale di Statistica), coupled with industrial loan data provided through the courtesy of the *Cassa per il Mezzogiorno*, the key development agency for southern Italy.† Manufacturing employment statistics were computed on a comparable basis for the three study years for nineteen sectors, while the loan statistics were only available for eleven sectors. Ideally, the study would have been enhanced by use of data on value added by manufacturing capital investment, power and materials consumed but such statistics are not collected in Italy at the regional detail required.

† The author acknowledges his thanks to Professor Gabriele Pascatore, President of the *Cassa per il Mezzogiorne*, for providing special tables of loan data which made possible the preparation of figures included in this text.

Fig. 9.1 Regional provincial divisions in southern Italy.

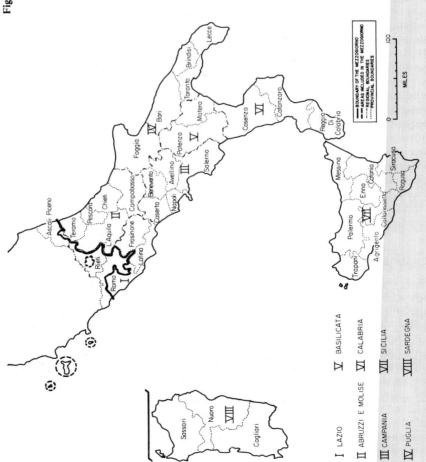

The data were employed at two geographical scales, first, for the thirty-four provinces and second, for the 2636 communes of southern Italy. Portions of the provinces of Rome, Reiti, Ascoli Piceno and Livorno, which are jurisdictionally part of the Mezzogiorno and as such entitled to aid offered by the development laws, are omitted from study.

The industrial pattern in 1951

The economy of southern Italy in 1951 was dominated by a depressed agriculture resulting from difficult physical environment and an inefficient, backward economic, political and social system. Only one person in eleven of the active population in the Mezzogiorno worked in manufacturing; the comparable ratio for northern and central Italy, hereafter termed the *North*, was one in four. Yet even these data exaggerate the role of manufacturing in the South as most industries were mainly of minute scale, with limited capital and low productivity.

Figure 9.2 illustrates the distribution pattern of manufacturing employment by provinces in Italy in 1951 when the Mezzogiorno had less than 600 000 industrial workers, about one-sixth of the total compared with nearly two-fifths of national population. Naples was the only notable centre, with nearly 100 000 persons engaged in manufacturing (62 000 industrial workers in the city excluding industrial suburbs) but its industrial employment equalled merely one-third that in Turin, one-sixth that in Milan. The only other nodes of even modest industry in the South were Bari in Puglia, Palermo and Catania in Sicily.

Table 9.1 illustrates several key facets of the structure of Mezzogiorno industry in contrast to that of the North. The relation of manufacturing employment to population (of working age), size of firm, motive power, and type of industry, clearly demonstrate the backwardness of manufacturing in the Mezzogiorno prior to the development programme. To this should be added its further handicaps: its lack of significant resources, an excessively illiterate and unskilled labour force, deficiencies in local entrepreneurial initiative, limited capital availability and the absence of an adequate infrastructure.

The development programme

From this base development has proceeded, the programme progressing through several phases, all presumed at the time to be consistent with development theory, but in fact responding to political pressures. Although expansion and modernization of manufacturing were recognized as fundamental, the development agencies first called for the 'pre industrialization' of the Mezzogiorno: drastic improvement in regional infrastructure prior to direct investment in industry itself. Relatively soon, however, political pressures forced a shift of resource allocation to industry. It was argued that the development of large-scale modern industry in southern Italy could only be achieved by 'outdrawing' the attractive power of the northern centres with their more ready market availability, greater entrepreneurial initiative and lower costs resulting partly from agglomeration economies.

Given the obstacles, however, creation of large-scale, modern assembly-line establishments in the Mezzogiorno was extremely difficult. The solution chosen was both direct and indirect government subsidization of industry. First, the 'laws' for developing the South required the building and expansion by State agencies of in-

Fig. 9.2 Manufacturing employment, by province in Italy in 1951.

dustrial plants there with the level of such investments constantly increasing over time. Second, the programme included diverse incentives for private industrial concerns, the most widely publicized being provision of long-term low interest loans and more recently direct subsidies for working capital and equipment. It was hoped that such inducements would stimulate 'northern' and foreign investors to locate facilities in the Mezzogiorno.

The programme, over two decades old, has involved expenditure of billions of lira. Yet the locational design, at least for the first decade, was a paper effort which relied far too heavily on the market mechanism to stimulate regional industrial development. A location *policy* was initiated in 1959 and reinforced in

Table 9.1 Manufacturing employment characteristics by province and region in Italy, 1951

Province and region	Proportion of working age population engaged in manufacturing† (%)	Proportion of manufacturing employment of firms‡		Proportion of manufacturing employment in firms lacking motive power‡ (%)	Proportion of manufacturing employment in first stage industries‡ (%)
		less than 11 employees (%)	greater than 99 employees (%)		
Milan	31.3	16.3	57.0	8.3	46.0
Turin	28.3	15.3	65.7	7.6	42.5
Northern Italy	16.6	25.1	50.4	14.2	61.9
Naples	7.5	34.2	41.8	32.2	66.8
Bari	3.4	61.1	18.2	36.1	85.9
Palermo	4.7	62.2	18.6	47.7	81.0
Southern Italy	4.6	63.9	19.2	48.7	87.3

† *IX Censimento Generale della Popolazione, 1951*, and *III Censimento Generale dell'Industria e del Commercio, 1951*, Vol. I, various pages. The working age population was defined as the resident population between 15 and 65 years of age.

‡ *III Censimento Generale dell'Industria e del Commercio, 1951*, Vol. I, various pages. First stage sectors comprised food and tobacco processing, lumber products, textiles, clothing, leather and shoes, machine repair shops, and the stone, clay and glass industries. The division was necessarily arbitrary. Artisan employment not included.

1965. Nevertheless, there remain officials of stature in the development banks and agencies who still regard as outmoded the notion that geographical location is a central variable influencing investment profitability within the South. They argue that technological progress has widened the range of potentially profitable locations so with obvious exceptions – such as regions plagued by difficult terrain, inaccessibility and long histories of depopulation – many areas of the Mezzogiorno, by their criteria, were equally capable of sustained and profitable growth. Such developments could only take place if the regional environment for industry, as it is perceived from the 'outside', could be altered.

Figure 9.3 depicts the distribution of industrial loans granted from 1953 to 1968 at the communal scale. Since there are often lags of two to three years from the time of granting a request for funds until its implementation in a functioning plant, such data can be correlated meaningfully with shifts in industrial employment. Although statistics on the anticipated industrial employment to be derived from such loans were also available these tended to be exaggerated and unreliable. The relationship between the volume of loans and various measures of employment growth depends on the type of facilities supported. Thus centres with highly capital-intensive industries – such as those supported at Brindisi in Puglia, Gela and Mellili in Sicily, and Porto Torres and Cagliari in Sardinia with their massive chemical complexes – are all notable on the commune map. Yet employment in these plants is low considering the investment involved. By contrast, centres like Naples and its neighbouring communes gained new industries which are relatively labour-intensive.

The impact of development efforts

What then have been the effects of these investments on the changing industrial employment pattern of the Mezzogiorno? It is assumed that, given industrial incentives of the dimensions and attractiveness of those available in the Mezzogiorno, all firms seeking to build plants or to expand existing facilities in southern Italy would have taken advantage of such inducements. In fact, a very large share of the loans were disbursed to establishments built by State holding companies like I.R.I., E.N.I. and E.F.I.M.-B.R.E.D.A. and to giant industrial corporations like Fiat, Pirelli, Olivetti and Monte-Edison. Such firms probably have had access to other capital sources but presumably none so attractive as the government-supported long term low-interest loans and direct subsidies.

Table 9.2 shows that, between 1951 and 1971, industrial employment in the South grew by 200 000 to nearly 774 000 workers, yet the growth rate fell far behind that in the North. Indeed, the South experienced a decline in its relative share of national industrial employment and would appear to support southerners, or 'meridionalists', who argue that not enough has been done by industrialization for their impoverished region. The same statistics may also provide additional ammunition for those northerners who contend that subsidy of the Mezzogiorno has retarded national economic growth. What Table 9.2 reveals is that the overall 1951–71 figures cloak two distinct periods of change which are surprisingly disparate in their values. The decade 1961 to 1971 saw relatively more rapid growth in the Mezzogiorno than in its northern counterpart, but this did not offset the unbalanced growth of the previous decade (31.4 per cent in the North, compared to 13.1 per cent in the South).

Table 9.2 Changes in manufacturing employment in Italy from 1951 to 1971

Region	Industrial employment 000s			Absolute change 000s			Relative change (%)			Share industrial employment	
	1951	1961†	1971	1951–61	1961–71	1951–71	1951–61	1961–71	1951–71	1951	1971
North	2925	3844	4513	919	669	1588	31.4	17.4	54.3	83.6	85.4
South	574	649	774	75	125	200	13.1	19.3	34.9	16.4	14.6
Italy	3499	4493	5287	994	794	1788	28.4	17.7	51.1	100.0	100.0

† Data for 1961 derived from the *IV Censimento Generale dell'Industria e del'Commercio, 1961*, Vol. 1 (Rome 1962), various pages.

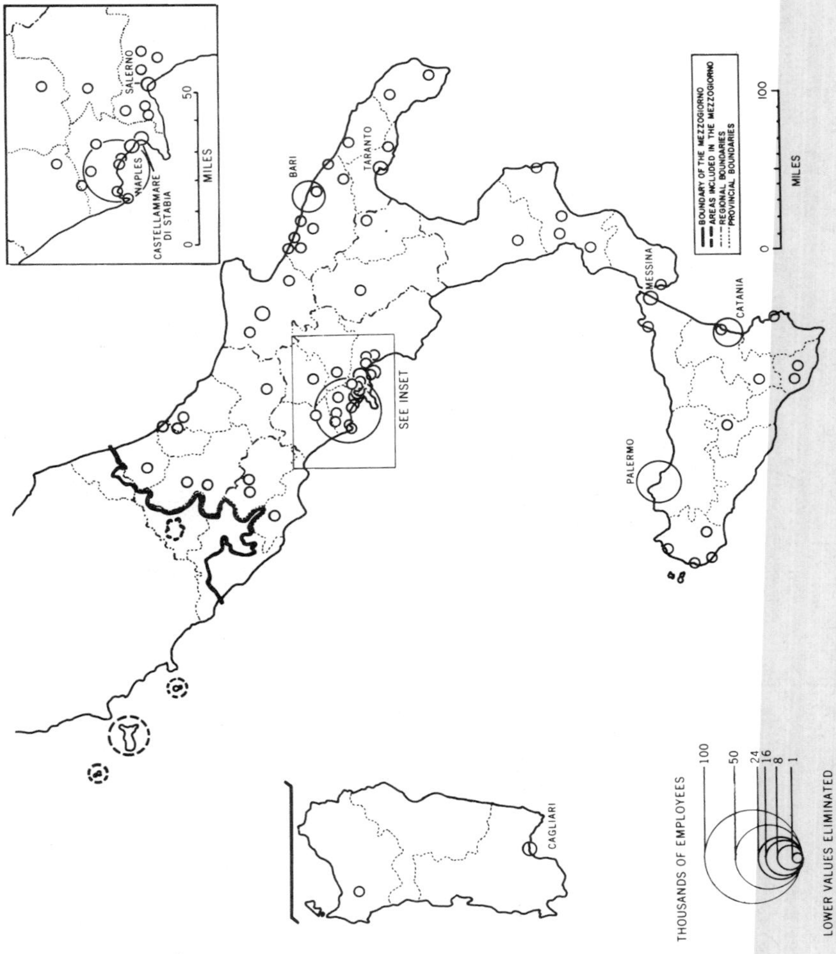

Fig. 9.3 Manufacturing loans, by commune, in southern Italy from 1955 to 1968.

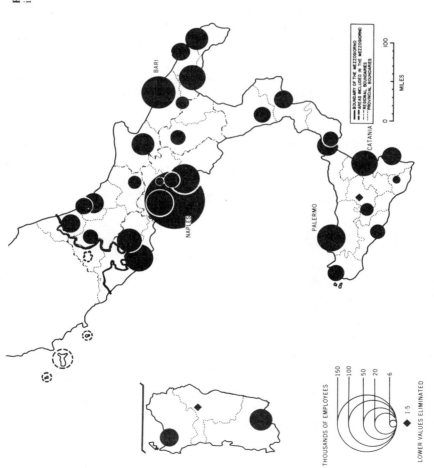

Fig. 9.4 Manufacturing employment, by province, in northern Italy in 1971.

A comparison of the data in Tables 9.1 and 9.3 provides clear evidence of a more positive shift in the structure of southern industry. Although the area is 'a highly industrialized region', there is strong evidence of the increasing scale and modernization of southern plants and of increased productivity resulting from changes in entrepreneurial initiative, higher literacy levels and from a growth in technical skills among young workers. The local industrial environment is clearly changing, but it is debatable if such changes are proceeding sufficiently rapidly to counteract the dramatic effects of the current Italian recession.

Figure 9.4 shows the manufacturing employment pattern in 1971. A comparison with Fig. 9.2, despite differences in scale, illustrates two decades of development. There were clearly two growth regions: the northwest coast (Latina, Frosinone, Caserta and Campania) and the southeastern mainland (especially Bari and Taranto). However, employment actually declined in several provinces located mainly along the Appenine spine, but none experienced *major* losses in the two decades.

Table 9.4 relates per capita (working age population) manufacturing employment on the provincial level (using the average for southern Italy as a base) to the share of manufacturing employment for the same areas for 1951, 1961 and 1971. The table is too detailed for an in-depth analysis here, yet the overwhelming importance of Naples is apparent as is the striking growth of several of the provinces cited earlier. The change in per capita levels of employment is also instructive because it partly reflects net out-migration from the Mezzogiorno from 1951 to 1971. Table 9.5 summarizes the geographical shifts using coefficients of variation. The changes in these coefficients are not striking, but the trend was evidently towards polarization rather than dispersion.

Shift–share analysis

Given the apparent differential in employment shifts between the two intercensal periods demonstrated by Tables 9.2 and 9.4 and the availability of sectoral data for the three census years, it was decided to use shift–share procedures to appraise the locational changes. This technique, widely used in regional planning and development, has been subject to substantial criticism particularly regarding its utility as a forecasting tool (Ashby, 1964; Brown, 1969; Dunn, 1960; Houston, 1967; Lasuen, 1971). Since the technique is used here mainly as a descriptive mechanism for examining past locational changes such criticism appear inappropriate. Southern Italy also provides a useful laboratory for testing its utility.

The technique ultimately adopted follows the 'American' rather than the British approach (Ashby, 1968; Stilwell, 1969, 1970). In its simplest form shift–share analysis uses a national rate of industrial growth as a base level. This rate is applied to the actual employment values for individual regions in the base year to arrive at an 'expected' value for employment in the terminal year. From this point, positive and negative shifts are calculated using actual employment levels at the end of the study period. Since concern here was with differential internal growth in the Mezzogiorno, the values for the South are used as a base level, not those for Italy. The available data for nineteen manufacturing sectors in thirty-four provinces for the three census years permitted calculation of industry mix and competitive shifts.

The industrial mix effect for each sector (e.g. foods) was computed by mul-

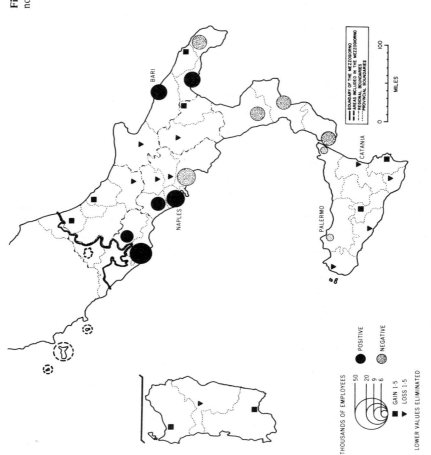

Fig. 9.5 Net shift in manufacturing employment in northern Italy by province, from 1951 to 1971.

Table 9.3 Manufacturing employment characteristics, by province and region, in Italy, in 1971

Province and region	Proportion of working age population engaged in manufacturing	Proportion of manufacturing employment in firms‡		Proportion of manufacturing employment in first stage industries‡
		Less than 10 employees	Greater than 99 employees	
	(%)	(%)	(%)	(%)
Milan	28.8	14.3	55.4	31.4
Turin	29.4	9.5	72.4	17.1
Northern Italy	17.1	20.6	47.1	52.3
Naples	8.8	25.6	48.5	52.7
Bari	8.4	39.5	32.0	73.5
Palermo	4.8	45.2	30.3	66.8
Southern Italy	6.2	39.6	33.8	68.3

† *XI Censimento Generale della Popolazione, 1971*, Vol. I (Rome, 1972), various pages and *V Censimento Generale dell'Industria e del'Commercio, 1971*, Vol. I, Tomo I (Rome, 1972), various pages.

‡ *V Censimento Generale dell'Industria*, op. cit., various pages. The working age population was defined as the resident population between 14 and 65 years of age. First stage sectors (as in 1951) comprised food and tobacco processing, lumber products, textiles, clothing, leather and shoes, machine repair shops, and the stone, clay and glass industries. Artisan employment not included.

tiplying the provincial employment in that sector by the differences between *the growth rate for that activity* and *the growth rate for all manufacturing* for southern Italy. Mix effects arise because some manufacturing sectors expand more rapidly than others: those provinces that specialize in slow-growth industries experience net outward shifts, while those that specialize in rapid-growth industries experienced net inward shifts. The competitive component is clear. Negative shifts here mean the failure of specific industries to keep up with the employment gains of their broad regional counterparts at the provincial level, or, in a reverse view, local industry may have grown at a faster rate than that of the Mezzogiorno as a whole. The mix and competitive shifts are then cumulated into values called net shifts. Table 9.6 summarizes these calculations.

The analysis of net shifts between 1951 and 1971

Figure 9.5 demonstrates the pattern of net shifts that occurred between 1951 and 1971. The gains or losses are only relative, having been computed as departures from the growth, by sector, of the Mezzogiorno treated as a single entity and as a closed system — which, of course, it is not. Aside from the two major growth areas that were apparent in absolute change, several provinces show relatively large negative values, including Salerno (Campania), Lecce (Puglia) and the three Calabrian provinces. Lesser negative shifts are also evident in northern Sicily. These variations are important, but the focus here is on the shifts during the two inter-censal periods.

The 1950s were 'the miracle years of the North' to some Italian writers. In contrast, limited industrial growth occurred in, while heavy out-migration occurred from, the Mezzogiorno. This lag partially results from the late 'take-off' of the loan programme after 1959 when direct grants just began. The consequence was a

Table 9.4 Share of manufacturing employment and per capita (working age population) manufacturing employment in Southern Italy for 1951, 1961 and 1971

Province	Share of Southern Italy manufacturing employment (%)			per capita manufacturing employment† Southern Italy = 100		
	1951	1961	1971	1951	1961	1971
Frosinone	2.39	2.45	3.49	92	105	158
Latina	1.20	2.28	4.08	76	135	206
Campobasso	1.81	1.35	1.07	79	68	63
Chiea	2.32	1.89	2.57	103	93	139
L'Aquila	1.56	1.49	1.54	75	84	98
Pescara	1.80	1.92	1.74	130	142	121
Teramo	1.47	1.71	2.02	95	121	146
Avellino	2.11	1.78	1.49	77	71	66
Benevento	1.53	1.23	0.86	82	73	57
Caserta	2.26	2.62	3.75	69	78	108
Naples	17.16	20.70	19.24	155	169	142
Salerno	7.31	6.95	5.24	160	147	107
Bari	7.18	8.01	9.10	112	125	134
Brindisi	1.63	1.59	1.95	95	89	106
Foggia	3.13	3.20	2.84	90	95	87
Lecce	4.36	3.35	3.17	128	95	89
Taranto	2.11	1.94	3.88	91	80	148
Matera	0.80	0.74	1.06	82	72	107
Potenza	1.95	1.41	1.31	81	61	63
Catanzero	3.49	2.78	1.96	94	76	57
Cosenza	3.27	2.57	1.87	88	73	55
Reggio Calabria	2.52	1.94	1.33	75	64	47
Agrigento	1.77	1.52	1.25	69	61	54
Caltanissetta	0.98	0.70	1.14	61	46	80
Catania	4.17	3.86	3.75	97	84	79
Enna	0.64	0.45	0.52	50	38	52
Messina	3.32	2.90	2.50	90	85	73
Palermo	5.40	5.75	4.47	97	100	77
Ragusa	1.16	1.12	0.95	88	86	73
Siracusa	1.41	1.95	2.10	80	107	112
Trapani	2.22	2.23	1.58	95	100	74
Cagliari	2.96	3.10	3.44	84	82	87
Nuoro	0.94	0.82	0.75	69	57	55
Sassari	1.68	1.55	1.97	88	79	97
Southern Italy	100.00	100.00	100.00	100	100	100

† Calculated from data in the 1971 Censuses of Industry and Population. Since no working age population data were available for 1971, age proportions, by province, for 1961 were used for all three periods.

significant *increase* in the disparity in manufacturing employment between the two regions: the southern share dropped from roughly 16 per cent in 1951 to 14 per cent by 1961. The net shifts for this decade show few areas with increases: Naples and, much less, Latina and Bari. Fifteen provinces, mainly in Sicily and the Appenines, experienced minor losses. Naples witnessed growth of varied labour-intensive industries and modernization of several State-owned enterprises (Rodgers, 1966). It was also the head-quarters of the industrial credit institution for the Italian mainland (Isveimer) and hence an early 'innovator' in the request for government-subsidized loans. Proximity to Rome stimulated industrial developments in Latina (Mori, 1955; Mazzetti, 1966) while Bari had long possessed a self-propulsive mechanism for further industrial development.

During the following decade, the loan programme finally blossomed. New plants were created, particularly by State enterprises which had been required by law to devote 40 per cent of their total and 60 per cent of their new, industrial investment to the South. These were complemented by private firms which, sometimes voluntarily and sometimes by public 'suasion', developed subsidiaries or branches in the Mezzogiorno. Many such investments were in capital – rather than labour-intensive industries. Nevertheless, the net shifts for the 1961–71 period (Table 9.6) shows more provinces with significant positive shifts in employment, including several new centres such as Taranto (with its huge new steel mill) and Frosinone. But, the negative values for Salerno, Palermo and Catanzaro should also be noted; in all, half of the Mezzogiorno provinces had negative shifts of over 1000 employees. Thus even when the South developed relatively faster than the North, growth was restricted to few areas. Notably, though Naples, which expanded industry quite rapidly before 1960, actually experienced a relative decline in the 1960s.

Table 9.5 Coefficients of variation of industrial employment on a provincial level for Southern Italy†

	1951	1961	1971
VC (employment share)‡	0.97	1.20	1.07
CV (per capita employment)§	0.26	0.33	0.40

$$\dagger \; CV = 1\sqrt{X} \quad \sqrt{1/N \sum_{i=1}^{N} (X - \bar{X})^2}$$

where N = number of provinces (34); $\bar{X}_i$ = value for ith province, and X = Southern Italian mean. The same formulation was used for the index numbers in the per capita data.

‡   These values are distorted by the disproportionate share of industrial employment in Naples in all three years.
§   Working age population proportions for 1961 were used for all three years.

Figure 9.6 synthesizes this information. The result is clearly qualitative in nature, yet instructive. Again industrial growth in southern Italy is shown to be polarized. The components of growth demonstrated in Table 9.6 expose a clear trend for the 'healthy' provinces (Fig. 9.6) which almost invariably had their growth concentrated in the competitive shift category. In contrast, the 'unhealthy' provinces are more difficult to classify. For some, negative values could be attributed to an undesirable mix, while in others negative values apparently resulted from the failure of local sectors to keep up with growth at the broader regional level.

Using industrial sector analysis the shift–share technique does permit a disaggregation of data and a comparison of provincial growth with that of the South as a whole. It also makes possible a study of the 'components' of change. Nevertheless, in moving from an examination of the growth patterns themselves to an analysis of the relationships between these shifts and other socio-economic variables, other measures of change produced more meaningful results. Moreover, absolute and relative change values proved to be better dependent variables when trying to explain regional variations in industrial growth in the Mezzogiorno.

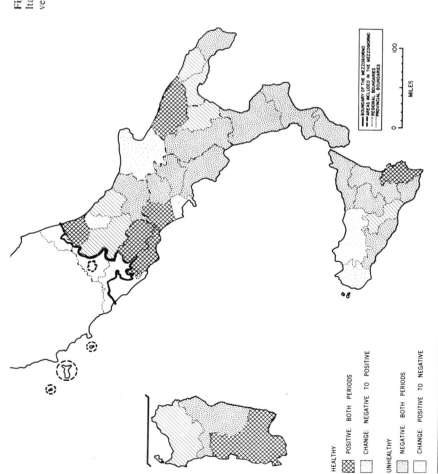

Fig. 9.6 Comparative shift–share analysis in southern Italy, by province, for the periods 1951 to 1961 versus 1961 to 1971.

Table 9.6 Summary shift–share analysis of manufacturing in Southern Italy from 1951 to 1971 (in thousands)†

Province	1951–61			1961–71			1951–71		
	Mix	Competitive	Combined	Mix	Competitive	Combined	Mix	Competitive	Combined
Frosinone	0.3	0.4	0.7	0.2	7.4	7.6	-0.2	8.7	8.5
Latina	0.3	6.8	7.1	3.4	10.3	13.7	-0.4	22.7	22.3
Campobasso	-0.5	-2.2	-2.7	-1.1	-1.3	-2.4	-2.4	-3.3	-5.8
Chieta	-0.6	-1.9	-2.5	-1.2	6.1	4.9	-3.0	4.9	1.9
L'Aquila	-0.6	0.3	-0.3	-1.2	1.3	0.1	-2.4	2.3	-0.1
Pescara	1.3	-0.3	1.0	0.6	-2.2	-1.6	2.3	-2.7	-0.4
Teramo	-0.1	1.8	1.7	-0.9	3.0	2.1	-1.2	5.4	4.2
Avellino	-0.7	-1.2	-1.9	-2.1	-0.5	-2.6	-3.2	-1.7	-4.9
Benevento	-0.6	-1.2	-1.8	-0.4	-2.5	-2.9	-2.4	-2.7	-5.1
Caserta	-0.7	3.2	2.5	-0.2	8.7	8.5	-2.8	14.3	11.5
Naples	14.3	-0.9	13.4	29.6	-29.8	-0.2	64.9	-48.8	16.1
Salerno	-2.9	1.4	-1.5	-8.7	-5.5	-14.2	-9.6	-6.4	-16.0
Bari	1.1	5.0	6.1	-1.2	8.6	7.4	2.0	12.8	14.8
Brindisi	-0.5	0.5	0.0	-0.9	3.5	2.6	-1.2	3.7	2.5
Foggia	0.7	1.5	0.8	-2.7	-0.5	-3.2	-3.2	1.0	-2.2
Lecce	-3.6	-2.5	-6.1	-4.5	2.7	-1.8	-10.4	1.2	-9.2
Taranto	0.1	-1.0	-0.9	0.0	14.9	14.9	1.9	11.8	13.7
Matera	-0.3	0.0	-0.3	-0.9	3.2	2.3	-1.3	3.3	2.0
Potenza	-1.0	-2.3	-3.3	-1.4	0.4	-1.0	-3.5	-1.5	-5.0
Catanzero	-0.8	-3.3	-4.1	-1.2	-5.5	-6.7	-3.2	-8.7	-11.9
Cosenza	-1.7	-2.1	-3.8	-2.9	-2.8	-5.7	-6.1	-4.3	-10.4
Reggio Calabria	-0.4	-3.1	-3.5	-1.5	-3.5	-5.0	-2.8	-6.5	-9.3
Agrigento	-0.9	-0.6	-1.5	-1.4	-0.9	-2.3	-3.1	-0.9	-4.0
Caltanissetta	-0.4	-1.3	-1.7	-0.5	3.8	3.3	-1.6	-2.8	-1.2
Catania	0.2	-1.7	-1.5	-0.3	-1.0	-1.3	-0.1	-3.1	-3.2
Enna	-0.2	-0.9	-1.1	-0.5	1.0	0.5	-0.9	0.0	-0.9
Messina	0.3	-1.7	-1.4	-1.1	-3.6	-4.7	-0.7	-5.6	-6.3
Palermo	1.5	1.4	2.9	7.5	-18.2	-12.7	5.0	-12.2	-7.2
Ragusa	-0.6	0.5	-0.1	-1.0	-0.5	-1.5	-2.0	0.3	-1.7
Siracusa	-0.3	4.0	3.7	2.1	-1.2	0.9	-1.3	6.6	-5.3
Trapani	-0.9	1.2	0.3	-3.1	-2.3	-5.4	-3.6	-1.3	-4.9
Cagliari	0.7	0.6	1.3	0.1	2.1	2.2	0.4	3.3	3.7
Nuoro	-0.4	-0.3	-0.7	-0.9	0.3	0.6	1.2	-0.3	-1.5
Sassari	-0.5	-0.2	-0.7	-1.6	4.6	3.0	-2.1	4.4	2.3

† Data calculated from the V Censimento Industriale, *op cit.*, Vol. I, various pages.

These results conflict with those of Fuchs' study of the growth of manufacturing in the United States (Fuchs, 1962). This author's research would appear to expose the weakness of shift–share analysis as a predictive tool. As Isard (1960) noted, the technique, among others, is a scaffolding for further analysis and interpretation. It does not heed changes in other major variables like regional realignments of population or income payments. Shift analysis may reveal certain statistical tendencies and aid in classifying empirical data; but it does not 'explain' nor identify the economic forces which interact to produce such tendencies.

Location policy

The first decade of the development programme lacked a meaningful locational design. Yet in the 1950s several key government officials working for the *Cassa per il Mezzogiorno* and the Comitato dei Ministri per il Mezzogiorno in collaboration with scholars associated with SVIMEZ (Associazione per lo Sviluppo dell' Industria nel Mezzogiorno) began promoting the formulation of a location policy which would restrict investment to a small number of viable regions within southern Italy. Their efforts came to fruition in the law of 1957, were first implemented in 1959 and further strengthened by Law 717 passed in June 1965. This legislation called for financial incentives to industrialization in long-term, low-interest loans allowing credits up to a maximum of 70 per cent of the proposed investment and direct grants for building costs and machinery up to 20 per cent of the fixed investment. Both sets of financial stimuli use criteria based on the industrial sector, the size of investment and the location. Attention focuses here on this last statement.

The first locational element is agglomerative in nature in supporting the creation of 'areas for industrial development', i.e. zones which are extensive in area, incorporating a number of communes, normally with a single focal centre, commonly a port (Fig. 9.7) Infrastructure should be reasonably well developed and improvements entirely State-financed. A large literate labour force and a significant number and variety of industrial plants should be present. Representatives of these areas must prepare regional plans analysing their present economic situation and detailing proposals for improving infrastructure and for industrial development. It is felt that with effective planning, better road and port facilities, these zones should act as magnets for further industrial growth. These 'areas for industrial development' must have a minimum population of 200 000, that of the principal commune being at least half that size. The second type of zone is the so-called 'industrial nucleus' (Fig. 9.7). According to current legislation population in such nodes should normally not exceed 75 000. Such small zones should have a relatively restricted number of economically-viable industries either in existence or in process of realization. This notion of industrial nuclei is diffusive in character and has strong political overtones.

Clearly the locational goal, as defined by development officials, is to secure the implantation of new plants within these 'areas' and 'nuclei', particularly inside the *agglomerati* or industrial zones to minimize the use of scarce capital for infrastructure improvements. The graduation of support in the current legislation encourages developments in these more favoured industrial districts.

The idea of planned industrial areas, particularly as it applied to the 'areas of industrial development', appears sound, and conforms with the policy recommen-

Fig. 9.7 Industrial development regions in the Mezzogiorno.

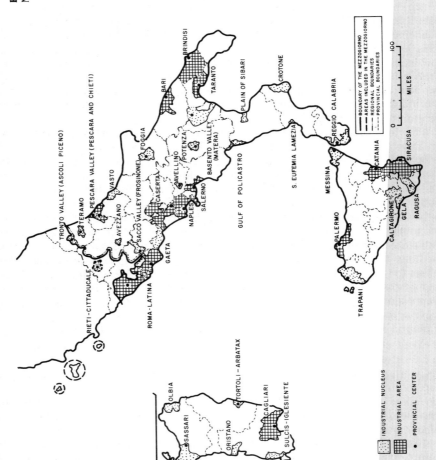

Table 9.7 Growth of manufacturing employment in the proposed 'areas' and 'nuclei' of the Mezzogiorno between 1951 and 1971†

Manufacturing employment				
Regions	1951	1971	Absolute increase	Relative increase (%)
Nuclei	58 119	96 684	38 565	66.4
Areas	218 382	368 014	149 632	68.5
Areas and nuclei of the South	276 501	464 698	188 197	68.1
Other regions of the South	297 005	309 127	12 122	4.1
Northern Italy	2 924 714	4 512 858	1 788 463	54.3

† Calculated from the Censuses of Industry for 1951 and 1971, op cit; various pages, and the communal limits of the areas and nuclei as given in materials provided by the Cassa per il Mezzogiorno. As indicated earlier, parts of the provinces of Rome, Rieti, Ascoli Piceno and Livorno, which are jurisdictionally considered to be part of the Mezzogiorno, were excluded from my tabulation.

dations of the growth pole literature. But the 'industrial nuclei' are questionable. If support for such areas were kept to a minimum there might be grounds for optimism. This has not proved to be so. There are now more than forty development zones and more than half of these are classified as nuclei (Fig. 9.7). Their area covers nearly 25 per cent of the Mezzogiorno, and includes more than 50 per cent of the Mezzogiorno population. Apparently political pressures have multiplied inordinately both nuclei and industrial areas, so impairing the effectiveness of the whole programme. To date unusual delays (even for Italy) have occurred in implementing this location policy: in fact few areas and nuclei are fully operational.

Table 9.7 confirms that the growth of manufacturing employment during the study period was confined predominantly to these areas and nuclei. In fact, their percentage rate of growth exceeded that of northern Italy. Yet nearly 50 per cent of the southern population lives outside of these zones. Location policy, if it is to aspire to more than a 'paper programme', must concentrate investment in a few viable growth poles. Such a policy, termed 'aree di sviluppo globale', is in course of implementation. First evisaged in the 1965 legislation, there are five such 'areas': southern Lazio and Campania; the southeast (particularly Bari, Brindisi, Taranto and Matera); the Canatia–Siracusa region; around Palermo; and around Cagliari (Sardinia). Given the limited resources now at the disposal of the development agencies and the State holding companies (because of the Italian economic depression), a policy of concentrated investment is essential to Mezzogiorno development. However, political pressures such as relatively recent riots in Calabria may make such *rational* economic planning unfeasible.

Conclusion

By 1971 commune data shows that the investment programme had clearly produced a far greater spread of industry than had been true in 1951, i.e. 'dispersed concentration' rather than concentration. Regional inequalities in industrial development still persist, however. Yet in channelling investment in the future, planners must not only focus upon the growth of a few viable centres within, but also upon the fate of the remainder of the South. Despite recession in northern Italy, the outflow of migrants northwards has not abated. This long-term flow has been a major positive factor in the economic growth of the Northwest and the whole nation and must be reckoned in future industrial policy.

References

Allen, K. and MacLennon, M. C. (1970) 'Regional problems and policies in Italy and France', *University of Glasgow Social and Economic Studies*, London.

Ashby, L. (1964) 'The geographical redistribution of employment: an examination of the elements of change', *Survey of Current Business*, 44, pp. 13–20.

Ashby, L. (1968) 'The shift and share analysis: a reply', *Southern Economic Journal*, 34, pp. 423–5.

Associazione per lo Sviluppo dell'Industria al Mezzogiorno, *Informazione SVIMEZ*, published irregularly.

Brown, H. J. (1969) 'Shift-share projections of regional economic growth: an empirical test', *Journal of Regional Science*, 9, pp. 1–17.

Dunn, E. (1960) 'A statistical and analytical technique for regionaly analysis', *Papers and Proceedings of the Regional Science Association*, 6, pp. 98–112.

Fuchs, V. (1962) *Changes in the Location of Manufacturing in the U.S. since 1929*, Yale U.P., New Haven.

Hamilton, F. E. I. (1967) 'Models of industrial location', in: R. J. Chorley & P. Haggett, eds., *Models in Geography*, Methuen, London, Ch. 10.

Houston, D. (1967) 'Shift-share analysis of regional growth: a critique', *Southern Economic Journal*, 33, pp. 577–81.

Isard, W. (1960) *Methods of Regional Analysis*, Prentice-Hall New York, pp. 266–81.

Instituto Centrale di Statistica (1951, 1961, 1971), *Censimento Generale dell' Industria e del Commercio*, Rome.

Keeble, D. (1967) 'Models of economic development', in: R. J. Chorley and P. Haggett, eds., *Models in Geography*, Methuen, London.

Lasuen, J. R. (1971) 'Venezuela: an industrial shift-share analysis, 1941–1961', *Regional and Urban Economics*, 1, pp. 153–220.

Mazzetti, E. (1966) *Il Nord del Mezzogiorno*, Milan.

Mori, A. (1965) 'Il limite della zona di intervento della Cassa per il Mezzogiorno come fattore d'attrazione e di localizzazione industriale', *Rivista Geografica Italiana*, 72, pp. 19–41.

Rodgers, A. (1966) 'Naples: a case study of government subsidization of industrial development in an underdeveloped region', *Tijdschrift voor Economische en Sociale Geografie*, 56, pp. 20–32.

Rodgers, A. (1970) 'Migration and industrial development: the southern Italian experience, *Economic Geography*, 46, pp. 111–35.

Stilwell, F. J. B. (1969) 'Regional growth and structural adaptation', *Urban Studies*, 6, pp. 162–78.

Stilwell, F. J. B. (1970) 'Further thoughts on the shift and share approach', *Regional Studies*, 4, pp. 451–8.

Chapter 10

Industrial migration in West Africa: the Nigerian case

J. Okezie C. Onyemelukwe

Although studies of West Africa in industrial geography have been few, the approaches used hitherto have followed three traditional paths. The first of these treats manufacturing as an essentially urban function which – along the lines of Harris (1943), Alexander (1954), Ullman and Dacey (1960) and Florence (1948) – can fruitfully measure urban functional importance within a system of cities. The study of industries in Ibadan province by Adeyanju (1969) and the locational analysis of the Ikeja textile mills by Akinola (1965) exhibit this approach in Nigeria. The second path examines factors of industrial location and processes of location decision-making, especially against the theoretical and conceptual background of Weber (1929), Lösch (1954), Isard (1956) and Hamilton (1967): work by Onyemelukwe (1974) and Kinpy (1969) provides examples. The third approach studies the spatial pattern and the processes of industrial concentration or dispersion like research by Aboyade (1968) and Mabogunje (1973).

Although West African studies have generally seen manufacturing as an end in itself, it should be more properly treated (Mabogunje, 1973) as one of the processes of spatial transformation, along with migration and information flows: such treatment is not only practicable but also meaningful and rewarding if properly conceptualized within the context of developing planning. Thus this chapter aims at identifying the patterns of industrial migration featured in the West African landscape and at analysing the peculiarities and causes of this type of transformation of the industrial geography of the region. To the extent that industrial migration has not been formally studied in West African milieux, it is more exploratory than exhaustive and more indicative of possible research paths than conclusive on the basis of the Nigerian case.

Industrial history and West African economies

Industrialization is a development process which is relatively new in West African economies. Like most other developing or transitional regions, West Africa provides ample evidence for questioning the frequently–assumed primary-secondary-tertiary development sequence. The tertiary component grew much earlier and faster in West Africa than secondary activity: data on occupational structure of the labour forces show that no West African country has less than half of its workers in the primary sector, none has more than 18 per cent in secondary industry, while tertiary activities everywhere employ more than four-fifths of the remainder, i.e. between 20 and 30 per cent.

Historically, planned industrialization is a post-Second World War pheno-

119

menon. Indeed, very little manufacturing pre-dates the political independence of the West African States. Liberia, the only country that has been independent since the last century, was in no sense any more industrial than were the dependent countries in the 1950s. Before then West Africa was essentially a source of industrial raw materials and a market for externally-manufactured consumer goods. There was neither the technology nor the capital to embark upon many forms of production of purely secondary order, mainly because the colonial relationship worked out by the metropolitan countries was not conducive to the development of the basic infrastructure necessary for industrial growth.

The economic boom that immediately followed the Second World War, and, more especially, the shift in political power in the 1950s, helped to bring manufacturing into the economic development scheme of most West African States. While the postwar economic boom raised the level of income and the invested capital of African primary producers, the sudden change to political self-determination for the people opened the way for decision-making favouring some degree of national structural economic change. The first official policy towards industrialization involved the simple process of export valorization and import substitution. Valorization increased the transportability and value-added content of raw materials through first-stage processing of agricultural products and beneficiation of minerals. Vegetable-oil processing, cotton ginning, saw-milling and hides-and-skin processing formed the bulk of such industrial activity. Import substitution, on the other hand, has involved domestic (often assembly-type) production of consumer goods mainly to save foreign exchange through self-reliance. Although this stage has meant appreciable structural change in most West African economies, a very wide gap remains between them and industrialized Europe, America or Asia. Largely as a result of scarcities of technology and capital, the industrial sector in West Africa is yet to develop a heavy-industry base for an appreciable stock of capital goods. Thus not only is the import substitution strategy much more costly and difficult than it would have otherwise been, but also the possibility for promoting exports of manufactures is still a distant hope.

Two important implications of the historical and structural characteristics of West African industrial activity are relevant to the study of industrial migration. First, because industries are essentially of the consumer goods–import substituting type, competition among firms is essentially intra-national in scope. Second, partly as a result, movement patterns of industrial establishments are largely responses to forces of competition within, rather than between, the countries constituting the West African region. Thus, besides the problem of data collection and comparability, a study of industrial migration in West Africa is likely to be more meaningful on a country-by-country basis. Nigeria is presented here as the first case, therefore, in an on-going study in West Africa.

Conceptual and theoretical issues

An in-depth study of industrial movements should identify the structural characteristics and the patterns of various movement subsets. The characterization of movement typologies may help to focus attention on what is essentially industrial migration. Substantial advantages for development planning at both regional (sub-national) and local scales increase the value of such an exercise. The research findings indicate possible lines along which official policy could help to encourage or to control plant movements in endeavouring to create a socially more fruitful organization of the entire space economy.

Movement type

Many studies of industrial migration describe it as involving the complete transfer (relocation) of productive capacity to, or the establishment of a branch factory in, a new location by an existing manufacturing firm (Brown, 1965; Cameron & Clark, 1966; Cameron & Johnson, 1969; Fagg, 1973; Griffith, 1955; Harris, 1974; Henderson, 1974; Keeble, 1965, 1968; Smith, 1970; Spooner, 1972, 1974; Townroe, 1975). But can it be rightly assumed that every new and separate location of a branch plant represents an act of industrial migration? Sometimes both the main and the branch plants are set up simultaneously, in which case there is no question of the main plant migrant branch relationship that would arise from the expansion process of the main plant. Even when there is a time lag between the establishment of the 'main' and the branch plants, the branch cannot be said to have been generated from, but is a result of decisions external to, the 'main' plant. Surely situations such as these do not reflect the ordinary expansion efforts of a main plant. Instead they are forms of marketing strategy common to firms in countries much of whose industrial development is exogeneously controlled. The need to protect a distant market from the decision-maker's (investor's) home base often leads to setting up a regional 'main' plant, or headquarters, as well as several branch plants with sub-regional scope.

Although this practice is common in developing economies with a large foreign investor control, it occurs in all industrial regions of the world where in-migration by foreign firms is feasible. This process represents more of a 'splash' than a sequential movement across the market area of the firm concerned. The concept of *industrial splashing*, which suggests the element of simultaneity in the development of both 'main' and branch plants within the spatial system, seems more appropriate than the concept of industrial migration which, by definition, has been applied hitherto to this phenomenon. Too elaborate further, one can say that 'industrial splashing' occurs at the national level, while migration, as traditionally conceived, occurs at the *international* level.

Patterns of industrial migration

Patterns of industrial migration may be studied regarding: forces behind the moves, factors relating to the distance and the directional characteristics of such moves; and the industrial landscape emerging as a result of such moves. Forces inducing industrial firms to move to other places include the following.

1. Need for additional *factory space* is often growth-induced. Moves that are growth-induced have a number of important characteristics. First, they are mainly a result of constraints to *in situ* expansion. Such constraints range from lack of space for *in situ* expansion for modernization, high cost of adjacent land, prohibitive congestion (or environmental) costs, to relatively high costs of labour. Second, growth-induced moves more often involve establishment of a branch plant than movement of the main plant. Since the need for expansion is itself not only a sign of prosperity but also an indication of good industrial environment at the location of the main plant, most firms would hesitate to relocate. This is also likely because of the fear of disrupting production and

losing markets, a large proportion of the vital labour force as well as local patronage badly needed by plants with relatively high non-basic components (Alexander, 1954; Smith, 1972; Ullman and Dacey, 1960). Moreover, the uncertainty risk in relocations and a fresh start is often greater than the risk of taking a branch plant to a new location

Another important characteristic of growth-induced movement is that it is more associated with old than with new manufacturing firms. In other words, if all the manufacturing firms within an economy were to be placed along a time scale, growth-induced migration would be more frequent *ceteris paribus* among the older firms. Thus in economies where industrialization is a relatively recent development, industrial migration of this kind is likely to have a low frequency of occurrence.

2. Another force behind migration is the *industrial infrastructure pull factor*. As new centres increase their potential for industrial promotion – especially through improvements in transport, communications, power and financial institutions – manufacturing units from other areas move in to take advantage of the relatively more favourable environment. That such industry-promoting facilities are still very scarce in developing economies suggests that they are more critical for industrial location in developing than in industrialized societies (cf. Ch. 5). Much of the polarization process and the lop-sided or primate structure of the urban system in developing lands derives from this. West African capital cities basically have the best of such industrial facilities and thus in 1970 accounted for the following percentage of their respective nation's industrial activity: Abidjan (Ivory Coast), 62.5 per cent; Accra (Ghana), 30.4 per cent; Bathurst (Gambia), 100 per cent; Conakry (Guinea), 50 per cent; Cotonou (Dahomey), 16.7 per cent; Dakar (Senegal), 81.5 per cent; Freetown (Sierra Leone), 75 per cent; Lagos (Nigeria), 35 per cent; and Monrovia (Liberia), 100 per cent (Mabogunje, 1973, p. 16).

3. Besides its indirect control of private sector industrial location through the spatial distribution of industrial facilities, *official policy intervention* may be a direct and an important factor in industrial migration. However, in developing economies where the technology level is still very low and a large share of factor stock in manufacturing belongs to foreign investors, much depends on cooperation from the foreign investor in being able to apply government policies effectively for regional or spatial equalization.

4. *Insecurity* for the plant and its personnel often constitutes a push factor encouraging industrial relocation. Insecurity arises from situations like war, drought, floods and hostile environment. The case study that follows shows that this factor is an important force in the West African context.

5. Particularly in economies where manufacturing has not yet approached the scale and level highly demanding of skilled manpower, and where, as a result of raw material rooting of plants, agglomeration economies are missed, there is a great tendency for *promoter's personal considerations* to override other economic issues in the choice of plant location. The temptation for special recognition among his people does lead to a decision to move a plant or its branch to the promoter's home area. This would seem economically irrational for effective industrial promotion; but, as will be shown, there is much more to it than mere effort to promote non-economic ends. Although cases of this nature are few at present, they will probably increase over time as the current campaign for rural industrialization gathers momentum.

The range and directions of migrant plants

Another dimension of migration patterns concerns the range and the direction of plant movements. On the range or distance scale, three broad divisions are considered: intra-city (main-plant relocation), inter-city (intra-regional, usually branch plant transfer) and inter-regional migration ('splash' of main and branch plants). A fourth category – international or intercontinental (locational shifts at industry level) – falls outside the scope of this study.

Plant movements at these scales can exhibit interesting directional bias. Factors underlying such bias seem to vary with migration types on the distance scale (Fig. 10.1). The main direction of intra-city movements is to the urban periphery for

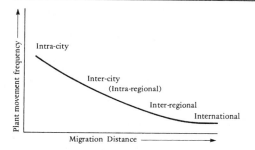

Fig. 10.1   Hypothetical relationship of plant movement frequency and distance of migration.

more land space at cheaper rental. Such movements are generally growth-induced and are selective, being most marked amongst expanding industries which are the most likely to hit the local (inner city) 'ceiling' (Henderson, 1974). Problems of noise, city pollution and effluent disposal may also explain this contrifugal tendency. But they are probably less important in developing economies where industrial congestion is, as yet, limited, and more important is the factor of externalities: official policy decisions in favour of urban expansion or renewal have played important roles, especially through the establishment of industrial estates to which plants shift.

Inter-city or intra-regional migration has wider directional scope than intra-city movements in response to migration forces – like infra-structural facilities, security and favourable cost differentials – which one urban destination exerts vis-à-vis other towns within the region. Those influencing inter-regional movements are not essentially different. A distinction does not seem to lie so much in kind as in degree. Plants require a stronger movement stimulus (like substantial tax or cost advantages) for inter-regional movement, still much more to generate migration between regions or nations: a strong distance decay element is present in industrial migration patterns (Fig. 10.1). And since the types of high positive differentials sufficient to induce long-range relocation are rare, cases of plant redirection between regions are likely, under normal conditions, to be few and far between. The following key hypotheses need to be investigated in a case study of Nigeria. First, in West African countries, where industrialization is a relatively recent phenomenon, industrial migration, particularly the growth-induced type, is still rare and second, much industrial migration is largely induced by public policy. And third, socio-political factors constitute an important force in industrial migration.

Patterns of industrial migration in Nigeria

The data problem

There is no official record in Nigeria to furnish information on changes in plant location: the Federal Office of Statistics and the Ministry of Industry do not gather such information. Equally the Office of the Registrar of Companies cannot be helpful since changes in location are never communicated to the Registry. There is also the problem of ascertaining whether or not registered firms are active in manufacturing. Thus migrant firms and branch plants had to be identified from a series of Industrial Directories and newspaper reports. Evidence of main plant relocation was sought by comparing firms' addresses in the 1971 edition of the Industrial Directory of Nigeria with those in earlier directories. Such information was supplemented by personal interviews. Respondents in all centres were requested to identify any industrial establishments known to have either newly entered the area or left it, or set up a branch in any part of the country.

Although the Industrial Directory of Nigeria (1971) uses the four-digit International Standard Industrial Classification (I.S.I.C.), it included mining and repair establishments which, by definition, do not belong to manufacturing industry. Such establishments were omitted in this analysis. As a result some 746 of the 832 establishments shown in Table 10.1 were studied. Of these only 47 were functioning before 1940, 21 of them concerned with processing, 26 with finishing stages. Most were in cotton-textiles (10 units), printing and publishing (7) and food-processing (8). The increase from 47 establishments before 1945 to 746 by 1970 (Table 10.1) indicates exponential growth and was itself the direct result of mid-1950 economic boom in cash-crop economy and of political self-determination since 1960. Yet still 93 per cent of all establishments engage in either processing or consumer-goods import-substitution. The near-absence of intermediate and capital goods industries plants with high potential for promoting inter-factory linkages and agglomeration tendencies would suggest that the industrial structure of Nigeria has little positive impact as yet on plant migration.

The extent of and explanation of plant migration in Nigeria

The hypothesis of a low frequency of plant migration has its rationale in the very short history of industrial development in West Africa: older firms or plants have more cause than newer ones to relocate or to expand by branch plant transfer. Table 10.1 and Fig. 10.2 clearly show that manufacturing industry is a relatively new sector in Nigeria's economy: in 1970 47.8 per cent of the 746 industrial establishments were less than ten years old!

Table 10.2 summarizes the results of an interview and questionnaire to determine the frequency, cause and type of movement of industrial facilities. The evidently small figure of forty-two units suggests a low rate of plant migration as compared with movement rates in industrial and post-war industrial societies. To discover the reasons for moving interviewees and respondents were asked to rank the following in order of importance:

1. The need for expansion through the establishment of a branch plant.
2. The lack of space for *in situ* expansion, so necessitating relocation.
3. Poor safety conditions at the original location.

Table 10.1 Manufacturing establishments by industrial group and start-up period

Type of industry	Total no.	By 1910	1911–20	1921–40	1941–60	1961–70
Meat processing and preserving	14	–	–	1	2	11
Dairy products	6	–	–	–	4	2
Fruit and veg. preserving	5	1			2	2
Vegetable/animal oil processing	60			3	50	7
Grain milling	7				6	1
Bakery products	92			3	35	54
Sugar refining	2					2
Confections	10				2	8
Animal feeds	5					5
Spirits, distilling	2					2
Bear and stout brewing	7				3	4
Soft drinks	11				6	5
Tobacco products	10				6	4
Ginning, spinning, weaving	50	2	2	6	12	28
Made textile goods (excl. apparels)	8					8
Knitting	11				4	7
Carpets/rugs	2					2
Weaving apparel	16				5	11
Tannery and leather processing	9				3	6
Footwear	14				5	9
Sawmills	53			2	31	20
Wood and cork	4			1	1	2
Furniture and fixtures	45				22	23
Paper container	8					8
Pulp and paper board	4				1	3
Printing and publishing	71	4		3	45	19
Basic industrial chemicals	6				1	5
Fertilizers pesticides	1					1
Paints, varnishes	7					7
Drugs and medicine	12				5	7
Soap and perfumes	18			1	8	9
Miscellaneous	7					7
Petroleum Refinery	1					1
Mis. products of petroleum	2				1	1
Tyre and tube	10				6	4
Other rubber products	21	1	1	1	11	7
Plastic products	11			1	2	8
Pottery, china	6				3	3
Glass	3					3
Structural clay	8				4	4
Cement	5				2	3
Non-metallic mineral products	9			1	2	6
Iron and steel basic industry	2				1	1
Non-Ferrous metal basic industry	4					4
Cutlery	7				2	5
Metal furniture	10				3	7
Structural metal products	16				5	11
Fabricated metal products	22			1	2	19
Agricultural machinery	1				1	
Machinery and equipment	2					2
Electrical industry	2				2	
Radio and TV	4					4
Electrical apparatus	2					2
Shipbuilding and repairing	5				3	2
Motor assembly	5				4	1
Motor cycle assembly	2				1	1
Jewellery	1					1
Miscellaneous products	16			1	6	9
Electricity, gas	1			1		
Vehicle repairs	67			6	42	19
Leather products	9				3	6
Total	832	9	5	33	366	419

Source: Federal Ministry of Industries, Industrial Directory of Nigeria (1971), Lagos.

Table 10.2 Type and explanation of migration of industrial units in Nigeria, 1974

Total number of moves: 42	Type of movement involved			
	Main plant relocation		Branch plant relocation	
	19		23	
Reasons for migration:	Topmost reason	Secondary	Topmost	Secondary
Need to expand in branch plants			13	4
Lack of space for *in situ* expansion	1	3	1	3
Better production prospects in a new place	1	2	3	2
Desire to be nearer home	2	1	4	5
Influence of government	8	2	2	3
Greater safety for plant in a new place	7	2		

Source: Field Survey and Questionnaire, May–July, 1974.

4. Better prospects for production in a new location.
5. The desire to be nearer the owner's home area.
6. To obtain lower production costs at a new site as compared with the original location.
7. The influence of government policy or decisions.
8. Other reasons.

Only the factors ranked top or second were considered to hold much significance. Table 10.2 shows that the questions of production cost variation and 'other reasons' were of minor importance, although perception of potentially lower production costs might have been implicit in those cases where respondents ranked 'better production prospects in a new location' as of topmost or second-most importance. Some firms had only one reason for moving: hence the disparities between the aggregate numbers of topmost and second reasons. Similarly other firms ranked more than two reasons as influencing their decision to shift production, so the total numbers of reasons given do not tally with the aggregate of plant moves.

What is clear is that government influence, need for expansion and problems of unsafe site seem to be the major forces behind plant migration in Nigeria. Government influence followed by high safety risks is most important in stimulating main plant relocation, but the need for expansion remains the paramount force behind branch plant transfers. However, a reason considered topmost is not necessarily the only motivating factor behind plant movements associated with it: other reasons, though less important, have helped to tip the aggregate balance of factors considered in decision-making in favour of migration. This is why the socio-political or personal factor (expressed in the desire to locate near home) can, for instance, be seen as a prominent – albeit subsidiary – factor in plant movement in Nigeria.

Government influence has taken two important forms. *Direct* influence operates through regional and metropolitan planning policies requiring evacuation from certain areas and concentration in other locations. *Indirect* influence, which has had greater impact, is well illustrated in regional administrative reorganization in Nigeria and in construction of industrial estates. The creation of the present

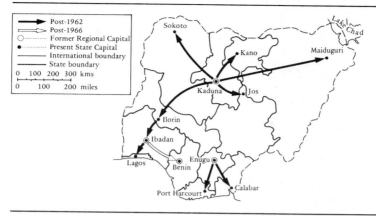

Fig. 10.2   The redistribution of State administration in Nigeria since 1967.

twelve States from the four pre-1967 regions of Nigeria has redistributed spatially (Fig. 10.2) the power centres of decision-making on public policy issues. This change in power structure has involved a corresponding realignment of political loyalties to State centres of decision-making. With the emergence of new State capitals and the consequent upgrading of their infrastructure facilities and increased population, manufacturing plants have moved in to serve the expanding demands of the State capital. Bakeries, furniture, block-making and printing plants have been among the first to relocate on these grounds.

The feeling of insecurity in certain States and places has prompted plant migration. Such movements have been more inter-regional than intra-regional and are not associated with any particular types or scales of industry. Some manufacturing firms moved immediately before, and also during, the Nigerian Civil War. The direction was mainly across the boundary between the East Central State and the rest of Nigeria, most notably from Port Harcourt in the Rivers State to Aba, Owerri and Enugu in the East Central State (Fig. 10.3). Fewer are as yet known to have moved from the northern States to the East Central State and only one case of migration, from Port Harcourt to Warri in the Mid-West State. Although the need for greater safety was paramount in each case, government decisions to redistribute political power through the creation of States has had an indirect influence on the pattern of inter-regional relocation of such plants, while the choice of capitals for the new States undoubtedly influenced the choice of site within the region chosen for movement destination.

Branch plant establishment to satisfy needs for expansion has been the commonest type of movement across the country. Mainly inter-regional in range, it has mostly reflected the desire of firms to protect their market. The breweries, the soft-drinks firms and the rubber (tyre) industries are the most prominent in this practice. With Lagos as their main plant location, Nigeria Breweries Ltd has, for example, set up two branch plants in the former Northern Region capital, Kaduna, and the former Eastern Region market centre, Aba. A similar pattern of inter-regional diffusion has been adopted by the Nigerian Bottling Co with a soft-drinks main plant in Lagos and branch plants in Ibadan, Kano, Ngwo near Enugu and Port Harcourt. Two tyre-retreading firms with headquarters in Lagos and

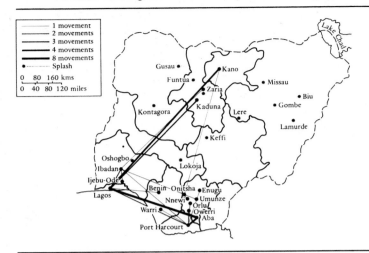

Fig. 10.3   Industrial plant movements in Nigeria 1960–70.

Onitsha respectively established branches in Ibadan, Kano and Port Harcourt. The Nigerian Tobacco Co began operation simultaneously in Ibadan and Port Harcourt and later set up another branch in Zaria.

Branch plant transfers and main plant relocation have been relatively important means of achieving the socio-political objectives of some industrial entrepreneurs. The bicycle tyre and tube plant at Ijebu-Ode, the foam mattress factory at Umunze (both branch plants), the meat-processing plant at Ukpor and the palm-kernel crushing-plant at Aro-Ndizuogu (main plant relocations) exemplify this practice. Employment in these establishments ranges from 20 to 320 workers and none had a start-up capital of less than $75 000. By Nigerian standards, each is a 'large-scale' industrial concern. The desire for an entrepreneur's close identification with his home community often has both short-term and long-term objectives. In the four cases cited here, the dominant short-term objective was social: the desire to bring development through factory employment, local resource-use and improved living standards. Stimulus to this has come from government policy to diversify the economies of rural areas, especially in the East Central State where large-scale factory activity has received significant official impetus particularly in areas with a minimum 'village-group' population of 8000 people. However, rewards for this behaviour are known to have come (as expected) from the community to the factory owner through special social recognition and sometimes political honours. Indeed, the desire to climb to, or retain one's position at, the top of the local political ladder has apparently been an important driving force behind what is, from maximum profit point of view, an irrational location decision for a relatively large manufacturing plant. Although the advantages of such a decision are socio-political in the short-term, enormous economic gains lie in the long-term expectations in a social setting where 'fringe benefits' are often mediated through political privileges.

On the whole, no significant directional pattern of intra-city industrial migration is yet in evidence, mainly as a result of the paucity of data, the small size of towns and embryonic stage of industrialization. However, five examples have been observed: Mazi Ejidike's and Sons bread industry, the Silas (baking) Works Ltd, the Ottibros jewellery manufacturing shop all in Onitsha, and two block-moulding plants, one each in Benin and Warri, Mid-West State, Nigeria. These indicate expansion-motivated centrifugal movement consistent with our earlier postulate. Also because of the small data sample, the distance-movement frequency relationship hypothesized earlier (Fig. 10.1) cannot be reliably tested. But if the existing information available is an adequate index then inter-regional migrations are much more frequent than intra-regional or intra-city migrations (Fig. 10.3). This results mainly, however, from branch plant transfers, and also from the factor of perceived insecurity during and after the Nigerian Civil War which was not a normal phenomenon. More research on plant relocations is required to draw valid conclusions.

Industrial splashing

The practice of industrial 'splashing' is common among expatriate firms most of which entered the country from the distributive trades sector but later adopted the strategy of zonal market consolidation through import-substitution. Their original network of product-merchandizing is often decided outside Nigeria. So is the decision to integrate manufacturing as a cost-reducing strategy for more effective competition in the various zones. The British Cotton Growing Association, operating thirteen cotton-ginning centres in the Northern States of Nigeria, is associated with this phenomenon of splash across the cotton-growing area of the country. But two petroleum refineries simultaneously being set up by the national government in Kaduna and Warri provide examples of an internally-controlled industrial splash. This is certainly not a case of industrial migration, since no branch–plant relationship exists functionally between the new refineries and the first (main) refinery near Port Harcourt in the Rivers State.

Conclusions

Any findings from Nigeria regarding the scale, types and patterns of plant movements are at the best preliminary and inconclusive in the wider West African context. The extension of similar enquiries to the other countries of West Africa is necessary and worthwhile. Evidence of industrial migration in Nigeria is very scanty. Yet since the main causal factors of migration are the need for plant expansion and government policies for urban renewal, solving congestion and creating new regional growth centres and since these are generally the outcome of long periods of industrial activity and modern forms of urbanization, the low frequency of plant movement in Nigeria is only to be expected. What is more interesting are factors of insecurity and of entrepreneurial desire for socio-political identification. The novelty and curiosity which industrial mechanization conjures in societies that are largely agrarian, and more important, the increasing demand for non-agricultural employment in a rural environment seem together to reinforce the quest of industrial entrepreneurs for social and political recognition through rural-industry promotion. This practice is probably not peculiar to Nigeria and may largely account for plant relocation or branch plant transfer in other countries of West Africa.

Industrial splashing, distinct from industrial migration in the traditional sense, occurs if main and branch plants are either established simultaneously or generated from outside a given economic system. Such 'splashing' is no more than international migration in a wider global context. In many cases the external centre of decision-making and control is essentially tertiary or quarternary in function and has no secondary (factory) establishment from which plants can be said to have migrated internationally as branch factories. Nigerian experience demonstrates that industrial splashing is not a random occurrence but a predictable feature of the economic landscape especially of countries whose industrial development is partly externally controlled. All West African countries fall within that category, though in widely varying degrees, so that further studies beyond Nigeria may fruitfully investigate the phenomenon of splashing.

References

Aboyade, O. (1968) 'Industrial location and development policy. The Nigerian case', *Nigerian Journal of Economic & Social Studies*, **10(3)**, pp. 1–16

Adeyanju, D. O. (1969) 'Transport cost and the location of industries Ibadan – a study in industrial geography', *University of Ibadan, Department of Geography*, M.A. dissertation.

Alexander, J. W. (1954) 'The basic–non basic concept of urban economic functions', *Economic Geography*, **30**, pp. 246–61.

Akinola, R. A. (1965) 'Factors affecting the location of a textile industry – the example of the Ikeja textile mills', *Nigerian Journal of Economic and Social Studies*, **7**, pp. 311–32.

Brown, C. M. (1965) 'Industry in the new towns of the London region: study in decentralization', *University of London M.Sc. dissertation.*

Cameron, G. C. and Clark, B. D. (1966) 'Industrial movement and the regional problem', *University of Glasgow Social & Economic Studies*, Occasional Paper 5.

Cameron, G. C. and Johnson, K. (1969) 'Intra-urban location and the new plant', *Papers & Proceedings of the Regional Science Association*, **29**, pp. 92–106

Fagg, J. J. (1963) 'Spatial change in manufacturing employment in Greater Leicester, '*East Midland Geographer*, **5(8)**, pp. 124–37.

Florence, P. S. (1948) *Investment, Location and Size of Plant*, Cambridge University Press, London.

Griffith, E. J. L. (1955) 'Moving industry from London, *Town Planning Review*, **26**, pp. 120–130.

Hamilton, F. E. I. (1967) 'Models of industrial location', in: R. J. Chorley & P. Haggett, eds., *Models in Geography*, Methuen, London, Ch. 10, expecially pp. 410–12.

Harris, C. D. (1943) 'A functional classification of cities in the United States', *Geographical Review*, **33**, pp. 86–99.

Harris, R. J. P. (1974) 'Intra-regional movement of manufacturing industry: a comparative evaluation of findings in the Nottinghamshire–Derbyshire sub-region', *Town Planning Review*, **45(4)**, pp. 431–43.

Henderson, R. A. (1974) 'Industrial overspill from Glasgow 1945–1968', *Urban Studies*, **11(1)**, pp. 61–79.

Isard, W. (1956) *Location and Space Economy*, M.I.T. Press, Boston.

Keeble, D. E. (1965) 'Industrial migration from North-West London, 1940–64', *Urban Studies*, **2**, pp. 15–32.

Keeble, D. E. (1968) 'Industrial decentralization and the metropolis', *Transactions, Institute of British Geographers*, **44**, pp. 1–54.

Kinly, P. (1969) *Industrialization in Open Economy, Nigeria, 1945–66*, Cambridge. U.P., London.

Lösch, A. (1954) *The Economics of Location*, Yale U.P., New Haven.

Mabogunje, A. L. (1973) 'Manufacturing and geography of development in Africa', *Economic Geography*, **49(1)**, pp. 1–20.

Onyemelukwe, J. O. C. (1974) 'Industrial location decision-making in Nigeria', in: F. E. I. Hamilton, ed., *Spatial Perspectives on Industrial Organization and Decision-Making*, Wiley, London/New York, pp. 461–484.

Smith, B. M. D. (1970) 'Industrial overspill in theory and practice: the case of the West Midlands', *Urban Studies*, **7(2)**, pp. 199–204.

Smith, D. M. (1972) *Industrial Location*, Wiley, London.

Spooner, D. (1972) 'Industrial movement and the rural periphery: the case of Devon and Cornwall', *Regional Studies*, **6**, pp. 197–215.

Spooner, D. (1974) 'Some qualitative aspects of industrial movement in a problem region in the UK', *Town Planning Review* **45(1)**, pp. 63–83.

Townroe, P. M. (1975) 'Branch plants and regional development', *Town Planning Review*, **46(1)**, pp. 47–62.

Ullman, E. L. and Dacey, M. (1960) 'The minimum requirements approach to the urban economic base', *Papers and Proceedings, Regional Science Association*, **6.**

Weber, A. (1929) *The Theory of the Location of Industries*, Chicago University Press, Chicago.

Chapter 11

Trends in industrial location in India

Mand Ranjan Chaudhuri

Industrial development has been very uneven among the world's nations, being a function *inter-alia* of their respective political power, natural resources, market, capital availability, technical skill, scientific and technological developments. The industrial map of some countries has changed substantially in recent years thanks to their intelligent use of national resources. Many still remain underdeveloped inasmuch as they have their special socio-economic and spatial problems. In these contexts this chapter highlights recent structural and spatial changes in Indian industry, constraints on development and measures adopted by government to correct unbalanced industrialization.

Planning and trends in industrial development

The industrial landscape of India has undergone spectacular changes in recent years. From a producer of mainly agricultural-based consumer products, despite ups and downs, a diversified industrial structure has been created. Table 11.1 shows trends in production in selected industries. Between 1950 and 1972 the output of coal has been more than doubled, that of iron-ore increased seven-fold, steel four-fold. Yet even now, Indian steel production meets only 10 per cent of needs. A chemicals industry has been created from virtually nothing to produce almost 1 million tons of nitrogen fertilizers and 1.4 million tons of sulphuric acid in 1971. There has been substantial progress, too, in engineering industries as Table 11.2 shows. As a wide range of industries has been innovated, so industrial complexes have emerged in several areas. Such growth, however, has been polarized excessively in some places so that in recent years the government has realized the need for measures to reduce the sharpening inter-regional disparities in levels of industrial development.

The many difficulties which India has passed through since independence have frequently meant under-fulfilment of plan targets. The *First Five-Year Plan* (1951–6) made a modest attempt to establish key industries, particularly heavy chemicals and electrical industries. Though progress was left generally to private sector investment, the State initiated or completed some industrial projects as a basis for more extensive industrialization in the second phase. The *Second Five-Year Plan* (1956–61) stressed heavy industrialization through cooperation between both State and private sectors. Three new steel works, each of 1 million tons, were constructed by the State while two existing private sector plants were doubled in capacity. A wide range of new industries were financed by State and

Table 11.1 The growth of production in selected Indian industries (figures in million tons)

	1950–1	1960–1	1971–2
Mining			
Coal (including lignite)	3218.0	55.5	74.0
Iron Ore	310.0	11.0	23.2
Metallurgical industries			
Pig iron	1.7	4.31	6.80
Steel ingots	1.5	3.42	6.41
Finished steel	1.0	2.39	4.79
Aluminium	0.004	0.018	0.082
Copper	0.007	0.008	0.009
Chemicals and allied industries			
Nitrogenous fertilizers (N)	0.009	0.098	0.952
Phosphatic fertilizers (P_2O_5)	0.009	0.052	0.278
Sulphuric acid	0.101	0.368	1.380
Soda ash	0.045	0.152	0.489
Caustic soda	0.012	0.101	0.385
Refined petroleum products	0.2	5.8	18.6
Paper and allied products	0.116	0.350	0.801
Cement	2.7	8.0	15.1
Cotton cloth (total)	4215.0	6738.01	7547.01
Jute	837.0	1097.0	1129.01

private capital for producing heavy electrical machinery, machine-tools, machines for cement and paper industries, basic chemicals, pharmaceuticals, synthetic fibres and engineering products like bicycles, sewing machines, telephones, textile and food processing machinery.

Aggregate industrial output increased by 94 per cent between 1950 and 1960 as a result. Nevertheless, delays in plan fulfilment meant short-falls in production. Two examples must suffice. The combined output of steel from the three new State mills at Bhilai, Rourkela and Durgapur reached only 600 000 tons in 1960 compared to a target of 2 million tons. Expansion of the Sindri fertilizer project and completion of three State-owned fertilizer factories at Nangal, Neyveli and Rourkela was delayed because of foreign exchange difficulties. Yet the aim at more balanced regional development did encourage greater dispersal of industrial plants through priority for location of public-sector plans in more backward areas. Similarly, the needs of such areas were considered in granting licences to private firms making decisions on the location of new plants.

The *Third Five-Year Plan* (1961–6) achieved an average annual industrial growth rate of 8.2 per cent as against an 11 per cent target. Though the first four years witnessed growth rates of 8–10 per cent annually, it slowed to 5.3 per cent in 1965 largely as a result of hostilities with China. Expansion was markedly un-even during the subsequent Annual Plans 1966–9 because of two successive droughts. Scarcities of farm and mineral raw materials and industrial components resulted and were accentuated by difficulties in sustaining an adequate inflow of foreign aid in those years. Nevertheless, significant industrial expansion did raise steel output to 4.7 million tons (though the 1966 target had been 6.8 million tons) and did fulfil the Third Plan's targets in the production of aluminium, vehicles, electrical goods, cotton textiles, machinery, machine tools, sugar, diesel engines and petroleum products.

The *Fourth Plan* (1969–74) has aimed at completing existing projects, expanding existing capacities, building new industries in areas with better infrastructure

Table 11.2 The structure of employment and value-added in Indian manufacturing, 1968 (percentages)

Industries	Employment	Value-added
All manufacturing	100.0	100.0
Textiles		
Spinning, weaving and finishing	27.8	21.2
Power		
Electricity and gas	8.7	10.6
Metallurgy	8.4	9.1
Iron and steel	7.7	7.4
Non-ferrous metallurgy	0.7	1.7
Engineering	18.2	18.6
Machinery	5.1	5.3
Electrical machinery	3.9	4.7
Railway equipment	4.9	3.3
Motor vehicles	2.3	3.3
Metal products	2.0	2.0
Food processing and tobacco	11.2	9.1
Sugar and gur	3.0	3.6
Miscellaneous foods	5.6	3.0
Tobacco	2.6	2.5
Chemicals	6.1	15.2
Miscellaneous chemicals	2.3	5.6
Basic industrial chemicals	2.3	5.2
Rubber products	1.3	2.5
Petroleum refining	0.2	1.9
Other industries	20.5	16.2
Miscellaneous	14.4	10.5
Cement	0.9	1.6
Pulp and paper	1.6	1.9
Printing and publishing	2.6	2.2

Source: Government of India (1972), *Indian Pocket Book of Economic Information*, Delhi.

and developed industry as well as creating infrastructure for industry in un-industrialized areas. After the caution of the Annual Plans, the Fourth Plan was overambitious. Output expanded but was still significantly below target in coking coal, iron-ore, steel, non-ferrous metals, chemicals and commercial vehicles, some types of machinery and even cotton cloth. The recession in farm-based and engineering industries has been a basic factor in this situation and has expressed itself through a decreased, if fluctuating, annual rate of growth in industrial production: from 6.8 per cent in 1969–70 to 3.7 per cent (1970–1 and 1973–4) and 3.5 to 5.0 per cent (1971–3). Table 11.2 expresses for 1968 the outcome of planning in changing Indian industrial structure. It will be noted that although textiles remain the largest industry, engineering and electrical industries are collectively more important than the farm-based food and tobacco industries.

Constraints on growth

The Planning Commission (Government of India, 1974, pp. 131–4) has explained unsatisfactory growth by several factors. First, inadequate capacity hindered production expansion particularly in mining, fuel and power industries. Second, certain basic manufacturing activities like steel, cement and fertilizers experienced under-utilization of capacity which partly resulted from lack of maintenance or deficient designs. Third, unpredictable climatic fluctuations caused erratic performance in industries dependent upon farm supplies of materials, notably of sugar, cotton and jute. Fourth, insufficient capital investment slowed the growth in demand for machinery, so adversely affecting capital-goods production while shortages of steel and non-ferrous metals hampered the ability of engineering to meet even real demand. Fifth, electric power and coal movements to delivery points were held up periodically by bottlenecks in infrastructure, notably power transmission and railway transport, so causing shortfalls in use of manufacturing capacity. Finally, difficulties experienced in the initial processes of 'indigenization', through greater dependence upon domestic technology, design and equipment, have generally impeded the rate of investment and capital efficiency.

Measures to correct imbalances

Four measures have been adopted to correct deficiencies in privately-owned industries: (1) The Industrial Reconstruction Corporation of India Ltd has been established to assist firms which were threatened with closure as a result of outmoded equipment or poor labour health. (2) In January 1972 the government brought in a new Act which would encourage fuller use of installed capacity: this permits production, subject to conditions, in excess of the capacity licensed (by the government) in 165 selected industries. (3) To remove uncertainty from the industrial environment regarding government controls on the private sector in India – which had impeded large and foreign corporate investment – a modified industrial licensing policy was announced in February 1973. This defined more specifically the scope of activity and rights of large Indian and foreign companies which wished to expand or to establish industries in the sub-continent. (4) Finally a 'Secretariat for Industrial Approvals' has been set up within the Ministry of Industrial Development to expedite decisions on proposals for plant expansion, closure or innovation in India from national and foreign private enterprise.

Further steps have been taken to improve economic performance, increase expansion and rationalize location policy for industries under State control: a high-level committee to make recommendations to the Ministry regarding performance; a Public Investment Board to examine and to approve State-sector industrial projects; and the introduction of the Monopolies and Restrictive Trade Practices Act in June 1970 to curb concentration of economic activity and power by promoting development of small-scale units in 124 industries with a view to increased dispersion of industrialization processes to selected backward areas.

The development strategy outlined in the fifth Five-Year Plan (1974–9) is in keeping with the twin national objectives of self-reliance and greater social justice. An annual growth rate of 8.1 per cent is envisaged as the outcome of a combined emphasis upon rapid expansion in key fuel, metallurgical, chemicals and machinery industries and upon rapid development of small-scale labour-intensive ancillary industries acting as feeders to the large-scale, capital-intensive plants. Production of non-essential goods is to be curbed in favour of selected goods which are competitive in export markets. Backward regions are to receive some priority in the combined development of both large- and small-scale industries.

Recently a National Committee on Environmental Planning and Coordination

Fig. 11.1   Industrial and total employment by States in India in 1971.

has been established to play an important role in the Fifth Plan in combating pollution, environmental damage and consequent health hazards. Industrialization in India has generated such problems especially in regions where plants emitting gases, smoke and effluent are mostly concentrated: the major cities of Calcutta, Bombay, Delhi, Madras and Bangalore and new heavy industrial centres like Jamshedpur, Rourkela and Durgapur.

The Planning Commission (1974, p. 138) has decided to establish larger unit size plans in such industries as can yield significant economies of scale. The Fifth Five-Year Plan programme stresses that substantial opportunities exist for achieving scale economies in manufacturing, particularly by increasing the scale of existing – or newly planned – chemicals, oil-refining, steel, paper, foods and textile industries and, for example, polarizing industries in select areas like Calcutta, Bombay, Delhi, Kanpur, Madras and Bangalore. About 80 per cent of all large-scale industries and 70 per cent of total Indian industrial employment is concentrated in six States: Maharashtra (19 per cent of industrial jobs), West Bengal (22 per cent), Gujarat (8 per cent), Tamil Nadu (10 per cent), Bihar (5 per cent) and Uttar Pradesh (7 per cent). That regional disparities in industrial development are great is shown in that all other regions virtually lack major industries, while two States alone – West Bengal and Maharashtra – localize two-fifths of all mining and manufacturing (Table 11.3).

Five types of industrial zones have emerged (Ahmed, 1956): (1) properly-

Table 11.3 Regional distribution of employment and value-added in Indian manufacturing, 1968 (in percentages)

States in rank order	Employment	Value-added
Maharashtra	19.85	26.95
West Bengal	18.80	19.29
Tamil Nadu	9.69	9.22
Gujarat	8.22	7.85
Uttar Pradesh	6.92	6.65
Bihar	5.53	6.26
Mysore	4.42	5.11
Kerala	4.34	3.63
Madhya Pradesh	4.23	3.61
Andhra Pradesh	5.91	3.35
Haryana	1.99	2.23
Punjab	1.95	2.28
Rajasthan	1.76	1.74
Orissa	1.86	1.71
Delhi	1.77	1.63
Assam	1.78	0.99
Pondichery	0.26	0.15
Himachal Pradesh	0.24	0.14
Jammu and Kashmir	0.25	0.14
Chandigarh	0.08	0.12
Goa	0.05	0.03
Andaman and Nicobar Islands	0.07	0.01
Tripura	0.03	0.00
Total	100.00	100.00

Source: Government of India, *India Pocket Book of Economic Information*, Delhi, 1972.

developed industrial areas with large and diversified industries like the Hooghly-side; (2) extensive zones with agricultural-based manufacturing, like the Ganges valley sugar belt that extends from Kosi to Jamuna in Bihar and Uttar Pradesh; (3) larger industrial nodes of limited geographic extent but diversified structure as in and around cities like Calcutta, Bombay, Madras, Kanput and Delhi; (4) smaller centres of metal-based heavy industries with rather specialized structure such as Jamshedpur, Rourkela, Bhilai and Durgapur; and (5) engineering centres like Ranchi, Bhopal and Bangalore.

More industrialized States have both larger and more diversified industries than less-developed States. But all are dominated by agricultural- and mineral-based or consumer industries, except Maharashtra, West Bengal and Tamil Nadu where capital-goods and footloose industries are also developed. Very backward areas like Orissa and Madhya Pradesh contain small industrial enclaves. Income distribution and relative living standards of people in different parts of India have been adversely affected by this lopsided industrial growth. An Industrial Policy Resolution of 30 April 1956 required a shift in emphasis in location policy towards greater inter-regional balance in growth: 'extension of benefits of economic progress to the less-developed regions and widespread diffusion of industry are among the major aims of planned development' (Planning Commission, 1961, p. 142).

Excessive concentration has resulted mainly from the unregulated freedom enjoyed by private-sector industrialists in promoting manufacturing in large urban areas. State control of industrial location is necessary as a counteractive measure and to ensure sufficient development in backward areas. The paucity of employment opportunities in such areas encourages out-migration of labour, creating over-congestion in industrial areas. Regionalization and control of location need to be related. Methods of developing the growth potentials of each region vary: while regional factors rooted in physical environment and geographic location cannot be changed, others can be influenced by raising levels of education and skill, power supply, and the application of science and technology.

Conditions in India differ from those in the western world. Natural resources and labour are widely distributed throughout many regions of India but entrepreneurial ability is available in few areas. Under such conditions balanced regional development would only be possible after proper assessment of resources has been made especially in areas where entrepreneurial ability is scarce. Development of industrial activities in such areas should be the responsibility of the State, by creating infrastructure, by selecting industries for development and by choosing their locations. Industrial planning in India thus aims at developing new industries from congested areas. In keeping with this policy the Government of India included a proposal in the Third Plan for establishing 'industrial development zones' in backward regions.

Every major project has to be regarded as a nucleus for integrated regional development. Around new irrigation schemes a whole series of projects are essential to link agricultural progress with processing and other industries serving local markets (Hamilton, 1967, pp. 406–9). Steel and other heavy industries provide conditions for developing small and medium-sized ancilliary plants and for generating educational and training programmes. Extensive regions such as Dandakaranya, the Rajasthan canal area, the Damodar, Tungabhadra, Nagarjunsager, Koyna, and Chambal valleys offer resources for exploitation. In States like Gujarat, Rajashtan and Assam which lack coal, hydroelectric, oil and atomic power stations can be developed. Large plants should be localized in select growth poles supported by dispersed small-scale processing and servicing.

Changes in industrial location

The interaction of government planning, State and private investment and changing industrial structure in India has produced some shifts in the location of industry despite much inertia. In a developing country like India, where an 'industrial revolution' began only in the planning era from 1951, migration results from: (1) the greater concentration of existing industrial production in larger-scale facilities, usually in existing urban centres; (2) the development of new plants in existing industries in places other than the original locations; and (3) the innovation of types of industries new to the country in new or less developed locations within the existing spatial system.

Industrialization in India began in 1854, with a jute mill at Rishra, 12 miles (19 km) north of Calcutta. Gradually the first cotton mill (1855) at Ghoosery near Howrah, paper mill at Bally (1887) and iron works at Kulti near Asansol (1874) were established. Subsequently, better advantages of site and infrastructure like power and transport induced movement of the paper mill to Titaghar, the blast furnace to Burnpur. Cotton textiles dominated the industrial scene in India as a cottage industry from early times. Traditional skill in spinning and weaving and marketing facilities located the industry in northern India. Overseas trading facilities and traditional skills located the industry also in the coastal areas of Surat, Broach and Manstipatan. But Japanese overseas competition and development of the local market altered its locational advantages and the industry migrated into the southern interior. As a result of their subsequent decline as administrative centres Agra, Lucknow, Allahabad and Patna have been replaced by Delhi, Kanpur and Calcutta in northern and eastern India as centres of cotton textiles.

The sugar industry, established in 1904, has tended to migrate from the traditional areas of concentration in northern, to southern, India – largely because of (1) better facilities for irrigating sugar cane production and (2) government licensing in favour of sugar manufacturing as a means of integrated farm-factory development in the more backward south. This trebled production and raised the contribution of southern tropical areas – Andhra Pradesh, Gujarat, Kerala, Madras, Mysore and Pondicheny – to total Indian sugar output from 27.8 per cent in 1950 to 56.1 in 1965, so replacing sub-tropical northern India as the major source of supply.

Indeed, government intervention has been instrumental in altering the spatial pattern of Indian industry since 1951: first, by providing subsidies to private-sector industries to establish branch plants in more rural areas; second, by developing infrastructure in such areas to give economic support to new industries; and third, by establishing nationalized industries in less developed areas. Thus, dispersion of growth has occurred around existing urban–industrial nodes and industries long localized in one particular state have been diffused to other states. Table 11.4 summarizes the major new centres of industry created since 1951. Two interesting aspects of industrial migration may be noted. First, iron and steel shifted its importance somewhat from West Bengal and Bihar to new steel centres created in Andhra Pradesh, Karnataka, Madhya Pradesh, Orissa and Tamil Nadu to satisfy government policy for balanced regional growth by exploiting available raw materials and superior infrastructure where possible and by serving the needs of backward regions where necessary and feasible. Second, shifts in the location of non-ferrous metallurgy industries resulted from mining and processing of copper and bauxite resources which were discovered in underdeveloped Orissa and Rajasthan.

Research on spatial industrial patterns in India

Reviews of research in industrial geography in India have been made by Chatterjee (1963), Shafi (1972) and Chaudhuri (1972). A very comprehensive bibliography of industrial location studies, analytical techniques, regional and urban industrial structure and spatial changes in industrial distributions in India in the period prior to 1968 is included in Hamilton (1970). The *location of industries* has attracted the most attention among economists and geographers. Rao (1942) stressed the need to study geographical environment before launching an industry and criticized Alfred Weber for neglecting the role of physical factors in industrial location. Krishnan (1952) analysed how raw materials influenced the location of mineral-based industries, while Tewari (1961) examined the impact of economic factors on the location of the sugar industry. Kuriyan (1962) studied the spatial distribution of textiles and steel, with emphasis upon the importance of employment in an urban centre and attracting labour from the countryside. Chaudhuri

Table 11.4 New industrial centres of India created in the planning era

State	Centre	Industries established
Andhra Pradesh	Ramchandrapuram Sanatnagar Secunderabad Vishakhapatnam	Heavy electrical machinery pharmaceuticals machine tools oil-refining, steel
Assam	NahorKatiya Nunmati	Fertilizers oil-refining

Bihar	Baruani
	Bokaro
	
	Ranchi
		Oil-refining
		iron and steel, coke and organic
		  chemicals, optical glass
		heavy machinery, coastings, tools,
		  insulators

Gujarat	Koyali	Oil-refining
Karnataka	Bangalore Vijaynaga (Hospet)	Machine tools, watchmaking steel
Kerala	Cochin Munnar	Oil-refining, new shipyards chemicals
Madhya Pradesh	Bhilai Bhopal Hoshangabad	Steel, refractory materials heavy electrical machinery paper-making
Maharashtra	Pimpri Trombay	Pharmaceuticals fertilizers, oil-refining
Orissa	Hirakud Rourkela	Aluminium steel, fertilizers
Punjab	Pinjore	Machine tools
Rajasthan	Khetri Kotah	Copper-smelting precision instruments
Tamil Nadu	Guindi Neiveli Ootacamund Salem Tiruchi	Surgical instruments fertilizers, briquettes, lignite, electrical power films and photographical products steel electrical power, boilers
Uttar Pradesh	Gorakhpur Ranipur Rishikesh	Fertilizers heavy electrical machinery pharmaceuticals
West Bengal	Durgapur Haldia Rupnarayanpur	Steel, machinery, tools oil-refining cables

(1962, 1964, 1970) has studied the growth and location of major Indian industries showing that the large population and natural resource base of Uttar Pradesh should be duly recognized in assessments of the future prospects for industrial development in India. Indeed, Tripathi (1968) stresses that rational planning of industrial growth in Uttar Pradesh is vital to balanced economic development in view of the State's pivotal location in the national spatial system. Industrial growth and migration have been studied by Chatterjee in the Howrah region (Chatterjee, 1968) by Karannaver (1968) in Bhadravati, by Sengupta (1958) in the Hooghly region while similar studies have been made of Bihar (Sinha, 1968),

Greater Ranchi (Pandey, 1969), Chotonagpur's industrial complexes (Mukherjee, 1970), and Orissa (Chaudhuri, 1971*b*). *Industrial complexes*, defined as a set of linked or ancillary activities grouped together to derive external economies from the use of common services, have attracted a growing literature. Mukherjee (1970) updates Ganguli's study (1949) of the Bengal–Bihar industrial belt of the Chotonagpur plateau. Ahmed (1956) examines complexes in India in contrast to specialized studies of steel complexes and of diversified complexes of the Greater Calcutta – West Bengal regions (Chaudhuri, 1964, 1969, 1971, 1972).

The gaps

Much research has been in a traditional vein. New fields need to be investigated particularly with regard to planning diversified spatial industrial structures. At the local level, yet of great practical significance for the employment and social involvement of the rapidly-expanding population, are small-scale and cottage industries: hitherto they have received far too little attention. Studies at the regional and national scales into the relevance of growth pole concepts for achieving some combination of large- and small-scale industries, for dispersing development to backward areas and for removing the great spatial economic disparities evident in India today. None of this research, however, can be insulated from broader socioeconomic studies of methods to overcome national economic recession, underutilization of installed capacity, underemployment of labour and shortages in materials and energy supply. More account must be taken of the spatial economic and social trade-offs between inputs and outputs. The Planning Commission itself admits that balanced regional growth has been difficult because of inadequate infrastructure provision. Thus the Fifth Plan proposes to create machinery to identify industries suited to the needs and potentialities of the backward areas by technical, economic and feasibility studies and to undertake integrated planning and construction of infrastructure. Selected growth centres should be located in the backward areas to provide a package of financial, marketing and other services to attract potential entrepreneurs to set up new units there.

Bridging the gap

The task of aiding the Planning Commission to bridge these gaps is not easy. First a detailed national and State-wide inventory is required of existing industrial patterns and detailed evaluation of future structural and spatial potentialities. A meticulous study of the potential role of industrial complexes in developing the country should be made, by research on geographical association or linkage, sources of inputs, destinations of outputs, costs of transport and investment, problems of technology transfer and improvement of marketing, the social consequences of large-scale industries and complexes and resultant urbanization.

A major difficulty is the inadequacy of statistical sources and is a partial cause of a dearth of literature on the application of quantitative analysis to Indian industrial problems; yet even existing statistics can yield useful insights into given problems and to suggest possible lines of remedial action. An example is the magnitude ratings for the locations of the nitrogen fertilizer industry in 1972. The author calculated the magnitude rating for each location as a percentage of the average magnitude for all fifteen locations where nitrogen fertilizers are produced in India. The results are given in Table 11.5. A plant of average capacity would

Table 11.5 The 'magnitude rating' for locations of the Indian fertilizer industry, 1972

Plant locations	Nutrient nitrogen and phosphate capacity (thousand tons)	Average nutrient capacity per factory	Magnitude rating (column 1 as a percentage of column 2)
	1	2	3
Total	1916	127.733	
A. Public sector			
Madras	249		194.94
Rourkela	120		93.95
Trombay	117		91.60
Travancore	109		85.33
Sindri	90		70.46
Gorakhpur	80		62.63
Nangal	80		62.63
Neiveli	70		54.80
Total	960	106.000	
B. Private sector			
Gujarat	266		208.25
Kanpur	200		156.58
Vizag	153		119.78
Kota	110		86.12
Ennore	26		20.35
Varanasi	10		7.83
Total	956	159.333	

receive a 'magnitude rating' of 100 per cent so that it is immediately apparent which plants in which locations are below or above average size. Two major points emerge. First, six plants in the private sector concentrate as much capacity as do nine State-sector plants and are of higher average scale. Second, these private-sector fertilizer plants have high magnitude ratings (over 100.00) as opposed to only one nationalized plant, which suggests the dominance of contrasting locational criteria, i.e. greater importance of productive efficiency through economies of scale for privately-owned firms developing fertilizer manufacture as compared with greater spatial dispersion of smaller nationalized plants to activate backward areas. Of course, the magnitude rating method can thus be used to assess where it is appropriate to locate new capacity if locational policy is striving to achieve greater spatial 'evenness' in development, but it does not of itself indicate optimal plant scales which should act as the criterion in investment decisions. Since the method can be applied to industrial location patterns at different times, though, it may be useful in measuring spatial-temporal shifts. The application of this, and other methods, in the future is feasible since Indian data provide information on numbers of plants, their employment levels, consumption of raw materials, installed capacity and output. Frequently all measures are required to avoid bias in evaluating distributions.

References

Ahmed, E. (1956) 'Industrial zones and centres of India', *Proceedings of the Eighteenth International Geographical Congress*, Rio de Janeiro.

Bellerby, J. R. (1964) *Economic Reconstruction*, Kegan Paul, London.

Chatterjee, S. P. (1963) *Progress of Geography: Fifty Years of Science in India*, Indian Science Congress Association.

Chatterjee, S. P. (1968) 'Changing patterns of industries in Howrah', *Abstracts of Papers, 21st International Geographical Congress (New Delhi)*.

Chaudhuri, M. R. (1962, 1970) *Indian Industries: Development and Location*, Oxford & I.B.H., Calcutta.

Chaudhuri, M. R. (1964, 1975) *The Iron and Steel Industry of India*, Oxford & I.B.H., Calcutta.

Chaudhuri, M. R. (1969) 'Growth patterns and problems of Durgapur industrial complex', *Proceedings of the Indian Science Congress, Session 56*, Part III.

Chaudhuri, M. R. (1971*a*) 'The industrial profile of Orissa: an economic-geographic evaluation', *Industries in India*, **7(4)**, pp. 11–15.

Chaudhuri, M. R. (1971*b*) *The Industrial Landscape of West Bengal*, Oxford & I.B.H., Calcutta.

Chaudhuri, M. R. (1972) 'Industrial complexes: a trend report', in: *A Survey of Research in Geography*, Indian Council of Social Science Research, Bombay, pp. 80–83.

Chaudhuri, M. R. (1972) 'Industrial activities in the Greater Calcutta industrial complex', *Industrial Situation in India*, **1(1)**, pp. 3–15.

Dayal, P. (1964), 'Industrial location in India', *Transactions of the Indian Council of Geographers*, pp. 73–84.

Government of India Planning Commission (1974), *The Fifth Five-Year Plan* (Delhi).

Hamilton, F. E. Ian (1967) 'Models of industrial location', Ch. 10 in: R. J. Chorley and P. Haggett, *Models in Geography*, Methuen, London.

Hamilton, F. E. Ian (1970) *Regional Economic Analysis in Britain and the Commonwealth: A Bibliographic Guide*, Weidenfeld and Nicolson, London, / Schocken Books, New York, 1971, pp. 326–61.

Karannavar, M. D. (1968), 'Industrial landscape in Bhadravati', *Abstracts of Papers, 21st I.G.U. Congress*, New Delhi.

Krishnan, M. S. (1952) 'Geographical control of mineral industries', *Bulletin of the National Geographical Society of India*, **16**.

Kuriyan, G. (1962) 'An analysis of the spatial distribution of industry in India with special reference to population', *Indian Geographical Journal*, **37(1)**, pp. 1–7.

Lokanathan, P. S. (1931) 'Migration of labour with special reference to South India', *Journal of Madras Geographical*, **6(1)**, pp. 1–10.

Lokanathan, P. S. (1932) 'Localization of industries in India', *Journal of Madras Geographical Association*, **7(1)**, pp. 1–17.

Mukherjee, M. (1970), 'Aspects of recent industrialization in Chotonagpur', *National Geographical Journal of India*, **16(2)**, pp. 121–36.

Pandey, P. (1969) 'Industrial landscape of Greater Ranchi', *Geographical Outlook*, **6**, pp. 6–15.

Rao, V. L. S. P. (1942) 'The geographer and the localization of industries', *Journal of Madras Geographical Association*, **17(3)**, pp. 216–21.

Sengupta, P. (1958) 'Some aspects of industrial growth of the Hooghly region', *National Geographical Journal of India*, **4(1)**, pp. 7–15.

Shafi, M. (1972), 'Industrial geography', *A Survey of Research in Geography*, Indian Council of Social Science Research, Bombay, pp. 62–9.

Sinha, B. N. (1972) *Industrial Geography of India*, Oxford & I.B.H., Calcutta.

Sinha, R. P. (1968), 'Growth of industries in Bihar', *Abstracts of Papers, 21st I.G.U. Congress (New Delhi)*.

Tewari, R. N. (1961), 'The location of sugar mills', *National Geographical Journal of India*, **4**, pp. 61–8.

Tripathi, V. B. (1968), 'Trends and planning of industrial location in the Kanpur region', *Abstracts of Papers, 21st I.G.U. Congress (New Delhi)*.

Chapter 12

The Australian environment and industrial location analysis

G. J. R. Linge

Geographers can contribute greatly to the information available to decision-makers who are faced in Australia – as elsewhere – with long-term changes in demographic, labour force and industrial trends. Yet research of this kind should pay more attention to the way that policy decisions in one country can impinge on the structure and location of manufacturing activities in other countries.

The Australian environment

Four aspects of the overall Australian environment are basic to any analysis of industrial location. First, 30 per cent of the vast continent (7 680 000 km²) is too arid, under present technology, for either man or beast; 59 per cent is used for extensive livestock raising, though at very low stocking rates on the margins of the dry interior; 6 per cent is under crops, lying fallow or sown to pasture; and 5 per cent is forested. A mere 0.15 per cent (11 000 km²) is urban.

Second, Australia has one of the most urbanized, spatially-concentrated settlement patterns in the world. At the census in mid-1976 about 60 per cent of the 13 548 000 population (including Aborigines) were in the capital cities of the six States and two Territories, and 30 per cent were in the 500 other urban places (defined as concentrations of 1000 or more people). Australia lacks medium-sized towns: apart from the capital cities, only eight other places have more than 50 000 inhabitants (Fig. 12.1): Newcastle and Woolongong in New South Wales; Geelong and Ballarat in Victoria; Gold Coast, Townsville and Toowoomba in Queensland; and Launceston in Tasmania. The largest, Newcastle, has just reached 250 000. Over wide areas, even in the more populous east, southeast and southwest, population density is less than 1.5 persons per km²; and beyond 300 km from the coast it quickly diminishes to an average of less than one person per 10 km².

Third, the wide separation of the main concentrations of population around the periphery of this extensive continent (see Fig. 12.1) generates costs, delays and difficulties of overcoming the distance between them. There are no inland waterways. Although coastal shipping accounts for 46 per cent of the tonne-km performed by all transport modes, this largely results from long hauls of bulk ore, petroleum and sugar cargoes. Rail transport (34 per cent of the tonne-km) is divided into six State systems, two main lines owned and operated by the Commonwealth, and privately-owned coal and iron-ore lines. In most States the rail network developed largely during the nineteenth century by pushing outwards from the capital city, so that the links become increasingly tenuous towards the

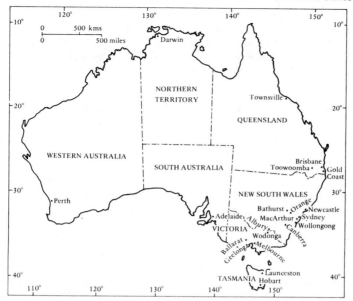

Fig. 12.1   Map of places named in the text.

border areas. Lack of coordination over the choice of gauges has long handicapped the inter-State movement of goods, although a standard-gauge line linked Sydney with Brisbane in 1930 and Sidney with Melbourne in 1962. Each State system charges a tapering rate so that, per tonne-km, long hauls tend to be cheaper: goods passing over a border, however, are usually liable for the sum of two tapering rates than one covering the whole distance. Road transport (performing about 20 per cent of the tonne-km but uplifting four-fifths of the tonnage consigned) is subject in four States to weight–distance taxation or specific licensing controls on intra-State movements (to 'protect' the railways); it is penalized on journeys across borders by differences in State legislation relating, for instance, to maximum axle loadings and vehicle dimensions (Gilmour, 1974).

A fourth institutional feature is the division of the continent into six States and two Commonwealth-controlled Territories. Australia was settled between 1788 and 1836 in the form of separate political units, each of which (except Western Australia) gained control over its destiny to all intents and purposes during the 1850s. When the six colonies federated on 1 January 1901 (and became known as States), all internal tariff barriers were dismantled and replaced by a consolidated external tariff. While the States were happy enough to see the Commonwealth handle problems like defence, external affairs and postal services, they retained very important rights – including the control of taxation (until 1942), land minerals, forests, water and railways. Even after Federation, therefore, the States maintained many of their competitive attitudes and policies while the Commonwealth could exert relatively little overall influence on the spatial arrangement of economic activity. Indeed the Constitution specifically states that 'the Commonwealth shall not, by any law or regulation of trade, commerce or revenue, give preference to one State or any part thereof over another State or part thereof'. Thus, the Commonwealth, through its control of taxation (since 1942), tariffs, overseas borrowing, immigration and the management of the economy generally, provides the overall Australian context within which each of the States retains considerable power to organize itself spatially. The Commonwealth has more control over the affairs of the Australian Capital Territory and Northern Territory, but together these contain merely 0.5 per cent of the nation's factory workforce.

Structure and characteristics of Australian manufacturing

During the 1950s and 1960s the manufacturing sector more or less kept pace with the expansion of the Australian economy: factory employment grew at about the same rate as total population, the share of the total labour force working in manufacturing establishments remained at between 27 and 28 per cent and the annual contribution of this sector to gross national product ranged from 26 to 28 per cent. Since 1970–1, however, its relative position has declined.

In 1973–4, 37 000 manufacturing establishments were operating in Australia and employed 1 338 000 persons, 28 per cent of whom were female. The details in Table 12.1, using the Australian Standard Industrial Classification (A.S.I.C.), emphasize the importance of metals, metal products, vehicles and appliances. Nearly 90 per cent of manufacturing establishments employ fewer than fifty workers (including those directly engaged in selling and distributing products). Although a high proportion of small factories is not uncommon in industrialized countries (as in Japan), in Australia it stems from the fragmentation of the relatively small economy between six States and the substantial distances separating the main internal markets (the capital cities and nearby areas), with consequent high transport and communication costs. For instance, the freight rate per tonne on a standardized high density cargo from Sydney to Townsville (1200 nautical miles) is considerably greater than that to overseas destinations like London, Kobe and Vancouver. This has led many larger companies to set up several factories, making more or less identical goods, in different regions of Australia. In this way the productive capacity needed to serve the relatively small domestic market is further fragmented and unit costs are increased. In the case of cars, for example, the Industries Assistance Commission (I.A.C.) calculated the minimum efficient scale of a plant to be 110 000 vehicles a year: in fact the Australian output of 485 000 units in 1973 was divided between four manufacturers and three assemblers together operating twelve plants. The Commission concluded (I.A.C., 1974*a*) that 'inability to exploit scale economies is the most important single factor contributing to the high cost of the Australian industry and accounts for about half of the assessed cost disadvantage against Japanese producers and a greater proportion of the disadvantage against North American and European manufacturers'.

By contrast 360 manufacturing enterprises (comprising all Australian operations of single legal entities) had more than 500 employees: between them these accounted for 43 per cent of the factory labour force and 49 per cent of the value added. This points up the high degree of ownership concentration. In 1968–9 there were twenty activities (including steel, motor vehicles, rubber types, pulp and paper, beer, concrete pipes and asbestos cement) in which the four leading enterprises were responsible for four-fifths of turnover. This can be explained partly by the lack, until recently, of anti-trust legislation comparable to that in the USA, but mainly it arises directly and indirectly from the relatively small-sized Australian economy.

Table 12.1 Summary of operations of manufacturing establishments, Australia, 1973–4

Industry group	†A.S.I.C. sub-divisions	Establishments operating at 30 June 1974		Persons employed		Males per female	Value added	
		Number	%	Number (000)	%		$A (m)	%
Food, drink, tobacco	21, 22	4249	11	204	15	2.61	2126	16
Textiles, clothing, footwear	23, 24	4077	11	165	13	0.49	1157	9
Wood, furniture, paper, printing	25, 26	9721	26	194	14	3.58	1863	14
Chemicals, petroleum and coal products	27	1169	3	67	5	2.64	1076	8
Glass, clay, other non-metallic mineral products	28	1911	5	55	4	8.43	664	5
Industrial metals, fabricated products	29, 31	6076	16	217	16	5.79	2418	18
Vehicles, transport equipment	32	1608	4	159	12	6.67	1337	10
Domestic appliances, industrial machinery	33	5001	14	199	15	2.63	1774	14
Miscellaneous, rubber and plastic products	34	3332	9	78	6	1.80	733	6
Total manufacturing	21–34	37 144	100	1338	100	2.63	13 148	100

† *Australian Standard Industrial Classification*

Source: Australian Bureau of Statistics, *Manufacturing Establishments: Details of Operations by Industry Class, Australia 1973–74*, Canberra, 1975 (ref. 12.29).

In the 1960s one partial solution to this problem of scale and high unit costs was seen to be increased exports. A sustained programme of trade promotion has led to a growth in exports of manufactured goods (*excluding* processed food products) from $A200 m in 1959–60 to $A1340 m in 1973–4, much of it sales of alumina, motor vehicles and machinery. Significantly, the six leading importers of Australian-made goods (New Zealand, Japan, United States, South Africa, Singapore and Papua New Guinea) all border the Pacific or Indian Oceans, reflecting the partial reorientation of Australia's total trade away from traditional European markets.

This enhanced interest in manufactured exports (20 per cent of total exports in 1973–4) has highlighted the need for greater investment in research and development (R. & D.). Expenditure on R. & D. is currently only 2 per cent of the manufacturing contribution to gross domestic product, or only one-third the proportion spent in the USA or UK. Moreover, much is undertaken by larger companies, mostly subsidiaries of foreign corporations. This again emphasizes the derivative nature of much of the manufacturing in Australia: few industries have been pioneered by mainly Australian finance, ownership, natural advantage and native technological ability.

Britain was the traditional source of overseas investment in Australian industry but since 1945 the flow from North America has become as significant. By 1962–3 (when adequate data were first collected) no less than 22 per cent of the value of production came from factories under direct foreign control. In 1972–3 the Australian Bureau of Statistics (1976) indicates that the 6 per cent of plants in Australia controlled by overseas interests produced 32 per cent of the value-added in all manufacturing. By this same measure overseas equity controlled 91 per cent of petroleum refining, 79 per cent of the non-ferrous metals industry and 78 per cent of both the motor vehicle and basic chemical industries.

Not surprisingly there has been much discussion recently about the benefits and costs of foreign ownership and control of Australian manufacturing. Arguments advanced are that foreign firms have better access to overseas sources of funds and up-to-date technology; are able and willing to take bigger investment risks; have encouraged healthy competition in the local environment and have been more active than locally-owned firms in seeking overseas markets. Yet problems have already emerged: increasing costs of servicing the investment, the progressive reduction in local equity, the extent of local borrowing and the absorption of existing companies without the injection of new or additional technology. Foreign firms also deliberately contrive to achieve political and economic influence, import technology that is not always suited or properly adapted to local conditions and may make worldwide decisions (like the imposition of franchise restrictions) which could be inimical to Australia's policies or ambitions. Transnational firms in chemicals, fertilizers, motor vehicles, domestic appliances and floor coverings have helped to fragment the Australian market and then successfully argued for tariff protection on grounds of limited sales and high production costs! The Commonwealth Government passed legislation in 1975 under which proposed acquisitions and arrangements, which would enable people overseas to determine the policies of Australian businesses, are to be examined and, if found to be against the national interest, prohibited (Department of Industry and Commerce, 1976). The basic objective of both policy and prescription is to ensure that the 'foreign investment . . . is on a basis of fair sharing of net benefits as between the foreign investor and the needs and aspirations of the Australian community'.

Notice must be taken, by contrast, of recent expansion of so-called 'offshore' manufacturing by Australian companies. In June 1975 Australian investment overseas in all activities including manufacturing totalled $A845 m, much of it being in New Zealand ($A220 m), Papua New Guinea ($A232 m) and countries like Indonesia, Hong Kong, the Philippines, Malayasia and Fiji (about $A200 m). In 1976 at least fifty-nine companies listed on the Sydney Stock Exchange had manufacturing operations overseas. The main reasons for this development are the limited size of the domestic market and the very rapid escalation of costs (especially direct and indirect labour costs) in Australia on the one hand, and the availability of cheaper labour, tax concessions and similar incentives offered abroad on the other. Ironically, some firms involved, especially in the clothing industry, have sought special treatment from the Commonwealth Government to enable them to send products into Australia under special tariff or quota concessions. This illustrates yet another of the problems of Australia's relationships with and responsibilities to the developing countries in the Pacific Basin.

Spatial distribution of manufacturing in Australia

The distribution of manufacturing is not hard to describe in outline. The five mainland State capitals contain 77 per cent of all factory employment and Newcastle, Wollongong, Geelong and Hobart 8 per cent (Table 12.2), compared with their concentration of 56 per cent of total population. The thirty-nine other urban places each having more than 1000 factory workers (none with more than 8000) account for a further 8 per cent of the total, thus leaving a mere 7 per cent throughout the rest of the continent. The evolution of this spatial pattern is detailed elsewhere (Linge, 1975), yet note that it had emerged basically by 1900 and has since been modified only in detail.

At first sight, the localization of so much industrial activity in a few centres seems to deny part of the aforegoing argument by suggesting that firms can achieve significant internal and external economies. In practice, competing companies in a wide range of activities have factories producing more or less identical goods in several capital cities, so the national market is divided spatially and then divided again commercially. The Tariff Board has noted (1963, p. 10) that the action of State authorities in competing for the establishment of industries by offering various incentives was one factor which had led to excess capacity. Of course, individual firms partly trade off the increase in unit production costs against the reduction in distribution costs that result from being nearer the largest markets; collectively, the firms in an industry can seek tariff protection against imports because of the small share of the market each can achieve. One effect of insulating Australian industry against the full rigours of overseas competition can be to postpone or lengthen the process of spatial, structural and market adjustment. For instance, economic production of whitegoods (refrigerators, stoves and washing machines) requires a minimum throughput per plant of about 500 000 units annually: in 1972 the nine refrigerator manufacturers in Australia were producing eighty different models at fourteen different locations while competing for a national market of only about 350 000 units a year (Tariff Board, 1973, p. 5).

Competition between the States has also helped to perpetuate the existing spatial distribution of manufacturing. Changes in the relative proportion of the

Table 12.2 Workers and value-added in manufacturing for selected areas, 1973–4 (percentages of Australian totals)

Industry group	Workers			Value added		
	Five mainland State capitals	Newcastle, Wollongong, Geelong, Hobart	Rest of Australia	Five mainland State capitals	Newcastle, Wollongong, Geelong, Hobart	Rest of Australia
Food, drink, tobacco	62.8	4.7	32.5	63.3	4.4	32.3
Textiles, clothing, footwear	80.1	8.1	11.8	84.8	6.5	8.7
Wood, furniture, paper, printing	73.7	3.8	22.5	73.2	3.3	23.5
Chemicals, petroleum and coal products	91.0	4.5	4.5	89.8	6.2	4.0
Glass, clay, other non-metallic mineral products	75.9	7.3	16.8	74.1	8.2	17.7
Industrial metals, fabricated products	62.5	25.4	12.1	53.6	23.3†	23.1
Vehicles, transport equipment	86.5	6.3	7.2	91.4	5.5†	3.1
Domestic appliances, industrial machinery	89.4	3.7	6.9	91.9	3.6	4.5
Miscellaneous, rubber and plastic products	95.9	0.9	3.2	97.7	0.4	1.9
Total manufacturing	77.1	8.3	14.6	76.2	9.4	14.4

Sources: Australian Bureau of Statistics, *Manufacturing Establishments: Small Area Statistics,* or equivalent publication for each State; *Manufacturing Establishments: Details of Operations by Industry Class.*

† Partly estimated

nation's factory activity in each State during the last forty years have been minimal: no State has lost or gained more than two percentage points. More significantly from a welfare point of view, such rivalry between the States has overshadowed the so-called 'decentralization' policies espoused since the Second World War to reduce the economic dominance of the five mainland capital cities by establishing employment-generating activities in other urban areas. During the 1950s and 1960s the packages of incentives and inducements offered by State Governments to persuade manufacturers to locate or relocate outside the capital cities did little more than to sustain the status quo. No State was willing to do more than offer 'carrots': they feared that the use of 'sticks' might cause potential investors to seek refuge in another State in Australia. Furthermore, no State Government was prepared to select a handful of non-metropolitan centres into which additional public expenditure could be channelled to upgrade their infrastructure, quicken their rates of growth and enhance their chances of attracting private investment – because of the risk of an electoral backlash in the areas not given such favoured treatment.

The Commonwealth Government, feeling fettered by constitutional constraints or reluctant to meddle in the affairs of the States, remained inactive until 1972. By then, Governments of both New South Wales and Victoria had come to the view that, if much were to be achieved, a few places would have to be selected for 'accelerated development'. Thus, when the Commonwealth Government under Prime Minister Whitlam was elected to office in December 1972 the political environment was ready to accept proposals for Commonwealth–State cooperation on a 'growth centre' policy. During the next three years four definitive projects emerged. These involved the investment of Commonwealth and State funds in, and the relocation of some government offices to, Albury-Wodonga (straddling the New South Wales–Victorian border), Bathurst–Orange (50 km west of Sydney), MacArthur (on the southwest fringe of Sydney) and Geelong (west of Melbourne).

Although these proposals had been barely initiated before the Whitlam government was dismissed from office late in 1975, the apparent determination by governments to finance a coordinated decentralization programme appears to have given manufacturers greater confidence in non-metropolitan locations generally. Thus during the five years to mid-1974 factory employment in Sydney, Newcastle and Wollongong (New South Wales) and Melbourne and Geelong (Victoria) increased by only 3.7 per cent (by 31 500 workers) whereas that in the remainder of the two States grew by 12.9 per cent (11 100). By now much of this business confidence in decentralization may now have evaporated: after a year of uncertainty during which public expenditure on a wide range of programmes has been slashed, the Commonwealth Government under Prime Minister Fraser indicated (in November 1976) that the growth-centre programme would be greatly restricted, although Albury–Wodonga would remain as a national 'pilot' project.

The future environment and industrial location

Several recent reports have together raised fundamental questions about the long-term future role, structure and spatial organization of manufacturing in Australia. They also suggest directions for research by industrial geographers that could contribute to public policy decisions before the year 2000.

The most significant was the report of the National Population Inquiry (1975). Till then many government and private enterprise decisions had been based on the tacit assumption that the annual rate of population increase of 1.92 per cent achieved during the 1960s would be more or less maintained and that Australia in 2000 would have a population of 22 to 24 million. The Inquiry argued that population, even after allowing for net annual immigration of 50 000 people, would be nearer 17.6 million – a figure substantially confirmed by the Australian Bureau of Statistics from provisional 1976 census data. As another example, a simple extrapolation of actual growth rates during the 1960s had suggested that Sydney and Melbourne would each have a population approaching 5 million by 2000: the Inquiry projected that the population of Sydney is more likely to be about 3.6 million and that of Melbourne 3.3 million. Thus expectations about domestic market growth in the next twenty-five years have been halved. On the same assumptions, the Inquiry noted that the annual addition to the total labour force is likely to fall from an average of 146 000 (1966–71) to an average of 102 000 in the 1980s and 87 000 in the 1990s. A related trend is that the work-force participation rate of married women has risen very markedly: of the 732 000 addition to the Australian labour force during 1970–5 379 000 were females (nine-tenths of them married).

Bennett (1976) notes that the 1970s have seen an absolute fall in manufacturing employment to only 24.7 per cent of the total labour force. This contraction may have resulted partly from short-term recessionary factors, but much of it is due to longer-term factors like reduced import protection, structural change, the slow growth of the domestic market, a lower rate of new investment and equal pay for women.

Lower import protection to induce structural change, and thus to promote greater efficiency, has been advocated by the Tariff Board and its successor the Industries Assistance Comission (I.A.C.). In a major study of all quantifiable forms of assistance available to each of the 173 A.S.I.C. manufacturing industries, the I.A.C. (1974*b*) argued that *effective* rates of assistance are generally higher for industries which are labour intensive and have a relatively low output per worker. On the one hand, manufacturing for which greatest assistance has been provided tend to be responsible for a relatively small proportion of exports; on the other, the existing pattern is of protection against industries in which Australia has an export advantage. Bluntly, 'the greatest assistance has been given to those industries for which the Australian environment and endowment of resources are least suited' (I.A.C., 1974*b*, p. 16).

The clothing industry, which enjoys a high effective rate of assistance (calculated to be 100 per cent), illustrates the dilemma facing decision-makers in Australia. First, nearly 90 per cent of the employees in this industry are women, most of them married; second, the clothing industry employs one-fifth of all female factory workers; third, labour-intensive industries like clothing are among the few 'footloose' ones that have been prepared to set up factories (or, more usually, branch plants) in non-metropolitan locations; and, finally, the clothing industry is one of the most sensitive to import competition. Thus any changes aimed as 'rationalizing' this industry, even if apparently desirable for national efficiency, would particularly affect both married women (the fastest growing sector of the labour force) and the viability of non-metropolitan centres (where alternative job opportunities are scarce). This conflict between national and local interests is already expressed by the 25 per cent across-the-board tariff cut made by the Commonwealth Government in July 1973 together with other decisions to lift quota restrictions and eliminate subsidies. Within a few months the Commonwealth had to introduce a scheme for Special Assistance for Firms in Non-Metropolitan Areas (S.A.N.M.A.) which was intended 'to sustain existing production and employment or to enable their phasing out without undue hardship to the local community'. By mid-1976 nearly 90 per cent of S.A.N.M.A. scheme funds had been paid to clothing and textile firms (I.A.C., 1976, p. 124); in short a 25 per cent reduction in tariffs necessitated support being given (for both political and social reasons) to firms employing perhaps a quarter of the female factory labour force in the non-metropolitan parts of New South Wales and Victoria.

These 'domestic' problems cannot be divorced from those confronting Australia in its relationships with the developing countries in the Pacific basin, particularly the Association of South-East Asian Nations (A.S.E.A.N.) which links Indonesia, Malaysia, Thailand, Singapore and the Philippines. These countries have expressed the hope that Australia will gradually reduce tariff and non-tariff barriers to trade from the A.S.E.A.N. group. But as indicated, many industries in which these countries have a cost advantage (such as clothing, textiles and footwear) depend for their existence in Australia on a high level of protection. In simplistic terms, a lower Australian tariff or enlarged import quota might lead to the expansion of the clothing industry in, say, Kuala Lumpar and to the decline of a country town in New South Wales or Victoria. In this way steps taken to promote international relations can have specific spatial consequences.

These long-run trends and the policy issues they raise suggest directions for research by industrial geographers. The relative decline in the importance of the manufacturing sector, the possible reallocation of resources from labour-intensive to capital-intensive industries and the large numbers of married women expected to enter the labour force are all likely to have, or require, spatial adjustments. But research is needed to find out, for instance, whether the growth of manufacturing towards the periphery of major metropolitan areas will be slowed or hastened; whether manufacturers will be more, or less, willing to locate away from the capital cities; and whether particular urban areas which at present largely depend on labour-intensive industries may need special forms of assistance if they are to remain viable. There are also wider ramifications. As one instance, the 'rationalization' of manufacturing industries may lead to changes in the use made of transport, warehousing and storage facilities and, in turn, on the organization of space in the urban nodes and on the nature of the linkages between them.

Although discussion has been confined to the Australian environment, its main thrust undoubtedly has more general application. Basically it suggests that there is scope for industrial geographers to undertake research which can contribute more directly to the formulation of national policy decisions since, to cite one example again, Australia is by no means unique in having a reduced rate of population growth and a changing labour force structure. But it is also suggested that industrial location analysis should pay more attention to the ways in which *decisions made by the government or one country can affect the organization of space within another country.* Geographers have failed to come to terms with the increasingly transnational nature of the industrial system.

References

Australian Bureau of Statistics (1976) *Foreign Ownership and Control in Manufacturing Industry 1972–73* [ref. 12.37], Canberra.

Bennett, F. N. (1976) 'Trends in the spatial distribution of the industrial labour force', in: G. J. R. Linge, ed., *Restructuring Employment Opportunities in Australia*, Department of Human Geography Publication HG/11 (1976), Canberra (Australian National University), pp. 13–39.

Department of Industry and Commerce (1976) 'New rules, new roles for foreign investment', *Developments in Manufacturing Industry*, No. 9, pp. 4–6

Gilmour, P. (1974) *Physical Distribution Management in Australia*, Cheshire Publishing Pty Ltd, Melbourne.

Industries Assistance Commission (1974a) *Passenger Motor Vehicles, etc.*, Australian Government Publishing Service, Canberra.

Industries Assistance Commission (1974b) *Annual Report 1973–74*, Australian Government Publishing Service, Canberra.

Industries Assistance Committee (1976) *Annual Report 1975–76*, Australian Government Publishing Service, Canberra.

Linge, G. J. R. (1975) 'The forging of an industrial nation: manufacturing in Australia 1788–1913' in J. M. Powell and M. Williams eds., *Australian Space Australian Time*, Oxford University Press, Melbourne, pp. 150–81.

National Population Inquiry (1975) *Population and Australia – A Demographic Analysis and Projection* (2 vols.), Australian Government Publishing Service, Canberra.

Tariff Board (1963) *Annual Report for Year 1962–63*, Canberra.

Tariff Board (1973) *Report on Domestic Appliances, Heating and Cooling Equipment, etc.*, Canberra.

Chapter 13

Manufacturing change, internal control and government spending in a growth region of the USA

John Rees

Recently, regional economic change in the United States has become a media event. The growth of the 'Sun Belt' South (Fig. 13.1) has been glamourized as heralding 'the Second War between the States' (*Business Week*, 17 May 1976), while the *National Journal*, 26 June 1976 saw the role of federal spending as a major causal factor in denying the Northeast of capital investment and indirectly subsidizing the Sun Belt growth process (Sale, 1975). This caused a political reaction at the national level typified by a Congressional coalition formed from delegates of the Northeastern and Midwestern states to protest about the flow of funds southwards and then a retaliatory Southern coalition. A change in the American regional economic system is taking place (Norton, 1977; Miernyk, 1977; Weinstein and Firestine, 1977) and such an issue is in need of research to sort out the 'myths from the realities' (Jusenius and Ledebur, 1976). Though the Sun Belt South is still dominated by low-wage manufacturing industries, the

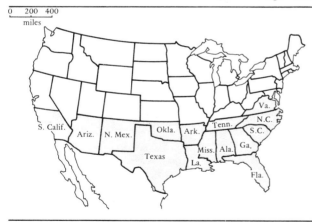

Fig. 13.1 The American 'Sun Belt'.

growth sectors are both high-wage and less energy-intensive industries. Such regional growth has serious public policy implications if indeed federal spending plays a role in these changes. Yet many question the traditional importance of the manufacturing sector as a generator of growth in the so-called post-industrial era: 'the explosive metropolitan growth of the South, Southwest and West was led by the tertiary and quaternary sectors (Berry, 1973, p. 5). Thompson (1975) finds a strong negative correlation between rates of growth of many metropolitan areas between 1970 and 1975 and their proportion of the labour force in manufacturing.

155

But suggestions regarding manufacturing based entirely on employment data tend to ignore the importance of increased productivity and capital intensity in manufacturing. To date, there are many unknowns though Thompson (1975, 8) may be closer to reality when he says, 'the south is going through the industrial and post-industrial age at the same time'. Advocates of 'unbalanced growth' suggest that shifts in the regional economy from the secondary to tertiary sector without technological change is a sign of possible economic weakness (Miernyk, 1977).

This chapter investigates two aspects of contemporary regional change: the sources of growth in manufacturing in one of the Sun Belt's fastest growing urban industrial areas, the Dallas–Fort Worth 'metroplex', and the effect of government spending on the manufacturing sector. It is part of a study of the impact of new, branch and acquired manufacturing plants on product changes, employment trends and linkage patterns in a growth region.

Behavourial components of manufacturing in the Dallas–Fort Worth Area, 1960–75

Structural changes in the Dallas–Fort Worth area need to be discussed using secondary data. A sample survey of manufacturing firms yields inferences about the sources and possible controls of growth, internal or external. Studies of industrial linkages permit further insights into regional economic change.

Dallas–Fort Worth manufacturing, 1963–72: a shift–share analysis

Shift–share analysis is a fairly simple descriptive device that can be used to show changes in the manufacturing structure of the Dallas–Fort Worth economy over the period 1963–72[1] relative to national changes (Ashby, 1965; Greenberg and Valente, 1975). Though a tool of some controversy when applied in a predictive sense, it does provide the necessary insights into manufacturing growth relative to national structure changes. Ashby's original formulation is used in the compilation of Tables 13.1 and 13.2 where: (1) the national component (n_{ij}) assumes that the expected change for a particular industry in a region duplicates the average for the national economy; (2) the industrial mix component identifies that proportion of change that is due to a region's share of fast and slow growing S.I.C. groups; and (3) the competitive component identifies changes due to regional industries growing at rates different from their national counterparts.

With all the publicity given to growth in the Sun Belt it may seem unusual to have a *negative* total mix effect for both value added and employment in Dallas–Fort Worth manufacturing. The analysis suggests, as it does for Texas as a whole, that the region had a substantial amount of industries whose growth rates nationally were *below* average. Food and apparel industries are particularly noteworthy as they are generally consumer-goods sectors regarded as potential growth sectors in a growth region (Hirschmann, 1958). And when the location quotients for 1972 are examined it seems that the Dallas–Fort Worth area specializes in industries which are declining nationally, especially electronics and transport equipment (mostly aircraft). But the definition of the industrial mix component is controversial: it compares *percentage* change in each two-digit S.I.C. group nationally to the national average. Thus a sector with a high *relative in-*

Table 13.1 Shift–share analysis of Dallas–Fort Worth manufacturing, 1963–72 (using value-added)

S.I.C.	Name	Dallas–Fort Worth 1963($m)	1972($m)	National component (n_{ij})	Industrial mix (m_{ij})	Competitive effect (c_{ij})	Location quotient 1972
20	Food	247.4	431.2	222.8	−69.7	30.7	1.05
22	Textile mills	3.8	3.9	3.4	−.05	−3.3	—
23	Apparel	85.7	180.3	77.2	−18.7	36.1	1.19
24	Lumber and wood	10.0	67.2	9.0	−6.1	42.1	.57
25	Furniture	32.0	77.5	28.8	−3.2	−13.5	1.12
26	Paper	46.4	107.7	41.8	−7.1	26.6	.703
27	Printing	111.2	270.9	100.2	−1.6	58.0	1.16
28	Chemicals	101.3	237.0	91.2	−6.0	50.4	.63
29	Petroleum	16.9	36.6	15.2	−5.7	10.2	.56
30	Rubber and plastic	20.4	86.0	18.4	−13.9	33.3	.62
32	Stone–clay–glass	59.9	157.2	54.0	−7.0	50.4	1.08
33	Primary metal	69.9	52.6	63.0	−25.3	−55.0	.20
34	Fabricated metal	83.5	261.9	75.2	−18.5	84.7	.84
35	Machinery	165.3	442.6	148.9	−40.1	88.3	1.02
36	Electrical	231.1	619.4	208.1	−27.6	207.8	1.76
37	Transportation	486.3	939.2	438.0	−29.5	44.4	2.01
38	Instruments	11.6	36.8	10.4	−8.3	6.4	.30
39	Miscellaneous	14.3	67.5	12.9	−12.4	52.7	.84
				1618.5	−117.3	777.3	

Table 13.2 Shift–share analysis of Dallas–Fort Worth manufacturing, 1963–72 (using employment)

S.I.C.	Dallas–Fort Worth 1963(000)	1972(000)	National component (n_{ij})	Industrial mix (m_{ij})	Competitive effect (c_{ij})	Location quotient 1972
20	19.4	17.7	2.4	−3.4	−0.7	0.94
22	0.7	0.4	0.1	−0.01	−0.4	0.04
23	13.9	19.7	1.7	−0.9	4.9	1.21
24	1.4	5.5	0.2	0.1	3.8	0.68
25	3.8	5.4	0.5	0.4	0.7	1.0
26	4.7	6.5	0.6	−0.2	1.4	0.73
27	10.5	15.6	1.3	0.2	3.6	1.2
28	4.2	6.1	0.5	0.01	1.4	0.59
29	1.5	1.6	0.2	−0.3	0.2	0.95
30	2.1	5.1	0.3	0.8	2.0	0.68
32	4.3	6.4	0.5	−0.2	1.8	0.86
33	5.4	3.0	0.7	−0.8	−2.2	0.22
34	8.7	18.9	1.1	1.6	7.5	1.05
35	13.3	22.1	1.7	1.6	5.5	1.0
36	21.8	37.0	2.7	−0.7	13.2	1.85
37	35.8	42.9	4.5	−0.5	3.1	2.04
38	1.2	2.4	0.1	0.4	0.7	0.43
39	1.5	3.3	6.2	−0.6	2.3	0.61
			19.2	−2.7	48.8	

crease but low *absolute* increase can appear with a highly positive mix effect whereas a sector with a greater absolute increase nationally can show a negative mix effect.

In fact it is the healthier competitive component which is of greatest interest as it facilitates identification of regional growth industries. The location quotients of Tables 13.1 and 13.2 show that the specialized manufacturing sectors of the region drew more industry competitively than other sectors. Only two sectors, primary metals and textiles (despite the near-by supplies of cotton and petrochemicals and the growing apparel market), register a negative loading for value added, whereas the large positive component for the electronics industry in particular shows that the region could be a seedbed of growth for that industry. The large competitive components for fabricated metals and machinery are also noteworthy: they show this region diversifying into producer-goods sectors usually associated with the traditional 'Manufacturing Belt'. For each sector with a positive competitive component some other manufacturing region in the nation has to show a negative component. This zero sum situation therefore suggests that the Dallas–Fort Worth area was extremely successful in attracting growth away from other metropolitan regions, be they Boston, Cleveland or Milwaukee.

Internal versus external sourcing of manufacturing growth

A definition of manufacturing change as an aggregation of firm location decisions – in-site expansions, new plants (both branches and births), relocations and acquisitions – have been compiled from secondary data sources.[2] For a fifteen-year period, 1960–75, the 5839 individual decisions for the Dallas–Fort Worth and Houston areas[3] provide an adequate data set for generalizing about the type of location decision. New plants accounted for 1128 or 37 per cent of all decisions in the Dallas–Fort Worth area, followed by 1105 expansions (34 per cent), 487 relocations (16 per cent) and 398 acquisitions (13 per cent). In Houston, by contrast, the 1225 expansions were the most common type of location decision (39 per cent of the total) followed by 974 new plants (31 per cent), 319 acquisitions (10 per cent) and 303 relocations (9.7 per cent). The type of location decision in the two urban–industrial areas appears to vary according to the existing industrial structure and its growth tendencies (Rees, 1978): the dominant sectors in Houston expansions are material-oriented sectors, especially S.I.C. 28 (chemicals) which accounted for 29 per cent of total expansion decisions over the period; much of the more frequent new plant decisions in the Dallas–Fort Worth area occurred in footloose sectors, electronics and aerospace-related industries accounting, for example, for 17 per cent of new plants.

The developmental implications are that if growth continues in material-oriented sectors like chemicals, Houston will continue to attract in-site expansions – particularly if environmental legislation facilitates the expansion of industry in existing industrial areas. The results will proliferate Houston's industrial complex where the 'spaghetti bowl' of interconnected petrochemical complexes may result in more pumping of underground water and resulting subsidence. But if growth continues in Dallas and Fort Worth, particularly in electronics and aerospace, their foot-loose nature may mean that other areas could more easily capture that growth, making the economy more vulnerable.[4]

That plant expansions and new plants are more frequent in these growth regions than relocations (and most relocation decisions were *intra-regional*, i.e. within the metropolitan area, as opposed to *inter-regional*, from other parts of the US) has important policy ramifications. The findings are contrary to the popular notion that firms relocating to and from areas play a major role in shaping the economic conditions of those regions. This is in line with evidence (Rees, 1972; Hamilton, 1974) that shows relocation decisions to be relatively infrequent within the firm, if not within a metropolis (Struyk and James, 1975). Findings here also concur with those of Allaman and Birch (1975) who have used the Dun and Bradstreet national directory to show that the primary cause of declining employment in the North has not been the relocation of firms from the Northeast but the death or closure of existing firms. In the South, however, the primary cause of increasing employment has been the expansion of existing firms and the birth of new ones. This suggests that at a more disaggregated level than the shift–share analysis, the process of regional economic growth in the USA is not a zero sum situation: *growth in the South does not necessarily imply decline in the Northeast.* Yet when a large multi-product, multi-locational firm has numerous plants over which it continuously makes decisions to expand and contract product lines, a regional demand factor would cause it to expand in one region and contract in another. It also suggests that the industrial area is a 'seedbed' for industrial growth in its own right.

More detailed study of manufacturing firms making location decisions in the Dallas–Fort Worth area between 1967 and 1975 shows that 61 per cent of the 551 new plants represented firm 'births' and the other 39 per cent were branch plants of multi-plant enterprises. During the same time period, 309 plants were acquired in the area which made acquisition more common than branch plant construction. Since the study region is one of the more dynamic growth zones in the United States it seems appropriate to define whether such growth is being generated from inside or outside the region. It was expected that manufacturing growth in Dallas–Fort Worth over the period 1967–75 had resulted because firms in traditional US manufacturing areas expanded vertically into the area to capture material sources and also horizontally to capture a new geographical market. This could be achieved either by building branch plants or by acquiring existing companies in the area, the latter strategy ensuring faster entry into regional market areas.

For firms involved in acquiring manufacturing plants and setting up branch plants in the Dallas–Fort Worth area from 1967 to 1975, the dominant states that housed their corporate headquarters are shown in Table 13.3. The data were compiled from *Texas Industrial Expansion* but without reference to firm size. Some 176 acquisition decisions or 57 per cent of the total were initiated by companies

Table 13.3 Major headquarters – states of firms setting up branches, acquisitions in Dallas–Fort Worth, 1967–75

	Number of branches	Number of acquisitions	Value added ($m) 1972	(000) Employment change 1967–72
California	20	14	31 195	−38
New York	15	15	30 404	−250
Connecticut	8	2	6828	−79
Illinois	7	14	25 849	−91
Indiana	6	4	14 112	−6
Ohio	5	6	27 171	−51
Missouri	5	1	8169	−18
New Jersey	4	7	16 409	−45
Michigan	4	5	23 376	−58
Rhode Island	3	2	1764	−4
Wisconsin	3	2	9443	−11
Minnesota	2	6	5524	+2
Pennsylvania	1	4	23 519	−132
North Carolina	2	2	2647	+101
Dallas-Fort Worth	102	176		
Rest of Texas	12	35		

with headquarters within the Dallas–Fort Worth S.M.S.A. while 102 branch plant decisions or 47 per cent of the total were undertaken by firms with headquarters within the S.M.S.A. This finding was unexpected since it showed a *dominance of local as opposed to external sources*, particularly for acquisition decisions. It runs contrary to the external control argument by displaying a strong localization or *'neighbourhood effect'*.

Both situations may reflect two tendencies. One is that smaller firms account for a larger proportion of decisions made in local headquarters while larger firms account for a greater proportion of the non-local decisions. Another explanation may be in the development of this urban-industrial area as a 'seedbed' for industrial growth with firms growing by opening branches or acquiring firms *closer to them*.

For acquiring or branch-plant firms with non-local headquarters one may expect a distance-decay factor to reveal itself and for the other major industrial area in Texas, Houston, to have an impact on industrial change in Dallas–Fort Worth. But only 15 out of 309 acquiring firms have headquarters in Houston and only 5 of the 215 branch plants. It is possible that geographic separation of Dallas–Fort Worth from the Manufacturing Belt and from California has influenced this pattern. That does not detract from the fact that most manufacturing growth in the study region between 1967 and 1975 seems to have been generated by firms from within the metropolitan region.

From Table 13.3, and excluding Texas, a high correlation is found ($r = 0.74$ which is significant at the 99 per cent level) between the State of origin of expanding firms and its importance in 1972 as a manufacturing state as measured by value added. California, with the highest value added for manufacturing, dominates with thirty-four, or 17 per cent of acquisitions and branch-plant decisions undertaken from States outside Texas. New York follows, ranked second in value added, and then other States in the traditional Manufacturing Belt of the United States: Illinois, Indiana, Ohio, New Jersey and Michigan. A distance decay effect then is not evident but there is a high degree of association between the amount of manufacturing that goes on in various States and the amount of acquisition of Texas manufacturing companies. A similarly high correlation (0.74) is found between the number of acquiring companies and branch plants initiated the larger manufacturing States, showing no significant difference between the state of origin of firms involved in these two types of decisions. A hypothesized relationship was also tested between the State of origin of the acquiring firm and those setting up branches and changes in the manufacturing sectors of those states between 1967 and 1972 because most of the aforementioned states lost manufacturing employment in that time period. But no significant correlation (0.236) was found. This tends to *disprove* the hypothesis that the greater the manufacturing employment loss of a State the more likely its firms are to acquire firms in the study region.

Some contrasts are also evident between local and non-local firms in their S.I.C. affiliations. In the more specialized Dallas–Fort Worth manufacturing sectors, that is those with location quotients greater than 1.0 in 1972 (Table 13.1), most branch plants and acquisitions were locally initiated by firms with local headquarters. The only exception was branch plants in S.I.C. 34 where the number of non-local plants was double the local number. Of the other eleven S.I.C. categories in the area which are not so specialized, six had a greater proportion of branch plants with non-local origins while five had more non-local acquisitions than locally-spawned ones. This shows that the specialized manufacturing sectors in Dallas–Fort Worth, which were also the major growth sectors between 1963 and 1972, exhibited a greater degree of local spawning than nonspecialized industries which tended to be non-local in their origins. Thus, while previous developments in the Southwestern hinterland of the American economy were controlled from the Heartland (Berry, 1973), in the late 1960s there was much internally-generated growth in one of the Sun Belt's major industrial areas.

The policy implications are obvious. Instead of trying to lure firms to relocate in the region from distant places, industrial development agencies should concentrate their strategies on fostering the area's existing industry. Firms surveyed also expanded by opening and acquiring plants in spatial proximity to their home base before extending their production space. Industrial growth in the Dallas–Fort Worth S.M.S.A., as elsewhere in the USA, also shows a strong suburban preference (Weinstein and Firestine, 1977). Such industrial decentralization implies that Dallas and other central cities of the Sun Belt may not be immune from the fiscal problems of older cities in the Northeast.

But an examination of the spatial distributions of acquired, new and branch plants among the three metropolitan sub-zones – central cities, adjacent suburbs and more removed exurban areas – show a distinct pattern. Between 1967 and 1975 more acquisition decisions were made in the central cities of Dallas–Fort

Worth (58 per cent) than in the suburban–exurban zones combined. This is expected since more plants exist in the central cities for acquisition purposes. Yet the suburban and exurban areas experienced a greater influx of branch plants (62 per cent) as opposed to the central cities. That 55 per cent of births of new firms were found in the central cities gives empirical evidence for Vernon and Hoover's (1959) 'incubator hypothesis'. The same tendency has not been found in the older cities of the Manufacturing Belt (Struyk and James, 1975) or in Canada (Steed, 1976) but this may be due to the larger areas and lower population densities of the newer Sun Belt cities. If fiscal disparities between central and suburban cities are to be minimized, central cities should foster their capacity to spawn acquisition and the birth of new firms. This is particularly the case since firms with headquarters in the Dallas–Fort Worth area were more likely to acquire plants in the central cities whereas non-local firms preferred suburban and exurban locations for both acquisitions and branches.

External or internal 'control' of growth?

Since the 1940s, concern has grown on the issue of external control in the US where centralization of economic power has supposedly increased regional disparities (Kefauver, 1947). Pred (1974) recently argued that the generation of non-local multipliers via external control mechanisms has reinforced the inertia of the existing economic system. His empirical work (Pred, 1975; 1976) shows that non-local intra-organizational job control linkages for certain metropolitan areas are dominated by ties with other national metropolitan complexes rather than with local sources. Yet, operational definitions of what external control actually means have been lacking (Dicken, 1976). There is a need to look at actual as well as potential control and *this cannot be done without regard to the structure and policies of different types of organizations, particularly the autonomy of company operating units, divisions, plants, or subsidiaries.*

So far, the argument has not incorporated the influence of firm size. An interview survey of a sample of 42 acquired plants, 15 branch plants and 18 births in the Dallas–Fort Worth area, however, throws further light on firm size and the issue of external control in the study region. A Mann–Whitney U test ($Z = 2.88$) showed that the 11 firms with non-local headquarters undertaking acquisition decisions in the area were significantly larger than the 17 firms with local headquarters. Also the larger firms establishing branch plants in the area had their headquarters outside the study region. Though manufacturing growth in the Dallas–Fort Worth area seemed to spawn from local sources, the more important acquisition decisions by size were made by firms headquartered outside the area. Thus non-locally based companies have had a greater impact on the economic health of the study region than locally-based ones, yet this does not necessarily mean greater external control over the local economy.

Indeed, the post-decision growth record of the plants surveyed does not reveal that larger, externally-based companies had a more detrimental effect on employment levels in the Dallas–Fort Worth area. The predominant patterns among the 42 acquired plants after acquisition was that *they were left to operate much as they had been prior to the location decision.* Most acquisition decisions proved to be of conglomerate type, in which firms acquired in unrelated product lines largely to boost their size (F.T.C., 1969): these acquired plants experienced increased production and employment. At least for the growth region under study, the survey suggests that acquisition in the short term leads to increased growth and not to consolidation and rationalization of production.[5] However, the regional growth environment may bias the results to such an extent that acquisitions can exacerbate employment consolidation and industrial decline in lagging regions.

The only evidence from the Survey of Manufacturers that can support any notion of external control in the Dallas–Fort Worth area was the predominance of cyclical employment changes in non-locally based firms: i.e. firms with local headquarters did experience more consistent employment increases. But the cyclical instability is probably due to the military industrial orientation of the non-local firms. Most of their output was sold to the US Department of Defence and their prosperity fell during the post-Vietnam era.

Thus little support can be given to the external control argument. So much seems to depend on the organizational nature of the firms. All but two had been involved in acquisition decisions at some stage of their development and the overall tendency was for firms that grew externally by acquiring others to have decentralized organizational structures where plant behaviour was hardly affected by the acquisition process.

Industrial linkages and import substitution

Initial concern over the process of regional growth and structural change led to the export base model which emphasized regional exports as the primary growth determinants. Recently the validity of this model has been questioned empirically by Moriarty (1976), though his findings are greatly influenced by the use of employment data which discounts the role of capital intensity in manufacturing and also the impact of revenue sharing policies. In his popularized five-stage development model, North (1955) suggested that consumer goods rather than producer goods are the first to respond to the success of the export sector. Gilmour (1975) later substantiated this for Ontario. Thus, one may expect import substitution to take place in consumer goods industries and then producer goods sectors.

The spatial pattern of backward linkages for 45 plants in the Dallas-Fort Worth area (Table 13.4) suggests a dependency on the more established manufacturing areas of the United States, the Manufacturing Belt (the Middle Atlantic and East North Central Census regions) and California which accounted for 42 per cent of all inputs. Thus just as the American industrial heartland once reached out to such peripheral regions for raw materials, now this maturing industrial area depends on that same heartland for manufactured goods for its own industries. One may expect import substitution to take place as a region develops, but this does not yet seem to be the case here. That this conclusion is drawn from a sample of firms in industrial sectors traditionally classified as producer more than consumer goods has to be borne in mind though these were major growth sectors in the region. Nevertheless, industrial diversification has taken place in Texas and in its major urban areas but from this *it cannot be assumed that industrial diversification is synonymous with import substitution.*

Backward linkage patterns were expected to vary by Census region according to two-digit S.I.C. product classification, but as Table 13.4 shows analysis of variance proved this not to be statistically significant.[6] Interviews indicated that the unique requirements of many manufacturers, particularly defence contractors, the lack of availability of inputs in the study region, and product quality in the

Table 13.4 Backward links by product type (%) – S.I.C.

	34(N=5)	35(15)	36(18)	37(7)	Mean% procurement (N = 45)	Value-added %73
New England	—	3.1	13.3	3.0	6.5	7.1
Mid Atlantic	22.0	7.9	12.1	12.4	12.5	19.2
E.N. Central	21.6	18.4	11.3	14.0	15.2	28.2
W.N. Central	9.4	1.6	2.3	2.6	3.4	6.8
S. Atlantic	1.0	1.3	1.9	1.3	1.7	12.4
E.S. Central	2.0	4.6	0.2	2.1	2.2	6.1
W.S. Central	21.4	55.0	34.7	37.9	40.1	7.0
(Dallas–Fort Worth)	19.4	37.7	31.3	24.9	32.4	
Mountain	—	—	1.3	0.6	0.6	1.7
Pacific	11.6	5.7	20.1	22.1	14.7	11.9
Foreign	11.0	2.0	4.7	3.3	4.3	

Analysis of Variance: d.f. = 3/40.
   F. Ratio = 0.03.

more established areas were factors which still outweighed the friction of distance. Yet surprisingly, as high a mean as 32 per cent of inputs even came from the Dallas–Fort Worth area, as this is very close to proportions found in the more mature manufacturing cities like Montreal (Gilmour, 1975) and Philadelphia (Karaska, 1969).

The federal role in manufacturing change

In contrast to the European experience where governments in post-Keynesian times have played direct roles in attempting to equalize regional opportunities, the role of the American government has been more indirect (Cameron, 1968; Hansen, 1974). In the 1960s concern grew over the direct effect of one type of federal policy, defence spending, as it affected the economic health of US regions (Bolton, 1966; Tiebout and Peterson, 1964; Karaska, 1967). Recently public attention has once again been directed to the role of defence spending and other forms of federal outlays, this time as instigators of economic growth in the Southwest. From the survey of manufacturers in the Dallas–Fort Worth area, where the growth industries (dominantly aircraft, S.I.C. 372) were also the sectors that sold most of their output to the Department of Defense (*Texas Input–Output Study*, 1970), one can infer about the effect of government spending on manufacturing change.

Industrial linkages in the defence sector

Five plants employing more than 4000 people each in the Dallas–Fort Worth area and supplying between 35 and 100 per cent of their output to the military, made procurement expenditures available by State for 1975. Table 13.5 shows the procurement patterns of four of these firms among the thirty-five major supplying States, together with national percentages of value-added per State in 1973 and prime military contract awards made to those states in 1975.[7] A correlation matrix of these data, percentage change in both value added and employment by

Table 13.5 Backward linkage patterns of three large defence contractors 1975

State	Per cent procurement				
	Firm A $670m	Firm B $160m	Firm C $47m	% value added 1973	$m Prime Military contracts
New Hampshire	1.0	0.14	0.25	.4	100
Vermont	0.5	0.01	0.05	.2	58
Massachusetts	1.5	2.1	2.5	3.0	1781
Rhode Island	.02	.06	.04	.5	98
Connecticut	1.9	1.3	1.0	2.0	2642
New York	27.5	7.3	4.8	8.2	2785
New Jersey	2.2	3.3	3.5	4.4	968
Pennsylvania	1.1	2.1	4.7	6.6	1307
Ohio	1.6	.4	1.7	7.7	994
Indiana	.2	.14	1.9	4.0	748
Illinois	1.5	.7	4.1	7.2	456
Michigan	.8	.36	.2	6.7	925
Wisconsin	.1	.01	.2	2.7	251
Minnesota	.6	1.2	1.1	1.7	408
Iowa	.3	.01	.4	1.4	158
Missouri	6.0	.9	.3	2.2	296
Kansas	.1	.4	1.6	.8	1373
Delaware	.04	.01	.09	.4	42
Maryland	1.1	.21	.3	1.3	743
Virginia	.16	5.3	2.3	1.7	953
North Carolina	.01	.1	.17	3.1	350
Georgia	.1	.14	.09	2.1	377
Florida	.5	.5	.2	1.6	790
Tennessee	.02	1.0	.6	2.2	329
Alabama	.1	2.0	.03	1.4	336
Arkansas	.4	.02	.01	.8	44
Oklahoma	.2	1.2	.3	.6	170
Texas	18.3	45.0	46.0	4.4	1914
Colorado	.12	.5	1.8	.7	239
New Mexico	.02	3.3	.01	.1	103
Arizona	.2	.3	.6	.6	479
Utah	.01	.03	.8	.3	193
Washington	.07	.25	.04	1.4	837
Oregon	.2	.01	.15	1.1	58
California	31.0	16.0	17.0	9.1	6917

State from 1967 to 1973 and defence spending *per capita* is shown in Table 13.6. The backward linkage distributions in the four plants are significantly correlated, with R greater than 0.33 at the 0.95 level, with absolute changes in value added by State from 1967 to 1973. The distribution patterns of three firms are significantly correlated with national percentages of value added by State in 1973; that of two firms is significantly related to employment percentage by State in 1973 while none of the procurement distributions show a statistically significant relationship to employment changes by State 1967–73. All firms show a negative relationship between their backward linkage patterns and employment changes largely because of a high proportion of supplies coming from New York State and Connecticut, two States which have a higher amount of prime military contract

Table 13.6 Correlation coefficients: State manufacturing capacity, defence spending and four firm procurement patterns

	VA Change 63–67	VA % 73	Empl. % 73	Empl. change 67–73	Firm D	Firm B	Firm A	Firm C	Military contracts
	C_1	C_2	C_3	C_4	C_5	C_6	C_7	C_8	C_9
C_2	0.969								
C_3	0.949	0.989							
C_4	−0.040	−0.270	−0.301						
C_5	0.549	0.478	0.412	0.287					
C_6	0.394	0.364	0.322	0.248	0.800				
C_7	0.588	0.624	0.602	−0.219	0.772	0.621			
C_8	0.345	0.318	0.279	0.239	0.781	0.986	0.643		
C_9	0.612	0.634	0.604	−0.178	0.789	0.466	0.820	0.461	
C_{10}	−0.089	−0.018	−0.038	−0.274	0.220	0.085	0.218	0.105	0.510

C_{10} = Defence spending per capita

df = 33

γ significant at 0.05 level if > 0.388 (underlined)

awards *per capita* than the national average, but States which also declined in total manufacturing employment between 1967 and 1973. In general, the backward linkage patterns of the four Dallas–Fort Worth companies show a high degree of reliance on the leading manufacturing states by value-added.

These States – particularly California, New York, Connecticut, Texas and Massachusetts – are those which receive the greatest amounts of prime military contracts from the Department of Defense and a greater degree of military spending *per capita* than the nation as a whole. But they are not all growth States, at least in employment terms. Of the five largest receivers of defence contracts, Connecticut, New York and Massachusetts are all States that lost net manufacturing jobs between 1967 and 1973, so questioning the argument that the States receiving the greatest amounts of defence contracts *per capita* were the manufacturing growth States. Significant statistical correlations are also seen between the backward linkage patterns of the four defence firms and the amounts of military contract awards made per State in 1975. This implies that defence-oriented firms in the Dallas–Fort Worth area subcontract to other States which are also receivers of large prime contracts. Table 13.6 also shows that the States increasing their relative proportions of value-added and employment in manufacturing between 1967 and 1973 were those which had a lower level of defence spending *per capita*. States which lost a relative proportion of value added and employment, especially in the Northwest and Middle Atlantic regions, had a higher degree of defence spending *per capita* as defined by prime military contract awards. This finding has important implications. It suggests that regional manufacturing growth in the US is related to dollar-value of defence spending but not defence spending on a *per capita* basis; States losing manufacturing from 1967 to 1973 were those with higher defence spending per capita.

Defence subcontracts from the southwestern Sun Belt therefore revert to the Manufacturing Belt. *This gives little evidence that any lack of defence spending in the traditional manufacturing areas proved detrimental to their economic health.* Since a significant degree of covariation exists in the procurement patterns of the four Dallas–Fort Worth defence-oriented plants, an inverse distance decay affect is implied, which compares favourably with an earlier study of defence subcontracting from Philadelphia by Karaska (1966, 1967). For the firms undertaking defense work in the Dallas–Fort Worth area a mean of only 25 per cent of the procurement came from the Dallas–Fort Worth metroplex, less than the mean California purchases (27 per cent). New York State followed with 9 per cent; the rest of Texas (8 per cent); Ohio, Massachusetts and New Jersey each supplied 2 per cent and Connecticut, 1 per cent, with the rest scattered among the States included in Table 13.5.

One important aspect other States do not have, however, is how such linkage patterns, particularly for defence-oriented firms, can fluctuate over time. The stability or lack of stability of industrial linkages can influence regional development, yet little is known about linkage fluctuations over time. The correlation coefficients of the procurement expenditures of one large defence contractor in three consecutive years shows a high degree of statistical significance (Table 13.7). But vast fluctuations occurred in proportions procured from some areas, involving large sums of money. The company's procurement from Texas only varied from 28 to 36 per cent in two consecutive years whereas that from California increased from 15 to 42 per cent in two years and that from Connecticut declined from 28 to 5 per cent. And these are based on total purchases of between

Table 13.7 Backward linkage patterns of one large defence contractor over time

State	Per cent procurement ($) Firm D		
	$372m 1975(C$_5$)	$393m 1974	$237m 1973
New Hampshire	0.1	0.1	0.1
Vermont	0.7	1.2	8.0
Massachusetts	0.8	1.5	0.5
Rhode Island	0.01	0.01	0.02
Connecticut	1.1	5.1	28.0
New York	1.5	2.8	2.0
New Jersey	1.3	2.1	2.1
Pennsylvania	.7	1.5	.6
Ohio	5.3	9.2	5.1
Indiana	2.4	4.8	3.2
Illinois	.5	1.3	.9
Michigan	.8	1.5	1.5
Wisconsin	.5	1.1	.9
Minnesota	.2	.9	.2
Iowa	.3	.7	.4
Missouri	.5	1.3	.7
Kansas	3.2	4.8	3.4
Delaware	.003	.001	.007
Maryland	.3	.3	.3
Virginia	.01	.02	.01
North Carolina	2.1	.2	.2
Georgia	.1	.1	.1
Florida	.2	.5	.2
Tennessee	.1	.1	.01
Alabama	.2	.03	.01
Arkansas	.1	.3	.3
Oklahoma	.1	1.5	.3
Texas	30.5	36.6	28.2
Colorado	.8	.4	.1
New Mexico	.01	.01	.003
Arizona	1.0	2.6	.9
Utah	1.4	1.0	.04
Washington	1.5	.7	.04
Oregon	.02	.14	.08
California	42.0	15.0	12.0
Correlation coefficients:		1975	1974
	1974	0.818	
	1973	0.595	0.776
	All significant at 0.05 level		

$237 million and $393 million and presumably involve numerous job changes. The same company disclosed that these changes involved inter-divisional transactions amounting to 9 per cent of procurements in 1973, 10 per cent in 1974 and 16 per cent in 1975 and requiring procurement of materials from their divisions in Texas, California and New York State. In 1973, the Texas division supplied 9 per cent of internal procurements, 43 per cent in 1974, and 40 per cent in 1975. The California division supplied 41 per cent in 1973, 32 per cent in 1974 and 47 per cent in 1975, whereas the New York division supplied 49 per cent in 1973, 24 per cent in 1974, and 13 per cent in 1975. From this it is easy to conclude that backward linkages fluctuate considerably on an annual basis *involving affiliated as well as non-affiliated suppliers.*

Such major changes in backward linkages, though based on only one example, have many implications for the process of regional change. Such massive changes must be detrimental to regional economic stability through their employment repercussions. The so-called 'Boeing recession' in Seattle, caused largely by over-commitments to short-run demand, may be typical of the American industrial system. Yet such rapid changes in purchasing patterns can be rationalized as contributing to the efficiency and competitiveness of the economy. The intra-company changes, in addition to the inter-company relationships, suggest that inter-divisional competition of branches and subsidiaries tends towards a system where intra-divisional transfers are not favoured and hence do not exist in many multi-plant firms even though they have a degree of vertical integration.

Employment implications

The survey of Dallas–Fort Worth manufacturers showed that 6 out of 11 defence-oriented plants showed large cyclical tendencies in employment while 3 showed consistent employment decreases between 1970 and 1976. Table 13.8 indicates the large employment changes in the five lead firms in the Dallas–Fort Worth area, all five of which are large defence contractors though the sales of any one defence firm make-up less than 35 per cent of its total sales. Correlation coefficients (Table 13.8) show relationships between the employment fluctuations of these firms with each other and also h local and national employment rates as coincident indicators of the business cycle. Six of the ten coefficients are significantly related though two are negative, implying that one firm – which was the more commercially-oriented – tended to increase its employment as that in others decreased. The coefficients relating the five employment trends to local unemployment rates also show a negative tendency, two to a statistically significant level: the local unemployment level increases as employment in these lead firms decreases.[8] Thus the employment potentials of the firms in this survey, all of whom depend on military contracts, have a major impact on the local economy.

When aggregate data on the manufacturing sector of the Dallas–Fort Worth area in the 1960s and early 1970s are examined a generally healthy picture tends to emerge (Tables 13.1 and 13.2). But behind the broad picture some contrasting processes are evident, reflecting the cyclical sensitivity of individual plants and individual firms, particularly if a large proportion of sales goes to the Department of Defence. Dependence on military contracting, particularly by the larger manufacturing employers in the area, could have resulted in large aggregated losses in employment to the Dallas–Fort Worth region and a far less healthy outlook, if it were not for two countervailing processes. One was the adaption of firms, particularly the defence contractors, to changing economic circumstances by reorienting themselves to commerical markets and international markets. The other process was a seedbed process which involved growth not from external sources but from within and with the emphasis on innovation and emergence of new product cycles leading to the expansion of existing, and the birth of new firms.

One final aspect of this process is worthy of note. The incidence of different types of location decisions in the Dallas–Fort Worth area, discussed earlier, was examined for the years 1960–75. The fact that new plants in the area were the only type of location decision not to show a negative relationship to the local unemployment rate ($r = 0.39$) suggests that *recessionary periods*, particularly those

Table 13.8 Lead defence firms' employment and unemployment trends

	Case C1	Case C2	Case C3	Case C4	Case C5	US unemployment	DFW unemployment
1965	10 500	6500	9000	13 750	17 000	4.5	4.4
1966	10 500	6500	9000	16 568	18 000	3.8	3.3
1967	10 600	6500	15 000	23 376	18 000	3.8	2.7
1968	10 500	6700	22 000	28 847	24 000	3.6	2.3
1969	10 600	6300	23 300	27 847	30 000	3.5	2.2
1970	10 900	6300	21 000	25 589	22 500	4.9	3.6
1971	8800	4500	15 000	15 818	23 500	5.9	4.4
1972	7300	3500	12 000	11 230	28 000	5.6	4.0
1973	6800	4000	12 000	9233	32 000	4.9	2.7
1974	7500	4300	11 000	7080	32 000	5.6	3.5
1975	9600	5300	12 000	7054	28 000	8.5	5.3
1976	10 000	4700	12 000	7050	27 000	7.6	4.3

Correlation matrix

	C_1	C_2	C_3	C_4	C_5	C_6
C2	0.912					
C3	0.387	0.387				
C4	0.640	0.726	0.820			
C5	-0.672	-0.679	0.149	-0.373		
C6	-0.285	-0.548	0.387	-0.742	0.371	
C7	-0.104	-0.336	0.562	-0.662	-0.074	0.826

r significant at 0.05 level if > 0.576

caused by the military spending cycle, *are opportunistic times for the birth of new firms*. Local recessions enable risk-taking entrepreneurs with available capital to tap unemployed skilled labour pools and to start their own companies. This was indeed confirmed in interviews with the personnel of seven of the fifteen new firms, people who used to work for the defence-oriented lead firms in the area. Though one might expect such 'off-shoots' to be more prevalent during times of relative prosperity, it is perhaps the salvation of the regional economy that recessionary periods in themselves lead to the spawning of industrial growth.

Such a seemingly dialectical relationship tends to recognize the counter-balancing forces that led to the complexity of the real world. It is apparent in the process of firm growth (Chamberlain, 1969) where certain forces tend towards coherence to hold complex organizations together through *inertia* and others tend towards disturbance and new developments to insure survival and adaptation in the future, *innovation*. Similar forces seem to generate the dynamic equilibria that prevail within the American regional economy where the *inertia* of the existing urban economic system (Pred, 1974) seems to be counterbalanced by the new *technologies* (Borchert, 1967) that create regional change. Indeed, such processes provide at least a *conceptual link between the product–cycle model*, the implications of which are evident among the growing firms of the study region, and the notion of *regional life cycles* as represented by the internal structural dynamics of the American regional system.

The findings and implications of this research remind us of the cautionary words of Jusenius and Ledebur (1976, p. 35): 'Rhetoric and biased studies which encourage a growing sense of economic competition between two regions do a disservice to the overall goal of balanced economic growth for both regions . . . the current debate which focuses on the rate of growth of the Sun Belt as a partial explanation of the economic difficulties of the Northern States is detrimental to the goal of achieving national policies that facilitate overall growth among all regions of the United States'. Their report saw the economic growth of the Sun Belt in a long-term context as the convergence of regional equality in a major economic system, i.e. as the kind of process that other regional economic theorists have said may take place (Myrdal, 1957; Hirschmann, 1958). Long-term structural changes in the American economy should not be confused with short-term cyclical fluctuations which, between 1970 and 1975, contained unusual cyclical characteristics, to say the least. Respondents in many interviews suggested that greatly increasing living costs and particularly labour costs were causing a long-distance decentralization process to small or non-metropolitan areas away from Dallas–Fort Worth and other large urban areas of the Southwest. If such 'filtering down' continues, it may result in the absorption of cheap labour pools in rural areas and halt the industrial invasion of non-metropolitan America. And since recent growth in the non-metropolitan areas may be related to that of the Sun Belt South in causation, that is they differ mostly in terms of *geographical scale*, it may well be the case that the economic growth of the Sun Belt turns into a short-term process. This may lead to decreasing regional disparities in the US and little more. Yet, this in itself will be a desirable goal that the 'invisible hand' may achieve in lieu of a myriad of planned adjustments.

Notes

1. The latest available *Census of Manufacturers* was conducted in 1972. At the two-digit level changes in S.I.C. definitions are minimal, and though the Dallas–Fort Worth S.M.S.A. increased in area over the period 1963–72, this involved non-manufacturing counties, so data are comparable.
2. Dominantly these were the annual *Directory of Texas Manufacturers*, compiled by the Bureau of Business Research of the University of Texas at Austin and updated monthly by *Texas Industrial Expansion*. These include an inventory of the above location decisions. Dun & Bradstreet Directories were used to cross-check data. Estimates of the accuracy of the data as confirmed by manufacturers themselves suggest 75 per cent reliability. There is no evidence to suggest that the degree of inaccuracy is biased towards any one type of location decision. One major drawback of the data source, however, is that no consistent definition of size of location decision exists either in terms of floorspace, employment or value of production. But it is a type of inventory and monitoring of industrial expansion that many States in the US lack.
3. Houston is included because a comparison of two urban–industrial complexes allows more adequate testing of hypotheses, while the two growth regions also reveal a complementarity to their industrial structures.
4. This is particularly the case since defence spending as a per cent of G.N.P. declined in the US from 1970 to 1976.
5. The fact that acquisition and branch plant decisions also resulted in *little* intra-firm linkage changes also leads one to question the argument that the multi-plant form of organization experience technical economies of scale at the firm level.
6. Firms disclosed $ value of procurements used in the manufacturing process by State location of original equipment manufacturers, not wholesalers. The aggregation, however, does conceal that many inputs of the same plant came from a multitude of sources.
7. The latest available *Annual Survey of Manufacturers* was conducted in 1973. Prime military contract awards as reported by the Department of Defence are included by State in *Statistical Abstracts*. Many of these prime contract awards are subcontracted out of State and this is not taken account of in data sources. Yet prime contract values can be used as proxies for defence spending since past studies (Tiebout and Peterson, 1964, and Karaska, 1967) have shown that roughly 50 per cent of prime contracts go out of State.
8. For the State of Texas as a whole between 1960 and 1974, a correlation coefficient of -0.88 shows a significant *inverse* relationship between prime military contract awards made to the state and the unemployment rate.

References

Allaman, P. M. and Birch, D. C. (1975) 'Components of employment change for States by industry group, 1970–72', *Working Paper* no. 5, Joint Centre for Urban Studies of the Massachusetts Institute of Technology and Harvard University.
Ashby, L. D. (1965) *Growth Patterns in Employment by County, 1940–50 and 1950–60*, Government Printing Office, Washington, DC.

Berry, B. J. L. (1973) *Growth Centers in the American Urban System*, Ballinger, Cambridge, Mass.

Bolton, R. E. (1966) *Defense Purchases and Regional Growth*, The Brookings Institution, Washington, DC.

Borchert, J. R. (1967) 'American metropolitan evolution', *Geographical Review*, **57**, pp. 301–32.

Cameron, G. C. (1968) 'The regional problem in the United States – some reflections on a viable federal strategy', *Regional Studies*, **2**, 207–20.

Chamberlain, N. W. (1969) *Enterprise and Environment*, McGraw-Hill, New York.

Dicken, P. (1976) 'The multi-plant business enterprise and geographical space: some issues in the study of external control and regional development', *Regional Studies*, **10**, pp. 401–12.

Federal Trade Commission (F.T.C.) (1969) *Economic Report on Corporate Mergers*, US Government Printing Office, Washington, DC.

Gilmour, J. M. (1975) 'The dynamics of spatial change in the export region', in: L. Collins and D. F. Walker, eds., *Locational Dynamics of Manufacturing Activity*, Wiley, London, pp. 59–82.

Greenberg, M. R. and Valentene, N. J. (1975) 'Recent economic trends in the major northeastern metropolises', in: A. Sternlieb and J. W. Hughes eds., *Post Industrial America: Metropolitan Decline and Inter Regional Job Shifts*, Center for Urban Policy Research, New Jersey, pp. 77–100.

Hamilton, F. E. I., ed. (1974), *Spatial Perspectives on Industrial Organization and Decision Making*, Wiley London.

Hansen, N. M., ed. (1974) *Public Policy and Regional Economic Development*, Ballinger, Cambridge, Mass.

Hirschmann, A. O. (1958) *The Strategy of Economic Development*, Yale University Press, New Haven, Connecticut.

Jusenius, C. L. and Ledebur, L. C. (1976) *A Myth in the Making: The Southern Economic Challenge and Northern Economic Decline*, Economic Development Administration, Washington, DC.

Karaska, G. J. (1966) 'Inter-regional flows of defense–space awards: the role of subcontracting in an impact analysis of changes in the levels of defense awards upon the Philadelphia economy', *Papers*, Peace Research Society, **5**, pp. 45–62.

Karaska, G. J. (1967) 'The spatial impacts of defense–space procurement: an analysis of subcontracting patterns in the United States', *Papers*, Peace Research Society, **8**, pp. 109–22.

Karaska, G. J. (1969) 'Manufacturing linkages in the Philadelphia economy: some evidence of external agglomeration forces', *Geographical Analysis*, **1**, pp. 354–69.

Kefauver, Senator (1947) *Statement Amending Section 711 of the Clayton Act*, Hearings before Subcommittee No. 2 of the Committee on the Judiciary, House of Representatives. 80th Congress, First Session, Washington, DC, US Government Printing Office.

Miernyk, W. H. (1977) 'The changing structure of the Southern economy', paper to Southern Growth Policies Board, North Carolina.

Moriarty, B. M. (1976) 'The distributed lag between metropolitan-area employment and population growth', *Journal of Regional Science*, **16**, pp. 195–212.

Myrdal, G. (1957) *Economic Theory and Underdeveloped Regions*, Duckworth, London.

North, D. C. (1955) 'Location theory and regional economic growth', *Journal of Political Economy*, **63**, 243–58.

Norton, R. D. (1977) *City-Life Cycles and American Urban Policy*, Ph.D. Dissertation, Princeton University.

Pred, A. R. (1974), 'Industry Information and City-System Interdependencies', in: F. E. I. Hamilton, ed., op. cit., pp. 105–42.

Pred, A. R. (1975) 'Diffusion, organizational spatial structure and city-system development., *Economic Geography*, **51**, pp. 252–68.

Pred, A. R. (1976) 'The interurban transmission of growth in advanced economies: empirical findings versus regional-planning assumptions', *Regional Studies*, **10**, pp. 151–71.

Rees, J. (1972) 'Organization theory and corporate decisions: some implications for industrial location analysis', *Regional Science Perspectives*, **2**, pp. 126–35.

Sale, K. (1975), *Power Shift: The Rise of the Southern Rim and Its Challenge to the Eastern Establishment*, Random House, New York.

Steed, G. P. F. (1976) 'Standardization, scale, incubation and inertia: Montreal and Toronto clothing industries', *Canadian Geographer*, **20**, pp. 298–309.

Struyk, R. J. and James, F. J. (1975) *Intrametropolitan Industrial Location*, Heath, Lexington, Mass.

Thompson, W. (1975) 'Economic processes and employment problems in declining metropolitan areas', in: Sternlieb and Hughes, eds., *Post-Industrial America: Metropolitan Decline and Inter-*

Regional Job Shifts, Center for Urban Policy Research, New Brunswick, New Jersey, pp. 187–96.

Tiebout, C. M. and Peterson, R. S. (1964) 'Measuring the impact of regional defense–space expenditures', *The Review of Economics and Statistics*, **46,** pp. 421–8.

Vernon, R. and Hoover, E. M. (1959) *Anatomy of a Metropolis*, Harvard University Press, Cambridge, Mass.

Weinstein, B. L. and Firestine, R. (1977) *Regional Growth and Decline in the US.*, Praeger, New York (forthcoming).

Index